Cambridge Studies in Chinese History, Literature and Institutions
General Editors
Patrick Hanan and Denis Twitchett

LAND AND LINEAGE IN CHINA

Land and lineage in China

A STUDY OF T'UNG-CH'ENG COUNTY, ANHWEI, IN THE MING AND CH'ING DYNASTIES

HILARY J. BEATTIE

Formerly Assistant Professor of History, Yale University

CAMBRIDGE UNIVERSITY PRESS

CAMBRIDGE

LONDON · NEW YORK · MELBOURNE

CAMBRIDGE UNIVERSITY PRESS
Cambridge, New York, Melbourne, Madrid, Cape Town, Singapore, São Paulo, Delhi

Cambridge University Press
The Edinburgh Building, Cambridge CB2 8RU, UK

Published in the United States of America by Cambridge University Press, New York

www.cambridge.org
Information on this title: www.cambridge.org/9780521219747

First published 1979
This digitally printed version 2008

A catalogue record for this publication is available from the British Library

Library of Congress Cataloguing in Publication data

Beattie, Hilary J.
Land and lineage in China.

(Cambridge studies in Chinese history, literature
and institutions)
Based on the author's thesis, Cambridge University,
1973
Bibliography: p.
Includes index.
1. Land tenure – China – T'ung-ch'eng hsien
(Anhwei) – History. 2. T'ung-ch'eng hsien, China
(Anhwei) – Rural conditions. I. Title.
HD929.T86B4   301.44'0951'225   77-91080

ISBN 978-0-521-21974-7 hardback
ISBN 978-0-521-10111-0 paperback

To my parents

CONTENTS

LIST OF MAPS AND TABLES

MAPS

TABLES

ACKNOWLEDGEMENTS

This work was written in the summer of 1973 as a Ph.D. dissertation at Cambridge University. It had originally begun as an investigation of conditions of landowning in one part of China but rapidly expanded to become a study of social structure and social mobility on the local level. I had intended to do much further research before publishing it, but a change of career has made that impossible. The study must therefore stand as it is, with only minimal alterations, in the hope that in spite of its imperfections, it will be of use to other scholars and stimulate them to carry on where I left off. Unfortunately, for the most part, it has not been possible to include references to relevant scholarly works published since 1973.

I should like to thank the staffs of the various libraries where I did most of the research, in particular Dr Greta Scott of the University Library, Cambridge who was extremely tolerant of and assiduous in meeting my endless demands for microfilms of rare works. The staffs of the Tōyō Bunkō, the National Diet Library and Tokyo University Library in Tokyo were also very helpful.

Financial support for the research and writing of the dissertation was provided initially, from 1968 to 1971, by the Department of Education and Science, and then by Newnham College, Cambridge, where I held a research fellowship from 1971 to 1973. In addition I was fortunate in obtaining a grant from the Universities' China Committee which enabled me to collect material in the Far East in 1971.

My major debt, however, is to Professor Denis Twitchett of Cambridge University, my dissertation adviser, for his initial suggestion that I take Chang Ying's *Heng-ch'an so-yen* as point of departure, for much advice and encouragement during the course of the research, and for furthering its publication. I am also grateful to Professor Ray Huang of State University College, New Paltz, New York, for his assistance with the translation of some of the highly technical material on taxation used in Chapter 3. Help from other scholars on one or two points is acknowledged in the appropriate footnotes. Other than that, the work was my own, and I alone am responsible for any errors of fact or interpretation.

New Haven, Connecticut, September 1977   H.J.B.

The Yangtze valley in the Ch'ing dynasty

1

THE CHINESE ELITE AND THE FOUNDATIONS OF ITS POWER

There are at present in the history of early modern China few more important controversies than that surrounding the nature and functions of the ruling class, the so-called 'Chinese gentry'. Some notable studies have been devoted to analysing its composition and economic basis, and few scholars working on any aspect of the history of this period have been able to resist offering their own modified definitions, theories and criticisms.[1] As this was clearly the key group in Chinese society, the one which enjoyed most wealth, prestige and influence on both the local and national scene, it is of crucial importance to arrive at some clear idea of how it was constituted and exactly how its access to wealth and power was maintained. Yet so far there has been surprisingly little consensus on these questions; opinions vary widely depending on the ideological predilections of the scholar and the range of material on which he has chosen to base his views. Thus for Chang Chung-li the gentry was a tiny and rather mobile group that owed its wealth and influence entirely to its possession of formal educational qualifications and office and was not based on the continued holding of large landed estates, whereas for most Chinese Marxist scholars it was a 'feudal' class of rack-renting landlords that monopolized access to education and therefore power by virtue of its dominance in the economic sphere.

These are two extreme positions and it is probable that the truth, as is usually the case, lies somewhere in between. The aim of the present study is to throw more light on some of these questions by examining a segment of 'gentry' society in one particular place over a lengthy period of time, thus to a certain extent avoiding the perils (to which many scholars appear to have succumbed) of generalizing broadly from a wide range of scattered and somewhat unsystematically collected evidence. As the title implies, attention will be devoted in particular to the subject of landholding and the precise role which it played in the fortunes and formation of the elite, that is, to elucidating the complex interdependence of wealth and power in Chinese society during the later imperial age. The other major, but closely related, purpose of the work is to investigate in an empirical fashion the composition of this elite (as far as possible leaving aside all preconceived notions and definitions) and to describe its social organization and internal stratification, in particular the role played by large kinship groups and by intermarriage among them.

The original starting point for the study was a small but cogently argued treatise on the desirability of long-term investment in landed property, *Heng-ch'an so-yen* (Remarks on real estate), by an exemplary member of the ruling elite, Chang Ying (1638–1708) from T'ung-ch'eng, Anhwei. This county, which lies in the central Yangtze valley, in the very heart of China, attained a certain renown in the Ming and Ch'ing dynasties for its production of notable officials, scholars, and intellectuals, most of whom left voluminous writings. In addition it offered three widely separated editions of its local gazetteer and an important biographical work on the famous men of the county, plus a truly remarkable number of genealogies compiled by local lineage organizations, not to mention other minor writings relating to the area.[2] Thus T'ung-ch'eng appeared an ideal focus for a study of this kind, through which it would be possible to evaluate Chang Ying's theories against the detailed background of their time, place and society. Assuming T'ung-ch'eng to be not totally atypical of the rest of China, it was felt that this might then throw some light on many of the keenly debated issues in the social and economic history of the Ming–Ch'ing period, some of which will be outlined in due course below.

Chang Ying has been considered a fairly typical example of a man who rose via the examination system to high office and distinction at court. He became a *chin-shih* in 1667 at the comparatively early age of twenty-nine and was immediately appointed a bachelor (*shu-chi-shih*) of the Han-lin Academy. In the course of his career he came to occupy several prestigious and influential posts, including those of director of the emperor's private secretariat (*Nan-shu-fang*), head of the Supervisorate of Imperial Instruction (*Chan-shih-fu*, which was responsible for the education of the heir apparent), chancellor of the Han-lin Academy, president of the Board of Rites and finally, in 1699, grand secretary. The details of his political career need not concern us at this point; suffice it to say that he managed to stay clear of most of the political feuds and factions of the K'ang-hsi reign and seems to have enjoyed the emperor's trust and favour throughout his period of high office, a twin feat that testifies amply to his own shrewdness and good nature. In general he is one of the more attractive characters to be found in Chinese government at this period and would appear to have deserved his success.[3]

It should not be forgotten however that he was by no means a completely 'new man' in government. As will be explained in more detail later, he came from a rather well-to-do family that had been settled in T'ung-ch'eng, a fertile and prosperous area, since the beginning of the Ming dynasty, and had evidently prospered through farming. At some stage, but certainly by the end of the fifteenth or beginning of the sixteenth century, Chang Ying's forebears were starting to acquire some education and in 1568 his great-grandfather, Chang Ch'un (1540–1612), finally became a *chin-shih*, later rising to provincial office. His uncle and his father's cousin both held high office, the latter as president of the Board of Punishments and of the Board of War in the early Ch'ing, and by the mid seventeenth century the family must have been held in considerable esteem locally. Chang Ying retained close links with his native place; he was fond and proud of his family and both his actions and his writings, as will be seen, bear witness to his anxiety that its success, prosperity and prestige be prolonged.[4]

Heng-ch'an so-yen was most probably written around the year 1697 when he was temporarily at home on leave from court duties. Its immediate audience was no doubt his own six sons (some of whom showed promise of emulating their father's career) and other young men of his family, but it may well be that he hoped it would reach a wider public also. If so, his hope was fulfilled, for it was many times reprinted, as a whole or in part, and seems to have enjoyed considerable popularity. A complete, annotated translation of it is presented as an appendix to the present work, but its main arguments will be summarized here in order to make clear their major implications and their bearing on some of the controversies already alluded to.[5]

Chang Ying's principal theme, reiterated over and over again, is that the only safe way of investing money is in land, for land is the only form of property that never depreciates, can be neither stolen nor destroyed, and can also be transmitted to one's descendants and be preserved in the family over generations. This he asserts has been the case ever since state ownership of land was abandoned and private ownership permitted, a change which he ascribes to the Ch'in dynasty (221–206 B.C.). He admits freely that the returns on land are far lower than the profits to be made from commercial enterprises such as trade, pawnbroking and usury, but argues that these arouse envy and resentment and are easily lost if kept in liquid form and not invested in land, the only secure asset. Only those who are immensely experienced, such as the merchants of Hsin-an (Hui-chou prefecture in southern Anhwei) and Shansi, are able to avoid such perils. He does not condemn trade as a socially inferior occupation and admits that it is permissible for a poor scholar to lend money for a time; his only substantial objection is to the risks involved in making this a permanent profession. To sell land in order to go in for trade, therefore, sooner or later inevitably means financial suicide, yet he notes with alarm that some of his contemporaries (especially young men given to extravagant pursuits and dazzled by the prospect of easy money) are tempted to do just this. Even if they do not sell their property they neglect it, and regard land management as a low and rustic occupation. Thus they lose touch with rural conditions and the fundamentals of economic life.

Such an attitude is foolish and shortsighted, for while the returns from land are comparatively low and may be further depressed, he implies, by low grain prices, they are steady and dependable. It is also possible to increase them by careful personal management. The wise landowner will promote the most intensive possible cultivation of his land (entailing the planting of a wide variety of crops, multiple cropping and good fertilization); select and supervise his tenants carefully so as to prevent laziness, carelessness and collusion with his servants to defraud him; undertake irrigation improvements, essential to any increase in productivity; and, finally, train his heirs in these principles of management. Moreover he should take care that their inheritance consist only of land and not cash, for the former is relatively hard to sell quickly whereas the latter is easily dissipated.

By these means, and by careful budgeting of expenditures against income, avoiding all extravagance, it is perfectly possible, he asserts, to avoid falling into debt and losing one's land to powerful and wealthy neighbours. (Interestingly, he never once mentions taxation as one of the problems besetting the landowner, which would seem to imply that it was not oppressive enough to constitute a great disincentive.)[6] In this way it is quite easy to live comfortably on the rent from one's land, which can of course be augmented by further purchases. He shrewdly observes at this point that poorer land is far cheaper than good land and thus brings greater returns on capital investment, if efforts are made to improve it. All this he reveals has been the practice in his own family for at least five generations and is still going on. He assumes moreover that it will continue, as is evidenced by his statement that the descendants of the careful landowner, even if they are reduced to being 'poor commoners', will still own land which they do not work themselves and will have a servant to collect their rents for them.

This brings us to the crux of the whole work, contained in its final section, namely the argument that investment in land is an essential part of a long-term strategy whereby a family can maintain its position among the well-to-do and influential sector of society. 'Wealth and honour', the universal social goals, cannot be counted on to last of themselves; the only way to renew them is by a joint programme of systematic land investment coupled with education. The former, needless to say, provides the wherewithal for the latter, which with luck and application will lead eventually to an official post.

The enlarged income which this implies will permit the family to live in the city for a time, but office (and the high standard of living it brings with it) cannot be expected to last for ever. It is essential therefore to maintain a close interest in property in the countryside so that after a generation or two the family can return to this and continue the work of conserving and building up their resources, ready for another spell of official life. This he apparently envisages as a cyclical process that will continue indefinitely provided that the strategy is properly carried out. The key to it however is, above all, land.

If Chang Ying's arguments are taken at face value they are seen to contain some implications of considerable significance. The first is that land was not merely a desirable but also an essential security for any individual or family that wished to remain prosperous, for it was the only sure way to preserve and transmit financial assets over any length of time. Secondly, it was not merely a security but a productive investment that could provide its owner with a safe and respectable living. The periodic division and gradual fragmentation of landholdings due to the absence of primogeniture, usually cited as a disadvantage of exclusive reliance on land, was apparently not necessarily so, for it seems to be assumed that a man's heirs would be able to build up their holdings anew on the basis of what they had inherited, as Chang Ying himself did. Though the wherewithal for this might, it is true, be provided by a spell in office, it is not stated that this was the only way to do it, and it is clear that in Chang Ying's scheme it is landholding that initially precedes office and not the other way around. In other words, what he is saying is that the social position of the educated elite is, or should be, based on the long-term ownership of land. With this asset its members ought to be able to survive temporary fluctuations of fortune and periods out of office and yet remain in the literate, leisured and relatively affluent stratum of society.

The only way to discover whether Chang Ying's assertions are an accurate reflection of the realities of his times is to investigate carefully the economy and society of his home area and the history of his own family, of which record survives from the late fourteenth century down to 1933. It is to this that the following chapters will be largely devoted. It should be noted at the outset however that his statements conflict with some influential views on the Chinese ruling class and its economic foundations in the Ming and Ch'ing period. It will therefore be as well at this stage to give a brief account of the historical background to Chang Ying's work and the conflicting theories that have arisen, in order both to explain the reasons for his preoccupations and to set them in a much wider context.[7]

When applied to the earliest period of Chinese history, from the very beginnings down to around the first half of the T'ang dynasty (618–906) Chang Ying's views, though nostalgic, are almost undoubtedly correct; the wealth and power of the ruling elite at this time were indeed founded on the ownership of land. In the almost entirely agrarian economy of the North China plain, characterized by comparatively sparse population and low agricultural productivity, primitive communications and as yet slight use of money, this was only to be expected. Though trade did begin to develop, particularly in the period of unification under the two Han dynasties (206 B.C.–221 A.D.), it was mainly on a limited, local level or else in a few high-cost luxury items like silk or, in the case of salt and iron, necessities with a limited area of production. Much of the agricultural surplus available was drawn off by taxation and thus did not enter the commercial sphere. Even this limited commercial development was considerably set back during the centuries of invasion and disunion that followed the collapse of the Eastern Han and the profession of merchant continued to be the lowest in the social scale. In the absence of a highly developed exchange economy it was there-fore necessary to maintain a certain degree of self sufficiency, and so the rich and powerful in China, as in early medieval Europe, established the basis of their wealth in land.

This accounts for the perennial problem, which Chang Ying acknowledges, whereby the attempts of the rich to accumulate large holdings resulted in the gradual dispossession of the poorer peasants. In periods of unified govern-ment spasmodic efforts were sometimes made to check this, usually justified in terms of the precedent of state ownership and allocation of land that was held to have existed under the Chou dynasty. Thus in the Western Han proposals were made by Tung Chung-shu around 100 B.C. for a limitation on land ownership and the usurper Wang Mang instituted a short-lived nationalization of the land in 8–23 A.D. Private estate building flourished unchecked throughout most of the period of disunion, however, until a further ambitious attempt at land equalization, the *chün-t'ien* system, which was inaugurated by the Northern Wei (386–535) and continued into the T'ang dynasty. Though part of its purpose was perhaps initially to promote the opening of new lands, the major aim, especially later, was undoubtedly to limit the formation of large estates.

It must be emphasized however that the ruling elite of this era was by no means the same as that of Chang Ying's own times. Though society in the Han dynasty was relatively mobile (or at least not characterized by strict status distinctions) that of the period of disunion became strongly hierarchical. The ruling class came in fact to resemble a hereditary aristocracy composed of clans and families of varying age and prestige whose position and influence in the government depended less on imperial patronage than on their independent prestige and power, the latter being based on their landed wealth.[8] In the conflict between their duty as officials of the state and their interests as private landowners it was almost inevitable that the latter would win out, and this was in fact one of the complex of reasons for the abandonment of the *chün-t'ien* system in the later eighth century. Thereafter attempts at state ownership did finally give way to the free market in land that Chang Ying obviously considered one of the most crucial features of economic life. This permitted an even more rapid building up of estates, particularly in the more recently colonized and immensely fertile Yangtze valley and southeast. After the An Lu-shan rebellion (755–763) this was being done by a much wider variety of people, including military men and parvenu officials in the service of local military governors, and by no means only the old aristocracy.

It was at this period and in the centuries following that there gradually took place two momentous and closely interrelated changes that were to transform Chinese society and the economy, and to alter in subtle ways the nature of the ruling class and its hold on wealth and power. The first was the gradual disappearance of the old aristocracy, which was replaced by a bureaucracy recruited by and large on the basis of proven ability rather than hereditary status, and thus drawn from a much wider sector of society. Henceforth wealth and status would give no automatic access to office and political power; the vital intermediate stage was now an intensive literary education and ability to pass a series of elaborate and highly artificial competitive examinations. A family's continued predominance in government could thus no longer be assured.

The second major development was the growth and diversification of commercial activity (paralleling the progressive breakdown in the hitherto rigid social structure) that began in the second half of the T'ang dynasty with the gradual trend towards a money economy and the disappearance of the state-controlled marketing system. This process, as is well known, was enormously accelerated in the Sung dynasty by the heavy southward shift of population to the rich Yangtze valley and delta, where continued reclamation and drainage work plus improved agricultural techniques and seed varieties produced high yields and large food surpluses. These, and better transportation by water, permitted the growth of markets, towns, and cities on a scale hitherto unknown. The increased urban demand for goods and services proved an immense stimulus to trade, industry and the development of commercial institutions and credit facilities. From now on money and goods circulated more widely and a national market was created in the sense that probably no area of China remained any longer completely isolated and self-sufficient. There was even a certain degree of regional interdependence in the provision of foodstuffs, particularly rice to feed the great cities of the south, and the role of merchant lost some of the stigma hitherto attached to it.[9]

Despite this unprecedented degree of commercialization it seems unlikely that it resulted in any immediate and fundamental change in the economic base of the ruling elite. There is certainly evidence to show that the broader social group from which Sung officialdom was drawn did take advantage, albeit covertly, of the new commercial opportunities open to them, in that they loaned funds to merchant enterprises, invested in urban property and warehouses, went in for discreet usury and so on. Many of them moreover, especially in the lower Yangtze area, came to live in towns or cities, and extravagant urban standards of living could perhaps best be kept up by trade, as well as peculation while in office. Nonetheless the greater insecurity of their hold on power seems to have intensified their desire for solid financial assets and thus their need to invest in land. At this stage the population of the Yangtze valley and southeast was still not particularly dense, there was much fertile land lying waiting to be reclaimed and despite complaints of heavy taxation it seems certain that its profitability was considerably increased by commercialization and the growing demand for agricultural produce on the market.

The character of land tenure in Sung times and the nature of relations between landowner and labour force are still matters of considerable controversy into which it is not proposed to enter here.[10] It is clear however that large holdings in this period as later were in general worked not by hired labour but by tenants. There is moreover evidence to suggest that these tenants were frequently of rather low social status. In particular they might owe extra dues and services to the landlord in addition to their rent, and were apparently not allowed to rent land from more than one owner, nor transfer their tenancy at will. In some cases their disabilities were such that they were termed serfs (*nu-p'u*). Though conditions varied enormously with locality, and the geographical extent of serfdom is unknown, there are signs that in some areas a relationship of superiority and subordination between landowner and tenant did persist until much later times.

Private landholdings were of course always subject to fragmentation on the owner's death, though it should be borne in mind that property at this time and subsequently was never freely alienable by the individual owner; his immediate family and other relatives had rights of objection and preemption which did act as a brake on the rapid dispersion of estates among outsiders.[11] Nonetheless it is significant that attempts were made from the Northern Sung onwards to institute a type of family property that would be held jointly in perpetuity as an inalienable trust, thus avoiding the problem of fragmentation. This was the charitable estate (*i-chuang*) first devised by the statesman Fan Chung-yen at Soochow around 1049 in order to provide permanent maintenance and education for all the branches of his family. It came at a period of renewed interest in the promotion of large-scale kinship organizations and activities on the local level. The ostensible purpose of this, stressed by Neo-Confucian theorists, was to maintain good social order through the strengthening of hierarchical family relationships. One may speculate however that it may also have been an attempt by the new bureaucracy of Sung times, recalling the power wielded by the great aristocratic clans of the T'ang and earlier, to strengthen its own social foundations and to give itself greater security on the local level against the power of the state. How successful these efforts may have been in practice in later times will form one of the major themes of the present work.[12]

To recapitulate, the ruling elite by the end of the Sung dynasty was markedly different from what it had been in the early T'ang. It was now a much more broadly based social group with no automatic rights to office but enjoying easy access to education (now almost the exclusive route to office) by virtue of its wealth. This wealth, though undeniably augmented by commercial activities of various kinds and by the proceeds, illicit and sanctioned, of office holding, was still based fundamentally on land, which besides being lucrative was the safest and most socially acceptable form of property. Some mobility into the top status group of officials and degree holders was undoubtedly possible, but this must in almost all cases have been conditional on the initial independent acquisition and preservation of the wealth that alone permitted education.[13]

The major question to be asked at this point is therefore to what extent this situation may subsequently have altered in the Ming and Ch'ing dynasties, a period of relative peace and stable government, prosperity and rapidly rising population, when the social and economic changes under way in the Sung came to full fruition and the governmental system reached its most sophisticated level. This is of course the period to which Chang Ying's arguments relate directly, and it is significant that they seem to imply that in certain basic respects the economic foundations of the ruling elite were very similar to what they had been in Sung times. Was he in fact right? Or was he merely voicing the views of old-fashioned Confucian orthodoxy that were no longer entirely applicable in his own day and even less so later? More detailed answers to these questions must be attempted in the following chapters, but enough work has been done on this period to permit a preliminary outline of the changes that did occur and the ways in which they may account for certain aspects of Chang Ying's theories.

It is clear, first of all, that the diverse commercial activity that had flourished in the Sung continued and increased enormously throughout the following centuries. The full extent and regional spread of these developments has yet to be determined but it seems probable, despite the assertions of some Chinese Marxist scholars that the 'sprouts' of industrial capitalism were being nurtured at this time, that the changes were of degree rather than of kind, that is, that they did not entail fundamental shifts in the economic organization of society.[14] Commercialization was facilitated by the rapidly rising population that both resulted from and further promoted the still more intensive exploitation of the rich, rice-growing lands lying along the Yangtze valley and to the south. This, along with improved irrigation methods and better seed varieties, meant higher yields and widespread prosperity, so that the rural population had more surplus to exchange on the market. The use of money became far more prevalent, partly owing to a large inflow of silver from the New World from the sixteenth century onwards.[15] By this time many labour services and even land tax payments were being commuted to silver, which obviously increased both the peasant's and the landlord's need to sell agricultural produce on the market.

This resulted in some commercialization of agriculture, in that farmers in certain areas began to specialize extensively in cash crops to supply the needs of urban centres. Such crops were not limited to foodstuffs—grain, vegetables, fruit, sugar cane, and so on—but included the raw materials for burgeoning urban and rural handicraft industries. Thus for example the peasants of Sung-chiang prefecture in south Kiangsu found it far more profitable at this period to grow cotton (by then the most popular clothing material of China) than grain, while those around Lake T'ai came to specialize in mulberry trees and silkworm-rearing — both to supply the needs of the local textile industries. In regions where cash crops were popular (and that seems to have included most of the lower Yangtze, Chekiang, Fukien and Kwangtung) less land, inevitably, was devoted to food grains. Thus grain had to be imported by water from the central provinces of China such as Anhwei, Hunan and Hupei. By the Ch'ing and perhaps earlier this was also true of raw materials such as cotton, which was obtained from Honan and Shantung, as demand in the delta area outstripped supply.

Urban manufacturing, greatly increased regional interdependence and a more complex marketing network meant that the role of the merchant in society became both more essential and more lucrative. Though the volume of long-distance trade was still undoubtedly limited by high transport costs, local trade proliferated. Business organization and techniques became more sophisticated and vast commercial fortunes were made, particularly in government monopolies such as salt. Certain areas became famous for their business men; one such was the prefecture of Hsin-an or Hui-chou in Southern Anhwei, a mountainous and overpopulated area whose inhabitants had been forced to rely on commerce for survival ever since Sung times. By the end of the Ming they came to dominate the grain trade of the Yangtze valley and were also prominent in the salt monopoly, pawnbroking, usury and other activities. It was their hereditary expertise and highly developed business ethics, evidently admired by Chang Ying, that enabled them to survive the all too real risks attendant on any form of commercial venture in traditional China. The absence of legal safeguards and resulting lack of business confidence, poor credit facilities and exorbitant interest rates, severe local price fluctuations and poor transport, and, above all, the ruthless squeeze of officialdom all combined to make trade a hazardous and speculative business that could easily, as Chang Ying warned, ruin the inexperienced or unwary.[16]

Even so there is ample evidence that officialdom itself and the educated elite from which it was drawn, seeing the profits to be made from business enterprises, were often avid to share them and quite willing to ignore the traditional Confucian prejudice against trade. Even in the late fourteenth century many high officials engaged in the salt trade, despite a prohibition against it, and some Ming officials came from a merchant background. Others put the profits of their peculation in office into ventures like iron smelting, pawnbroking and usury, while some of Chang Ying's colleagues in the early Ch'ing, like Kao Shih-ch'i and Hsü Ch'ien-hsüeh, had extensive interests in pawnshops.[17]

This does not necessarily mean that they gave up all interest in owning land, as Chang Ying feared. No member of the social elite in China would have considered it a respectable goal to become a professional merchant (rather, it was the merchant who usually aspired to the ranks of officialdom, or at least the respectability conferred by a degree) and it was probably always desirable to maintain some safe, profitable assets that would more or less look after themselves, permitting the gentleman to enjoy scholarly cultivation and to educate his sons. The real question is to what extent land was still able to meet this need throughout the period, that is, to what extent its long-term profitability and the propensity of the elite to invest in it might have been affected by commercialization, tax changes, population pressure and so on. If the effects of these were in the long term adverse, could land ownership indeed be entirely replaced by other sources of income and, if so, which?

It is impossible to give a definite answer to the question at this point and may long continue to be so, for the simple reason that too little is known. Undoubtedly there must have been enormous regional and local variations across the country as a whole, but a great deal of information on conditions before the twentieth century comes from the highly developed areas of the

Yangtze valley and south-east coastal provinces where tenancy and commercial agriculture were most prevalent and which cannot be entirely typical
of the rest. Even here the evidence is fragmentary and often contradictory.

As far as is known at present it appears that in the early Ming and later
commercialization in general had the fairly predictable effect of increasing
the profitability of land. Most manufacturing was after all still limited to the
processing of agricultural products and urban populations depended on
outside supplies of foodstuffs.[18] Some large landowners by the sixteenth
and seventeenth centuries apparently took to commercial farming on an
extensive scale, using hired labour, but this seems on the whole to have
been rather rare.[19] Most, as will be explained shortly, probably let it out
and collected rent. Concentration of ownership, particularly in the lower
Yangtze valley, was a problem from the very beginning of the dynasty. The
first Ming emperor is reported to have had 59,000 rich families transported
from their estates in Chiangnan and Chekiang to the capital and their lands
converted to government property. Various reasons have been given for this
move, but even assuming that his aim was to break down large estates and
halt the dispossession of the peasantry (as may have been partially the case)
it seems to have had little effect, for there were continuous complaints of
estate building in this region throughout the rest of the Ming.[20] By the mid
seventeenth century Ku Yen-wu could assert that in Soochow prefecture
for instance nine out of ten persons were tenants and oppressed by heavy
rent payments.[21]

To what extent tax pressures may have constituted a disincentive to landownership throughout the Ming is still a debatable point. As has been recently demonstrated by Ray Huang, the official level of land tax was actually
fairly low.[22] The major burden of government exactions was the miscellaneous labour services which taxpayers were called upon to perform in
person and which were assessed progressively on the basis of property and
household size. These were greatly increased in the fifteenth century and
appear to have been onerous. Officials and degree holders were however
given a generous series of graded exemptions from them and in practice
might evade the remainder, thus increasing the burden for those not so
privileged.[23] In some areas at least this apparently did deter even the well-
to-do from landownership; in one part of Fukien in the early sixteenth
century it was said that 'these hardships [of heavy labour service] ruined
families; even the local official households could not avoid them and so the
rich and noble did not buy much land'.[24]

This situation appears to have been effectively eased by the so-called
Single Whip reform, carried out piecemeal in many parts of south China
in the second half of the sixteenth century, whereby in general most labour

services were combined into one, commuted to silver, and assessed as a small surcharge on acreage or existing tax assessment.[25] There is some evidence to suggest that this move to lighten the burdens of landowners and reduce tax evasion did actually stimulate further the demand for land. Ku Yen-wu directly attributed the rapid growth of absentee landowning around Nanking in the later sixteenth century to the fact that from that time onwards 'labour service was not an unfair burden and people began to realize the profits to be had from cultivating land; rich families from the cities became eager to buy land and poor people in the countryside were unwilling to surrender it lightly'.[26]

It may well be, given the fairly low level of basic tax assessment at this time in all regions except the Yangtze delta, that it actually did not constitute any great disincentive to large-scale land acquisition. It could in any case be evaded by the really influential. Sources for the late Ming are full of accounts of rapacious land-grabbing and tax evasion by great families. In Chiangnan some of them, like that of Grand Secretary Tung Ch'i-ch'ang, are asserted to have had holdings of hundreds of thousands of *mou*. This is in fact highly improbable in view of the increasingly acute competition for land due to population pressure in this region. Huang estimates, plausibly, that in Chiangnan by this time holdings of over 10,000 *mou* were rare and most large owners may have had no more than 2,000 or so.[27] On the whole it seems likely that there was a steady downward trend in the average size of large estates throughout the Ming and Ch'ing, owing to increased population and competition for land.[28]

Rapidly increasing population and commercialization between them seems also to have brought about some changes in land tenure and in the relations between owners and labour force. It is difficult to generalize about this owing to enormous regional variations and our ignorance of conditions in many parts of the country, but at present it seems safe to say that on the whole the social position of tenants was improving in the Ming and Ch'ing and that this may have affected the attitudes of those traditionally disposed to invest in land on a large scale.

It appears that in at least a few areas where large-scale landowning had been prevalent since the Sung, especially in south China, a hierarchy of superiority and subordination between masters and tenants persisted well into the Ming dynasty. This was certainly the case, as Fu I-ling has shown, in much of Fukien and in parts of southern Anhwei, notably Hui-chou prefecture (Hsin-an). Under this system tenants were still in effect little more than serfs and were indeed frequently termed such (*tien-p'u* or *nu-p'u*). Though they paid rent and could own property they were still bound hereditarily to the land and to one master, who might often supervise them personally. They owed him all kinds of extra dues, service and obligations beside their rent, such as presents of livestock and poultry at New Year, compulsory service in his household, particularly at festival times, and work on construction projects. In effect they were thought of as part of the landlord's household in the same way as domestic servants, and in ideal circumstances could actually benefit from his exercise of Confucian paternalism.[29]

There were signs however by the fifteenth century or so that this state of affairs was changing, especially in regions where commercialization was most advanced. Now that the landowner could obtain more goods and labour on the market there was far less need for him to maintain self-sufficiency on his estate and personal service from his tenants (it was for similar reasons that the state found it possible and more efficient by the sixteenth century to dispense with most corvée labour and to hire government workers instead). With the expansion of the rural population and therefore of the available labour force, it was no longer so important to tie the tenant hereditarily to the land and might well be advantageous to be able to change tenants at will. In any case in commercialized areas more landlords, attracted by the pleasures of urban life, were beginning to move to their local towns rather than stay on their estates. For this reason they were less able to supervise their tenants closely and perhaps took less personal interest in the working of the land. This could be advantageous for the tenant but equally it meant the gradual dissolution of the personal, almost family tie between him and his master, so that the latter was now more often disposed to exploit his labour force ruthlessly for the sake of commercial gain.[30] The apparently growing trend towards absenteeism also made it a matter of indifference to the landlord whether his holdings were concentrated or dispersed: this, along with increased competition for land due to population pressure, meant inevitably that the latter form of holding came to prevail.

The effects of all these changes on the attitudes of tenants were equally striking. Because individual holdings were becoming smaller they were now more anxious to retain or to acquire security of tenure and to hold on to as much of their produce as possible.[31] They also began to resent service obligations to their masters, their own subordinate status and their inability to change their tenancy at will. Though complaints and demands varied enormously in different parts of the country there is no doubt that serfs were becoming restive; in Fukien for instance by the mid fifteenth century cases of rent resistance were fairly common and occasional riots and revolts broke out.[32] As a result, the tenancy system was undoubtedly changing in many areas long before the end of the Ming. It became normal for tenants' obligations to be clearly stipulated in written contracts and in some cases they began to secure the right of permanent tenure on their land. This encouraged the development and spread of the system of 'two masters to one field' (*i-t'ien liang-chu*) and its variants, whereby the tenant in effect became the owner of the surface of the land he worked (the landlord retaining only the sub-soil) and could sell or mortgage it at will, all of which no doubt made it increasingly difficult for the original owner to have a say in its management.[33]

These changes were to come to an abrupt climax at the end of the Ming dynasty, when rural discontent was aggravated by the corruption and demoralization of local government and a series of seven extra levies on the land tax. These appear to have been largely evaded by rich landowners whose rapacious desire for land and exploitation of their tenantry are reported to have grown apace. They frequently extended their holdings by a kind of protection racket known as *t'ou-hsien* or *t'ou-k'ao*, whereby they assumed supposedly nominal ownership of the land of poor persons in return for protecting it from taxation. In these circumstances clashes were inevitable. As one late Ming landowner put it: '. . . people were in general acquisitive and aggressive . . . there arose conflicts between masters and serfs . . . and the violent ones opposed and insulted their masters . . . [all] the proper bonds were loosed . . .'.[34]

The outcome was the series of massive revolts that ravaged north-west and central China in the 1630s and 40s. At this time discontented serfs and tenants all over the Yangtze valley seized the opportunity to take violent revenge on their masters and to assert their equality and independence. There seems no doubt that these prolonged and bloody risings accelerated the disappearance of the old system of social relations in the countryside. Though in some areas harsh treatment of tenants and severe obligations did persist, serfdom was effectively ended by the eighteenth century, a fact recognized by the Yung-cheng emperor's edict of 1727 abolishing 'base' status. The relationship between master and tenant became on the whole a more purely commercial, contractual one, a matter of convenience rather than personal obligation. In general the tenant could now rent from more than one owner and could terminate his lease at will. Even if he did not have formal ownership of the surface (this system never became universal) he still often in effect enjoyed permanent tenure as a kind of customary right and proved increasingly difficult to shift even when in long-standing arrears with the rent. This was hardly in the long-term interest of the landlord, especially the absentee owner whose main interest in the property lay in the steady income it was supposed to provide. Memories of violent revolts and resistance no doubt discouraged landlords from taking reprisals against their tenants and there are some signs that a rather more humane or at least cautious attitude towards them was emerging.[35]

All this, coupled with the attractions of commerce and usury, may to some extent have discouraged the well-to-do from putting their money into land and made them more ready to rely on other sources of income. There were other reasons too, at this time, why land might have appeared a relatively less attractive prospect. One, alluded to by Chang Ying, was probably the low price of grain throughout the second half of the seventeenth century, consequent on a series of good harvests and a temporary improvement in the population—land ratio in many areas in the aftermath of the revolts.[36]

Another deterrent, though its effects are extremely hard to evaluate, may conceivably have been the taxation policy of the Ch'ing government in its early years. The Manchus naturally were anxious to alleviate the rural discontent that had had such catastrophic consequences and to this end restored the basic land-tax quotas to what they had been in the 1570s before the imposition of the surcharges. They also granted several years' tax exemption on devastated land. One major reason for rural unrest however had been widespread tax evasion and the high-handed behaviour of the local elite. It was essential to check this without at the same time alienating completely the stratum of society on which the new government depended for its supply of officials. It is therefore not surprising that in 1657 severe cuts were made in the generous tax exemptions hitherto permitted to officials and degree holders. Henceforward all exemptions assessed on the basis of the land tax were abolished and they were allowed a labour service exemption of only one fiscal individual (*ting*) each, a privilege that was not to be extended to their families.

Considerable efforts were also made to stamp out illicit practices like *t'ou-hsien*, to prevent the maltreatment of tenants and to check large-scale tax evasion by locally powerful persons. The most spectacular instance of this was the so-called Chiangnan tax clearance case of 1661 when no fewer than 13,517 degree holders and officials and 240 yamen employees were investigated for tax default and subsequently punished by dismissal, deprivation of degrees and titles, confiscation, imprisonment and flogging. The immediate effects of this were to spread shock and alarm among the elite of the lower Yangtze region; land was occasionally sold off as an unwelcome liability and in some places its price for a time fell sharply.[37] All official tax exemption moreover was in theory ended in 1728 when the individual *ting* labour service charge was finally merged with the land tax and assessed simply as a surcharge on it.[38]

Whether any of this really constituted a major long-term deterrent to landowners is, however, rather hard to say. (As was noted earlier, Chang Ying's silence on the matter seems to imply that it did not.) There is much evidence (some of it relating to T'ung-ch'eng, which will be discussed in detail in Chapter 3) to show that the local elite was still quite capable of defending its own interests in matters relating to taxation. One notable instance is the way in which the projected national land survey of the 1650s and 60s, which aimed at a fairer redistribution of the tax load, was finally shelved owing to local opposition.[39] That their ingenuity in finding ways of evading tax payments could be boundless has been amply demonstrated by the work of scholars like Hsiao Kung-ch'üan.[40] Ch'ing land tax rates more-over were actually fairly moderate and from the eighteenth century quite certainly failed to reflect the increase in agrarian population and pro-ductivity.[41] It may well be that the major effect of the Ch'ing measures, especially the severe cut in tax exemptions, was to help reduce the extreme disparities of wealth and privilege in the countryside that had characterized the late Ming. On the other hand this may also have been in part the effect of tenant assertiveness, increased competition for land and the trend in some areas towards fragmentation of property rights.

Conditions in the seventeenth century thus do help to explain Chang Ying's fears and preoccupations, especially his insistence on the need for reliable tenants, his castigation of extravagance and absentee landlordism, and his awareness of the counter-attractions of commerce and usury as alternatives to investment in land. He was nonetheless still absolutely con-vinced of the importance and profitability of landowning, and there is no question that interest in the acquisition of landed property did continue long after his own time. Innumerable cases can be cited throughout the Ch'ing dynasty of officials, merchants and others owning land on a fairly consider-able scale.[42] By the middle of the eighteenth century concern was being voiced over the renewed concentration of landownership in many parts of China, and in 1743 a proposal that individual holdings be limited to 3,000 *mou* had to be dismissed as impractical.[43]

The important point to be established however is not simply whether the social elite went on buying land in the Ch'ing dynasty but how important a role it can have played in their total financial position, given that it was now becoming more expensive and harder to obtain, could be rapidly divided up by the inheritance system, and that other, more profitable sources of wealth were certainly available. In other words, can it be claimed in any sense at all that ownership of land was basic to maintaining membership in the elite? Or did it form only a minor and dispensable part of their total economic assets? It is over this question that there has to date been most confusion and least agreement.

Some scholars, while not denying that interest in land-holding as a form of security did continue, consider that its attractions were greatly diminished by the late eighteenth century and that in highly commercialized areas far more capital went into trade, usury and so on, or else was simply hoarded in the form of cash, jewellery and antiques, etc.[44] Hatano Yoshihiro indeed postulates two distinct patterns of investment by officials, those who lived in the country still investing predominantly in land while those in cities or in urbanized areas preferred commercial ventures or making loans. The latter, he feels, was becoming much more prevalent in the nineteenth century.[45] On the other hand Muramatsu Yūji in some extremely well-documented studies, notably of landlord bursaries or rent-collecting organizations, has shown that even in highly commercialized areas like the Yangtze delta right down to the early twentieth century land could still bring sufficient returns to make it an attractive investment for the absentee owner. He therefore asserts that it was still 'the most easy, secure and respectable way of living a prosperous, independent and influential life', and that this state of affairs did not change much until the 1920s.[46]

The most extreme position on this question has been taken by Chang Chung-li in his two well-known studies on the Chinese gentry. Briefly, his contention is that by the nineteenth century the returns to be had from land were continually diminishing because competition for it pushed up land prices faster than those of grain. Increasing population and rural poverty also meant that rents became much harder to collect, while the corruption of local government officials and underlings further ate into profits. The only landowners who could avoid 'squeeze' (and also regular taxes) and had some chance to collect their rents in full were those who enjoyed the same privileges and status as local officialdom, that is, those who had an official position or a degree themselves.[47] Even they however could not maintain or build up holdings of land on any scale and avert the effects of division by inheritance without continued access to the opportunities for money-making afforded by examination success and official position. Land was therefore of comparatively little real importance to the social elite, many of whom, he asserts, owned none whatsoever.[48] Absolutely the only way to acquire a fortune and to maintain a high standard of living in his view was to obtain the formal educational qualifications which opened the way to lucrative official positions and other supposedly profitable careers such as teaching and the management of local projects. Even large-scale commercial activity by the end of the nineteenth century is said to have been monopolized by degree-holding 'gentry' who alone had the power to protect their interests.

By these means he arrives at a view of the ruling elite in the Ch'ing that is completely the reverse of that implied by Chang Ying's arguments (namely that it was essentially a landowning group whose landed income gave access to education and therefore, periodically, to office). In his scheme the social elite depended for its very survival on access to degree-holding, office and the wealth they alone conferred; without this privileged position no independent source of wealth could be maintained for long. This leads him in consequence to define the elite (the 'gentry', *shen-shih* or *shen-chin*) in purely formal terms as consisting of only those who held degrees or office and as a result enjoyed economic privileges denied to the rest of the population. In this way they constituted, he feels, a clearly demarcated social class the membership and mobility into and out of which can be very precisely measured.

Such a definition was implicitly accepted (albeit with considerable criticism on points of detail) by Ho Ping-ti in his influential study of social mobility in the Ming and Ch'ing. Owing to the highly competitive nature of the examination system and the successive division of wealth by inheritance it was obviously impossible for any individual family to preserve its place at the very top of the government and educational ladder for very long. By examining the immediate antecedents of *chin-shih* winners and the fate of the descendants of high officials he is therefore led to conclude that there was a considerable degree of mobility in the society as a whole (particularly long-range downward mobility) though this varied at different periods.

It is unfortunate that these important and stimulating studies, by starting out from an exceedingly narrow, formal definition of what constituted the upper class in Chinese society have in their different ways obscured some of the questions they set out to clarify. As D. C. Twitchett has already pointed out, there is a basic linguistic fallacy in the attempt to identify a Western concept like 'class' with the Chinese term *shen-shih*.[49] A class is usually defined above all in economic terms, whereas the *shen-shih* were a group whose prestige and privilege depended in the first instance on formal educational qualifications regardless of individual economic standing. They should thus be more appropriately regarded in Western sociological parlance as a status group (as Max Weber in fact defined them).[50]

The group of *shen-shih* at any one time was so small a proportion of the total population that it seems unlikely that it can ever have been synonymous with the whole of the affluent and leisured stratum of Chinese society.[51] There must surely have been wealthy persons who did not possess membership in the strictly defined *shen-shih* group and, equally, members of the latter who were far from affluent. To measure mobility simply in terms of this tiny elite (and particularly its top layer of office holders) is therefore not the same as measuring mobility between classes in Chinese society as a whole. The attempt is even more unreal when it fails to take account of the wider family groups to which almost all office and degree holders must have belonged. It is improbable that the relatives of an official would necessarily be members of a different social class from that to which he himself belonged, and possible that apparently 'newly risen' degree winners were in fact from extended families with a tradition of wealth and education.

The directly opposing view on all these questions has been put most forcefully by the Chinese sociologist Fei Hsiao-t'ung.[52] He considers on the basis of his own family experience and extensive fieldwork that even in the twentieth century, long after the abolition of the examination system, 'gentry' and peasantry constituted two distinct classes in Chinese society. The former, the 'leisure class' (about 20% of the population), was still maintained economically by owning land and politically by access to official positions – a view that accords well with that of Chang Ying in the late seventeenth century. Furthermore mobility between the two classes was, he feels, rather limited. In particular, gentry very rarely reverted to peasantry, that is, to a life of physical labour on the land. The major reason for this was the existence of kinship groups organized by the gentry for their own mutual security and protection (a view challenged however by some other authorities who feel that such gentry kinship relations were merely 'the accoutrements of wealth' rather than 'techniques of continuing aggrandizement').[53]

Historical study of the Chinese upper class and its economic foundations is as yet in the very early stages and it will be many years before definitive judgments can be made on the controversies outlined above. It should once again be emphasized that many of the more extreme views on the social and economic history of this period have arisen from overambitious generalization on the basis of patchy evidence collected from a few areas, in particular the prosperous and highly commercialized Yangtze delta and south-eastern seaboard which there is no reason to consider typical. In the study of a country as vast and varied as China the absence of precise regional definition is fatal, in that it leads the historian to assume a uniformity in social and economic activity that can by no means be proved. The only way to counteract this and to provide material for more valid generalization is by the study in depth of as many different localities as possible. The present work is offered as one contribution to this long-term project.

It will adopt as far as possible an empirical approach, avoiding the usual tendency to view the 'gentry' purely in terms of their formal status and relationship to the central government. The principal aim is to investigate the history of Chang Ying's home county throughout the Ming and Ch'ing dynasties in order to discover what was the real economic basis of local wealth, education and influence and to what extent this was correlated with formal elite status. It should thus be possible to ascertain just how the local elite was formed and constituted, how mobile or how exclusive a group it was, and by what means and with what success individual families attempted to preserve their position in the long term. This will also entail an examination of the role which the elite played in local administration and the ways in which it tried to defend its own interest against those of the government.

The chapters which follow will be devoted, first, to a description of T'ung-ch'eng itself, its history, economic, social and cultural development; second, to a discussion of landowning and taxation in the area; and third, to an examination of local kinship organization, in particular the history of the Chang family itself and others.

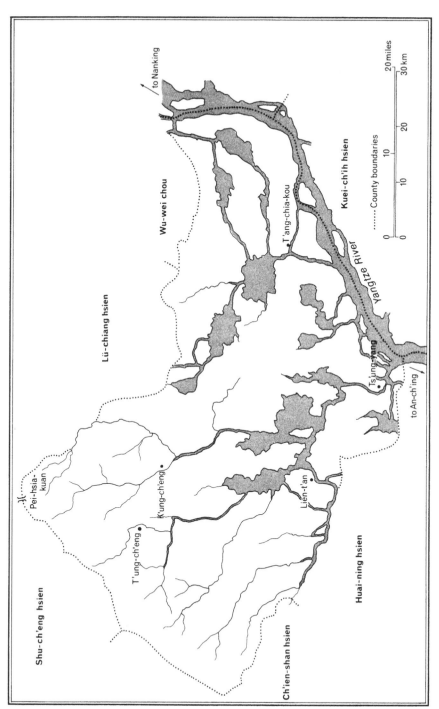

T'ung-ch'eng county (adapted from *Chiang-nan An-hui ch'üan-t'u*, 1896)

2
T'UNG-CH'ENG COUNTY

What follows is a sketch of the history, economic, social and cultural development of the area of Anhwei province from which Chang Ying's family came,
where he spent the first thirty years or so of his life and to which he retired
in old age. It is drawn largely from information found in the three available
editions of the county gazetteer, its genealogies and a variety of other sources.
Unfortunately, as is nearly always the case, contemporary chroniclers, compilers and scholars apparently took for granted and neglected to record much
that would have been helpful to the modern historian's understanding of
the area, so that the picture that emerges is still fragmentary and much less
clear than one would wish. It is sufficient however to give some idea of Chang
Ying's background and the ways in which this must have conditioned his
thinking, and thus to set in perspective the more detailed investigations
that will follow.

It may seem to those concerned with the great events and trends of
Chinese history in the past few hundred years that the affairs of one county
are of but trivial, parochial significance. Nonetheless, as has already been
indicated, T'ung-ch'eng did become a place of some importance in Chinese
political and intellectual life and was thus by no means outside the main-
stream of history. Though it would be dangerous to regard it simply as a
microcosm of Chinese society in this period (for no individual case can ever
be wholly typical) the study of a strictly delimited area does permit a sharper,
more precise focus than is ever possible in one on a nationwide scale. It is
only the assembly of many such investigations of individual localities in
widely separated parts of the country that can ever provide the means to
evaluate some of the ambitious generalizations already formulated on Chinese
economic and social development.

This kind of study is also valuable in that it forces the historian for once to
look at Chinese society as most Chinese themselves must have done, that is,
not from the vantage point of the central government but from that of the
local community. The sense of local attachment and intense local pride which
they felt is usually ignored or under-rated, but that it often existed strongly

cannot be doubted. The magistrate who sponsored the compilation of the first edition of T'ung-ch'eng's gazetteer in 1490 did so because of regret and indignation that the county received so little attention in the Ming imperial geography, the *Ta-Ming i-t'ung-chih* of 1461. He was quite confident that despite the locality's hitherto modest record of accomplishment its history and current achievements were still of sufficient interest and importance to warrant recording for posterity. Indeed, to neglect to do so was to court the indignation of posterity, for 'in later days they will look at the present as the present looks at the past', and failure to record events in full was to deprive future generations of knowledge that was rightfully theirs.[1] Such sentiments, and such pride, were fully shared by the compilers of later editions of the gazetteer and by those many scholars of T'ung-ch'eng who wrote about their home area. Thus the history of the county, which mattered intensely to those who lived there, may prove to have some intrinsic human interest besides providing a convenient focus for the study of Chinese economy and society.

The present-day county of T'ung-ch'eng is situated in south central Anhwei, to the north of the Yangtze, something over 100 miles up the river from Nanking. It is thus in the very heart of China, in the region of temperate, deciduous forest and mixed rice—wheat agriculture.[2] The Yangtze valley was not extensively colonized by Chinese settlers until T'ang times or even later, and thus the earliest history of the area is obscure. What is certain is that the name T'ung has long been associated with it, for in the Warring States period this region was said to be the state of T'ung (T'ung-kuo), part of the greater kingdom of Ch'u. In the Han it was known as T'ung-hsiang, an administrative district of Ts'ung-yang *hsien* in Lü-chiang *chün*, and it is recorded that the name was chosen because the area abounded in oil-bearing t'ung trees.[3] The precise boundaries of the Han district are unknown, though it quite possibly covered much more than the present county. It must however have been very different in character from what it became in later times, a sparsely populated area of hills, lakes and dense woods, with swamps and marshes extending all along the Yangtze.

The district apparently changed hands, and names, frequently throughout the period of division between Han and Sui. In the latter it re-emerged in the guise of T'ung-an *chün*, which at this stage seems to have been identical with the whole of the area that was later to become An-ch'ing prefecture. It was first clearly identified as a separate county, with the name of T'ung-ch'eng county and with the county seat in its present location, in the T'ang dynasty, in the years 756—7 (precisely the period of the An Lu-shan rebellion). The larger unit of which it formed a part was at this time called Shu-chou, but by the end of the twelfth century was designated An-ch'ing *fu*.[4] T'ung-ch'eng thus existed continuously as a county (though possibly within contracting boundaries, as administrative divisions proliferated in the Yangtze valley in this period)[5] from the T'ang right through to the Ming and Ch'ing. At the beginning of the Ming it was one of the six counties of An-ch'ing prefecture, part of the province of South Chihli or Chiangnan.

From descriptions in the two later editions of the gazetteer, as well as from the evidence of modern maps, it is possible to get a reasonably clear idea of the general topography of the area.[6] The county at this period was roughly fifty miles from east to west at its widest point and thirty-five miles from north to south. It had good east–west communications by water along the Yangtze, to the south-west and south via Kiangsi, and to the north by road to Lü-chiang county and so to Peking, about six hundred miles away. The seventeenth-century edition of the gazetteer describes it enthusiastically as 'the gateway to Anhwei province'.[7]

The terrain is varied, the major contrast being between the north-west and the south-east. The former is predominantly hilly or mountainous, with numerous watercourses, and remained fairly thickly wooded until well into the Ch'ing dynasty. What little agricultural land there was in the north of the county, on the boundary with Shu-ch'eng county, was said to be poor and the people simple and rough. The western parts, adjoining Huai-ning and Ch'ien-shan counties, were famous for their beautiful scenery; their deep caves and gullies also served the more practical purpose of a refuge for the population in times of trouble. Farming here too was difficult, the major products being timber and charcoal, as well as bamboo and tea. The county city is set in a small plain among these hills, away from the danger of flooding from the Yangtze, and on the main road from the north to the provincial capital.

The southern and eastern areas, though hilly in places, include much flat, fertile, alluvial land, covered with lakes, pools and streams. Many of the lakes in the centre and south of the county were annually connected up 'for a distance of a hundred *li*' by the spring and summer inundation of the Yangtze, whose waters receded again in the autumn and winter. To the east of these lakes was an area of extremely fertile land, said in the seventeenth century to be more expensive than anywhere else in the county. Along the banks of the Yangtze and to the east again stretched a long expanse of marsh, sandbars and reeds, also very fertile when properly drained. As will be shown, much of the good agricultural land in the county had originally been marsh, and was only reclaimed gradually in the Ming and Ch'ing as population increased and agricultural efforts intensified.[8]

It was no doubt the northern and western areas, away from marshes and floods, that were first settled in the remote past. The earliest inhabitants were probably a non-Chinese people, for they are described as being hard and fierce, with savage customs and beliefs; these persisted until the area was eventually civilized, presumably by Chinese settlers from the north.[9] It appears however that throughout the pre-Ming period it remained fairly sparsely populated and was never intensively exploited. As the early Ming edition of the gazetteer reports, it was fought over from the period of the Three Kingdoms down to the Yüan dynasty, and the people never had a chance to live in peace.[10] There are no contemporary records of this early period and rather little is known even of events in the Sung and Yüan.

The county, although reputedly prosperous, was certainly not in the least distinguished in the Sung, for it produced a mere 6 winners of the *chin-shih* degree and only one official of any note whatsoever.[11] When compared to the only outstanding area of Anhwei at this time, the rich and already highly commercialized prefecture of Hui-chou or Hsin-an to the south of the Yangtze, it was obviously a mere backwater; Wu-yüan county of Hui-chou alone produced 61 *chin-shih* in the Northern Sung and 124 in the Southern Sung.[12] Yet it should be noted that even at this time in T'ung-ch'eng there were some 'great' or 'powerful' families who were evidently landowners, for they took the opportunity during the fighting at the end of the Southern Sung to seize the land that had belonged to the Confucian temple and school.[13]

What happened to these families between then and the Ming dynasty is not clear. Warfare during the transition period between the Southern Sung and Yüan was prolonged. The county administration had to be moved from T'ung-ch'eng city itself first to Ts'ung-yang on the Yangtze and finally across the Yangtze. Meanwhile the city was sacked, the Confucian temple destroyed and the sons of the local elite (*i-kuan*) scattered like the common people. Some of them no doubt returned but it seems that not until after 1314 was the Confucian temple rebuilt, its land recovered and something like a normal state of civil administration resumed.[14] Peace was to be short-lived, for less than forty years later the whole area was torn once again, this time by the revolts and military campaigns that heralded the fall of the Yüan in its turn.[15]

There is no doubt that this was the great turning point in the history of the area. The whole Yangtze valley at this time was in a state of upheaval for the best part of twenty years. T'ung-ch'eng was damaged in the fighting but seems to have escaped more lightly than other places. As it was without walls its magistrate, a Mongol, judged it better not to waste lives on defending it and went instead to assist in the defence of An-ch'ing, where the governor held off the rebels for a long time.[16] Other places were not so fortunate. One of the areas worst afflicted was north Kiangsi, especially Jao-chou prefecture around the Po-yang Lake. Fighting went on here continually from 1352 and the future Ming founder himself campaigned here for several years. By the early 1360s, as one county gazetteer informs us, 'the waters of the Po-yang lake were completely red' and the whole area was in addition suffering from drought, famine and pestilence.[17] Another devastated region was the hitherto prosperous and populous prefecture of Hui-chou in south Anhwei, which was eventually taken by Ming T'ai-tsu in 1358.[18]

This prolonged turmoil appears to have caused a major redistribution of population along the Yangtze valley, a movement which, although it has never yet been adequately documented, was probably in large part responsible for the more effective exploitation of the whole region in the Ming and thus indirectly for much of the prosperity and cultural flowering of the era. It is certainly possible to trace a major movement of people to the T'ung-ch'eng area and surrounding counties at this time, and it is unlikely that this can have been an isolated case.[19] The move is explicitly described in the case of the 'first ancestor' of one of the county's later notable lineages, the Tais of Hsiang-shan. This man was Tai Chih-fu, whose family had lived in a village called Wa-hsieh-pa in Jao-chou prefecture on the Po-yang Lake for generations. When the fighting started many of the local population decided to escape. Hearing that the An-ch'ing area was well defended and had good grain supplies 'several tens of them and more took their old folk and children and went there in search of food and a trouble-free place to live; this gentleman was among them'.[20]

The Tais were not the only ones to arrive in T'ung-ch'eng in this way. As the county's greatest modern scholar, Ma Ch'i-ch'ang, observed: 'The families of our district for the most part moved here from other areas in the transition period between the Yüan and the Ming.'[21] A survey of all the genealogies available for local lineage groups shows that of their 'first ancestors' no less than 20% came at this time from the same village of Wa-hsieh-pa as the ancestor of the Tais, and about as many again from elsewhere in Po-yang county.[22] Among the latter were Chang Ying's own ancestors.[23] Of the rest the largest single group came from Wu-yüan county in Hui-chou prefecture, where the recorded population in the early Ming dropped to half what it had been in the Yüan.[24] This influx of refugees must have been large for it appears to have swamped the existing population. Of the families later famous in the county only a very few could trace their descent to ancestors who moved there before the late Yüan.[25]

When these enterprising settlers arrived at the beginning of the Ming they found an area of 'beautiful scenery and fine customs' where 'the inhabitants were few and the land empty and uncultivated'.[26] The expanded population, according to the first Ming registration (probably reasonably reliable), was 58,560 persons and 10,427 households, large for such an area by contemporary European standards but still only a fraction of what it later became.[27] It appears that many of the immigrants settled first in the west district of the county or around the county city, or else in the north and north-east, avoiding the low-lying and easily inundated parts of the south and south-east, most of which were probably still undrained at this stage.

Their first action in every case seems to have been to appropriate some land and to set to work to farm it. The 'first ancestor' of the Tais, mentioned above, opened up no less than 300 *mou*, all of it irrigated, somewhere in the west district of the county. This he must have done in a rather short space of time for by the 1360s he had amassed enough grain from it to be able to present 300 *shih* to the future Ming T'ai-tsu on his campaigns. (This prudent move in 1370 earned him a life-long remission from all labour services.) His household at this time consisted of only six persons, two adult males, two boys and two females, so it is certain that to work his land he must have had some tenants or serfs.[28] Similar actions are reported of other early settlers, for instance one P'an Jung-i, who also moved with his brothers from Wa-hsieh-pa and settled at Mu-t'ou-shan. 'From the beginning he raised his family through farming' and his offspring and those of his brothers also opened up land there, so that the whole area became settled by P'ans and 'there were no other families there'.[29]

Some of the settlers must have been forced to embark on quite ambitious irrigation and even reclamation projects if they were to exploit their new lands effectively. One case is that of the first recorded ancestor of the Ch'engs, another family that had moved from the Po-yang area. He left his original holdings in T'ung-ch'eng in alarm when Ming T'ai-tsu started moving great landowning families to Nanking, and went instead to live in the west district; here he was heard to complain of the expense of repairing dikes and building embankments for his land.[30] From the very beginning of the dynasty, under the pressure of this influx of population, efforts were made to promote irrigation on a large scale. (It seems though that pressures at first were not so intense as to force the reclamation of much marsh land along the Yangtze; this started in the following century.)

The first major public irrigation project was started by the magistrate Hu Yen, who held office in T'ung-ch'eng from 1399 to 1402. 'He taught the people to construct dams and embankments and to improve their efforts in farming; he diverted the waters of the T'ung river from the north to the south-west to irrigate 10,000 *mou* of land. It was he who started work on the T'ung dam.' This refers to the diverting of the T'ung river through the county city to irrigate elevated and parched land on the other side of it. The system was improved and repaired by an outstanding magistrate in the late fifteenth century, Ch'en Mien, and even two hundred years later was said to be the major irrigation scheme in the county.[31] In addition in the fifteenth century several large water storage ponds (*t'ang*) were built, on orders from the central government. By the end of the century there were twenty-six in all, long and rectangular in shape (one or two were as long as six thousand feet but only thirty or so feet wide). Innumerable private ponds were also constructed and by the late sixteenth century occupied approximately 4% of the registered acreage.[32] It is certainly not hard to see why Chang Ying a hundred or so years later insisted on their importance.

There is no doubt that, despite the county's proximity to China's major trade route, the Yangtze, and its comparatively short distance from the Yangtze delta and from Hui-chou, the economy of the area in the late fifteenth century was overwhelmingly agrarian. The list of local products in the 1490 edition of the gazetteer, in contrast to later ones, consists almost entirely of food crops (besides local flora and fauna). There is no section on commercial products at all and no readily identifiable cash crops. Tea is not mentioned nor, more surprisingly, is cotton, nor indeed any other textile fibre, though another source indicates that a coarse variety of hemp (*ko*) was anciently grown there. The most important crops were rice, wheat and barley, as well as pulses, fruits and vegetables of various kinds. Early ripening rice (*hsien*) was grown, along with the normal late variety and glutinous rice, so that double cropping of rice with a winter crop was obviously possible. T'ung trees, probably the major local source of oil, must have been found mainly in the northern and western parts of the county. The most important occupation besides farming was evidently fishing in the lakes and streams and along the Yangtze; here a heavy fish tax was levied, and also a reed tax on the inhabitants of the reedy sandbars.[33]

It must have been possible for the inhabitants at this stage to be largely self-sufficient and there is little sign that any were involved in non-agrarian pursuits (except, presumably, domestic handicrafts for home consumption). They were said to be sincere, honest and frugal and to work hard at farming, a stereotyped description but certainly not indicative of extensive commercial occupations.[34] A little trading must have gone on but was probably very localized or else in luxury goods, salt, metalware and so on. It is also possible that there was a limited exchange of products between the different parts of the county, perhaps timber and bamboo for grain and fish. Only two places outside the county city before the sixteenth century were actually termed market towns (*chen*). These were Ts'ung-yang, a port on the Yangtze and also the site of a tax collection office, and Pei-hsia-kuan, on the county's northern boundary with Lü-chiang county, on the major route linking T'ung-ch'eng with the north (here there was a police office). There was however a market at Lien-t'an, at a crossroads on the way to the prefectural and provincial capital at Huai-ning (An-ch'ing) to the south, where a hostel for travellers and merchants was rebuilt in the 1480s.[35]

In the fifteenth century then, the way to become prosperous in T'ung-ch'eng was to own and to farm land, and there is no doubt that the ancestors of those who were later to become illustrious in the county's history did precisely this. The ancestor of the Tais has already been mentioned; one of his descendants was the important and ill-fated scholar Tai Ming-shih (1653—1713) who recorded that their wealth, farming traditions and ownership of land continued throughout the fifteenth and sixteenth centuries, indeed to his own times.[36]

Records of individual holdings are unfortunately almost unobtainable, save in a few cases where the size of a holding is noted on the registration certificates of 1370, some of which are preserved in the genealogies. The first ancestor of the later Tso lineage for instance had fifty *mou* of land and a tiled house of three rooms, a modest enough beginning.[37] Most references to landowning occur in connection with such matters as the division of family property or the performance of charitable deeds. Some of the Yao family (one of the very few whose forebears moved to the county before the Ming) were definitely well-to-do landowners in the late fourteenth and early fifteenth centuries. This is shown by the case of Yao Hsien (1372—1432) who was renowned for his strictness and probity. He at first shared the paternal estate with his younger brother. 'His family had long been wealthy and when his brother asked for a division of the property he initially refused . . . [on the grounds that brothers should live together] . . . When the brother persisted Hsien selected the richest fields and finest houses to give to him, and kept the worst for himself. The local people thought him very righteous.'[38] A case of a somewhat similar nature occurred in the Fang family (whose descendants were also later famous in T'ung-ch'eng and even in China as a whole), showing that they too relied on landowning. A certain Fang Mao in the early fifteenth century was orphaned very young and forced to cede much of the family property to his father's elder brother. He worked hard to build it up again, however, and his family in consequence prospered.[39]

Aid to the poor, especially in times of famine, became something of a tradition in the area (note that Chang Ying emphasized it) and occasionally gives glimpses of the economic status of the families who carried it out. One instance is to be found in the Tso family (that of the later Tung-lin martyr Tso Kuang-tou, 1575—1625). At some time in the Ch'eng-hua reign (1465—87) some poor people who could not pay the heavy taxes on reed land were arrested and imprisoned. A certain Tso Lin and his wife planned to pay the arrears for them but did not have enough ready cash. They therefore decided to sell some rich land, and also to raise a loan for the purpose if that were not enough. The fact that in order to raise a large sum of money all at once they would have to sell land indicates that most of their wealth must have been in this form.[40] Chang Ying's own forebears had acquired property by the late fifteenth century, if not earlier, as is shown by his mention in *Heng-ch'an so-yen* of his fourth-generation ancestor Chang P'eng (Master Tung-ch'uan). According to the genealogy 'his times were peaceful and the family prospered'. He himself was at pains to stress that his land was poor and infertile but his anxiety lest it should be grabbed by some powerful family rather indicates that this was not the case, and one account says that he was 'known locally for his prosperity'.[41]

It is quite clear however that many in T'ung-ch'eng even at this early stage had greater ambitions than to be merely wealthy farmers, and perceived that education and official positions were the route to enhanced local prestige and possibly even greater wealth. Perhaps too they were inspired by the record of official success of Hui-chou prefecture to the south, whence so many of them had originally come. Some of the county's early magistrates (including Hu Yen, mentioned above) were keen to promote education there. One of them, Ch'ü Na-hai, early in the Yung-lo reign (1403–24) had the Confucian temple and school rebuilt on another site; the gazetteer notes that 'it was from this event onwards that the people of T'ung-ch'eng first began to distinguish themselves in examinations'.[42] How much effect these official efforts really had is uncertain but there is no doubt that in the fifteenth century, after the first *chin-shih* success in 1404, T'ung-ch'eng began to produce a steady trickle of degree winners and officials. Throughout the century there were twelve *chin-shih* and forty four *chü-jen*. Some of them subsequently became officials, in minor provincial or county posts.[43]

Though it was a portent of things to come, this record is undeniably modest, especially for the period when according to Ho Ping-ti the possibility of upward social mobility was at its highest.[44] What is important however is to note some of the names that appear in this list of degree winners and also the kind of family background they came from, for there are signs that even at this early stage Chang Ying's joint prescription of agriculture combined with study was being put into effect, and that some families were managing to do this fairly consistently over an extended period.

The family name which occurs most frequently in the list of examination successes for the fifteenth century is that of Fang. Five Fangs attained the *chü-jen* degree in these hundred years and two of them became *chin-shih*. As it turns out, all these men were related to each other in a direct line of descent.[45] The first of them, *chü-jen* in 1399, was Fang Fa (1368–1403) whose ancestors had moved to the area from Hui-chou at the end of the Sung and had thus had a long time in which to build up property there. Fang Fa's father died very early in his life and it was his mother (née Ch'eng, whose parents had insisted that she be married into a notable family) who made him espouse the civil arts and study as his father had done, in contrast to the generally militaristic tone of the times. After his success he obtained a post in the office of the regional military commissioner in Szechwan but got mixed up in the political feuds of the Chien-wen era (1399–1402) and drowned himself in the Yangtze on his way home to T'ung-ch'eng in 1403.[46] It was his elder son, Fang Mao, who was mentioned above as having built up the family property again so successfully after his father's death. (The land can hardly have been acquired by his father solely on the proceeds of three years in a minor office, however, and must have been in the family beforehand.) Fang Mao had no degree of any kind himself but educated his own five sons very strictly. It was from him that all the later Fangs of any importance were descended.[47]

Two of these five sons, Fang Yu and Fang Kuan, did well in the examinations in their turn, the former becoming a *chü-jen* in 1447 and *chin-shih* ten years later; he eventually became prefect of Kuei-lin in Kwangsi. The latter was a *chü-jen* in 1465 but held no office. The eldest son, Fang Lin, on the other hand, simply lived the life of a wealthy landowner in a large joint household with his brothers and two male cousins, and supervised the family strictly. Every morning he gave his instructions that some were to plough, others to study and others to help with the management of affairs. The Fang family rules were said in consequence to be renowned in the district. Fang Lin's son Yin continued these strict traditions and in 1477 reaped the reward of a *chü-jen* degree followed by a post as county magistrate. His family was still rich but it is emphasized by his biographer that he did not make any of his money through his office, in which he died after a few months.[48] The other *chin-shih* of the Fang family in this century was Fang Hsiang, a grandson of Fang Mao by another son, Yü (again a farmer), who won his degree in 1481 and also became a prefect.

I have digressed in such detail over these seemingly unimportant individuals partly for the reason that it was from them that all the branches of what was later to be the Fang lineage were descended, and its members continue to appear at intervals right through the county's history.[49] Another reason is that they exemplify so well at this early stage the growth of the tradition of agriculture and study that Chang Ying recommended. It is obvious that in their case landowning was indeed the basis of their educational success, for their official posts were often of minor importance or did not last long enough to be really lucrative. In two cases they actually found their official salaries so inadequate that they were forced to supplement them with their landed income. Fang Yu while in office got his brother Lin to send him some of the 'family wealth' to assist him and Fang Kuan had to resort to selling the rent grain from the family land for this purpose.[50]

Other examples of this will be found later, but one other fifteenth-century success that should be noted is the 1451 *chin-shih* degree of Yao Hsü, eventually followed by his rise to a post in the Yunnan provincial administration office. He was a son of the landowner Yao Hsien, mentioned above. Though no others of his family were so distinguished at this time, the name is another of those destined, as will be seen, to play a major role in T'ung-ch'eng's history.

Overall however the county's record of achievement in this period was but modest, a fact acknowledged rather regretfully by the compilers of the first gazetteer in 1490. One of them was the magistrate Ch'en Mien (in office from 1485), who made enormous efforts to improve the county's educational showing. He personally instructed the local *sheng-yüan* and repaired the Confucian temple. He also on central government instructions founded twenty-four schools throughout the county for the education of local boys; poor ones were to be supplied with paper and brushes and also a monthly grain ration.[51] Monuments to the county's degree winners were erected and re-paired, presumably to encourage emulation. The compilation of the gazetteer itself, with its detailed listings of all those who had in any way distinguished themselves, was no doubt intended to have the same effect. At all events the local *sheng-yüan* were reported to be delighted with the work.[52]

Whether these measures had any direct effects, or whether they were merely symptomatic of rising local ambitions, is uncertain. It is clear however that from roughly the early sixteenth century onwards T'ung-ch'eng began to undergo a gradual transformation, from a very minor backwater into a place known throughout China as the home of scholars and great officials. Though the reasons for this transformation, and in particular for the county's eventual pre-eminence over the surrounding area, were no doubt complex, the most immediately apparent cause was its rising population and prosperity. These in their turn were closely connected with the increase in commercial activity in the Yangtze valley at this time, something from which the local economy could not fail to benefit.[53]

The county's population figures after the first Ming registration are of very dubious value and for the most part greatly understated. The most obvious instance of this is that the figures given for registered households and persons in 1631 are identical, save for one digit, with those of 1383, two and a half centuries earlier. That the population was nonetheless increasing rather rapidly is hinted by the luckily preserved figures for 1481 which give a total of 109,650 individuals, nearly a doubling of the previous figure of a hundred years before.[54] This again may not be accurate but it is not likely to err on the side of over-statement. Thus the growth rate of population in the fifteenth century may well have been close on 1% per annum, high for a pre-industrial society without the benefits of modern medicine.

It is certain that in the generally favourable economic conditions prevailing in the county the population must have gone on expanding throughout the Ming, at least as fast as in China as a whole during this period.[55] This is confirmed by the fact that more and more attention began to be devoted to the large-scale drainage and reclamation of hitherto inundated and unusable land, an indication that the existing cultivable acreage was filling up. The first definite reference to this occurs in the mid sixteenth century when the magistrate Ch'en Yü-chieh (in office 1563—6) had dikes built to reclaim waterlogged land along the Yangtze; the resulting fields were so extensive as to yield an annual harvest of 10,000 *shih* of grain.[56] Much of this work was probably undertaken on local initiative, for the seventeenth-century edition of the gazetteer simply states that the people living by the lakes and creeks and in the polder lands (*yü-t'ien*) along the rivers were allowed to carry out their own construction and maintenance of water control projects.[57] By this time, evidently, reclamation was so commonplace as to be worth no greater mention. It looks too as if the sandbars (*chou*) and reedbeds along the Yangtze were being steadily extended and opened up to cultivation, to judge from seventeenth-century references to their being used as agricultural land and complaints of tax evasion on it.[58]

At the same time as the labour force and land acreage were increasing there are signs that agriculture in T'ung-ch'eng was becoming more diversified and more intensive, a trend that fits in with what is known of farming elsewhere in the Yangtze valley during this period. Thus by the seventeenth century there was a far greater variety of crops and products than there had been in the fifteenth. There was no apparent change in the types of rice grown but a greater emphasis on winter cereals like wheat (used to make flour and noodles), barley (valued as a standby in years of poor harvests), and buckwheat (said to be a good autumn fill-in crop). Many more kinds of pulses and vegetables were found (the latter including yams for the first time) and local fruits now included such delicacies as grapes, pears, cherries and loquats. Even new trees made their appearance (or were exploited for the first time); examples are the tallow tree, of which the oil was used to make candles, and other varieties the bark of which yielded dye or could be twisted into rope. Thus Chang Ying's statement that every scrap of land could be utilized to grow something and that three crops could be grown in one year is quite plausible.[59]

The county also had some commercial products by the seventeenth century. The most important was tea, grown in hill plantations in the west district, though only one variety was said to be fine. These wooded areas moreover yielded honey and beeswax. Several textile fibres were produced, including ramie, *ko*, hemp and cotton, as well as indigo for dye. Paper was made from the bark of the paper mulberry and all kinds of products from bamboo, notably writing brushes, rainhats and umbrellas.[60]

There were likewise unmistakable signs of expanding commercial activity. The number of market towns increased from two to five, the additions being Lien-t'an (for which see above), K'ung-ch'eng, on the main road east from the county city, and T'ang-chia-kou, a Yangtze port in the east of the county (the area where land reclamation was probably most intensive).[61] Markets came to be held daily in the county city, whose 'many good merchants' were 'both energetic and honest'; inside and outside the city were several street markets.[62] A further indication that T'ung-ch'eng was becoming part of the increasingly monetized economy of the Yangtze valley was the implementation of the Single Whip tax reform there in the years 1563–6.[63]

It is important however not to exaggerate the scale and intensity of these developments. One should not assume that T'ung-ch'eng was undergoing the same degree of transformation as for instance the Yangtze delta and parts of Fukien, where large-scale urban manufacturing and intensive specialization in cash crops and handicraft production for the urban market were well advanced. Anhwei as a whole (apart from Hui-chou prefecture) was not one of the most commercialized provinces in the Ming. It produced no important specialities apart from tea, and its markets are said to have been on a smaller scale than those in neighbouring Kiangsu, or in Chekiang.[64] T'ung-ch'eng's commercial products, with the exception of one kind of tea and the umbrellas made at Lien-t'an, were not of outstanding quality. Most were probably produced domestically as off-season, unspecialized means of supplementing farm income, and were very likely sold locally rather than exported any distance, for all the surrounding counties produced similar things themselves.[65]

There is practically no evidence to indicate that very many of T'ung-ch'eng's inhabitants actually became professional merchants or artisans in this period, nor that any of its notable officials came from families whose fortunes were founded on large-scale trade or manufacturing.[66] The sources, particularly the genealogies, are in general remarkably silent on the subject of commerce. This does not necessarily mean that it was shunned or despised. Chang Ying, as was noted earlier, did not condemn it as a socially worthless occupation and few of the later lineage rules actually ever forbade it outright. Trade was a necessity of economic life and the later gazetteers mention the activities of merchants in the county with pride as an indication of local prosperity.

So far only three documented cases have come to light of people in T'ung-ch'eng taking up trade in the Ming, and it is significant that in two of them the activity was still closely tied to agriculture. Towards the end of the dynasty one Fang Hsiao (probably though not certainly a descendant of the Fangs described above) was forced by his stepmother to work at farming while her own sons were allowed to study. He found an outlet for his abilities in trading during the agricultural slack season, by which means he increased the family wealth tenfold in thirty years.[67] The other case, in the sixteenth century, was that of P'eng Chung-tao, who apparently had indifferent success in his studies and instead decided to trade his surplus grain down the Yangtze, something that proved highly profitable.[68]

These examples and the other available evidence suggest strongly that most local and large-scale trade, both inside the county and across its boundaries, was still in staple items of food, particularly grain, and also fish and salt. In the county city for instance the merchants were described as being good at 'selling grain dear and buying it cheap'. In the prosperous central district boats and carts were said to come and go continuously and rice supplies mount up. Much the same was true of the eastern districts, where carts and boats laden with fish and salt went to and fro, and supplies of fish and rice were conveyed for sale at T'ang-chia-kou, the second most important market town (after Ts'ung-yang) of the county. In the west district the people traded timber and charcoal, tea and bamboo, bracken and bamboo shoots, presumably in exchange for grain and other food supplies.[69]

In immediately adjacent counties the picture was the same. In Wu-wei *chou*, somewhat further east along the Yangtze, though most of the people were farmers, those who did become merchants traded largely in grain; as to other local occupations like 'collecting firewood, catching fish and growing vegetables, only poor people support themselves by these means, so how would they be sufficient for traders [to make a living from]?'[70] In Lü-chiang county to the north-east even at a much later date the major local product was still grain but it was mostly outsiders who traded it; the rich of the area did not go in for trade but occupied land and lived on rent.[71]

Thus it seems reasonable to infer that in T'ung-ch'eng the immediate effect of greater commercialization was not to divert people away from traditional agrarian occupations but to increase interest in them. Rising grain production, the proximity of a huge grain market in the lower Yangtze region, good communications by water and the presence of numerous merchants (especially those from Hui-chou) may well have meant an agricultural boom in the area from the mid Ming onwards. There was no great need for landowners to look for extra sources of income if selling rent grain could be highly profitable, and it is quite likely that those with large surpluses over consumption needs could prosper exceedingly. That this may have begun to be so even in the late fifteenth century is hinted by the case of Fang Kuan, referred to above, who sold his rents to augment his official salary.[72]

It is therefore hardly surprising that, of the many natives of the county who distinguished themselves in the second half of the Ming dynasty, just about all appear to have come from families whose major assets consisted of landed property, and that the tradition of education financed by farming that had taken root in the fourteenth century continued unabated thereafter. As a member of the Tso family was later to put it, quite unequivocally, when writing of the wife of a seventeenth-century forebear who had lived on the proceeds of his land: 'All families distinguished in official life were built up through farming . . .'[73]

Examples are numerous and would be tedious to cite at length. One of the most interesting, however, in view of the family's later prominence, is that of Yao Hsi-lien (1514–62), a great-grandson of the Yao Hsü who became a *chin-shih* in 1451. Yao Hsi-lien had studied in his youth but after prolonged disappointments eventually gave up examinations and devoted himself to managing his property and promoting the education of his six young sons. In his enthusiasm he went so far as to sell some land in order to engage the best possible teachers for them. Nonetheless 'he put great energy into farming and in the end became prosperous'. On his death his eldest son coached his brothers strictly in order that their father's hopes might be fulfilled. After getting them all through the first degree he himself gave up exams and spent the rest of his life farming. Many of Hsi-lien's descendants did well for themselves. Two of his grandsons, Yao Chih-ch'i and Yao Chih-lan, attained the *chin-shih* degree at the beginning of the seventeenth century and subsequently held provincial office (the former was the grandfather of Chang Ying's wife). It was later declared: 'Those persons in the Yao family who passed examinations and those who to this day are renowned and prosperous are all his descendants.'[74]

As will be seen in more detail later, there were precisely similar traditions in Chang Ying's own family. His great-grandfather, Chang Ch'un (1540–1612), the first of them to become a *chin-shih* (in 1568), could only afford to devote himself to his studies because he had inherited a large amount of property from his father. He became an official, but his only brother, Chang Chien, remained in the country looking after the land his father had left him.[75]

This is not to assert however that landed income could not be augmented by other means when opportunity arose. The fact that more and more men of the county began to pass the higher examinations and to obtain official posts of greater importance meant that new sources of wealth were opened to them. There is every sign that a great deal of this wealth, besides being used to finance a more affluent and even extravagant style of life, was channelled directly back into land. A clear case occurs among the sixteenth-century ancestors of the modern biographer Ma Ch'i-ch'ang himself. One of them was said practically to have 'ruined his family through philanthropic deeds' and his son, Ma Fei, continued this practice. 'In the Chia-ching reign [1522–66] once when there was a bad harvest he issued the contents of their granary and made gruel of it to feed the hungry, but it was not sufficient. The family had land east of Chu-ch'eng-tsui, so he mortgaged this to a rich man' and spent the proceeds on relief. This rich man, assuming that the Mas would be unable to redeem the land, started to build a house on it. On hearing however that one of the family, Ma Meng-chen, had in 1597 passed the provincial examination, he stopped, realizing that their fortunes would soon improve. Later Ma Meng-chen did indeed redeem the land with the proceeds of his office (though his descendant states firmly that it was with legitimately acquired salary, rather than unauthorized extras).[76]

This may have happened too among members of the Fang family in the late Ming. Fang Ta-mei, a fifth-generation descendant of Fang Kuan (on whom see above), became a *chin-shih* in 1585 and subsequently spent forty years in censorial and other office at the capital. On retirement when he divided his property among his sons he made out a complete inventory for them, saying: 'I have bought an extra 350 *mou* of land and also amassed 1,700 taels of silver. This was not acquired through office but resulted from gifts and bequests of friends and your mother's care and frugality.' His own great-great-grandson, Fang Pao (1668–1748), who liked to tell the story, explains that he was afraid that his sons would assume all this to be the ill-gotten gains of his official career and would despise him for it.[77] Ma Ch'i-ch'ang comments on how small his bequest was in comparison with those of other officials who were intent on accumulating wealth for their descendants.[78] It is not hard to deduce from this that it became fairly common in T'ung-ch'eng for officials to make sizeable fortunes and to invest at least some of the proceeds in land.

Another way to add to landed assets in this period was certainly usury, of which Chang Ying disapproved so strongly, and the mortgaging of other people's land. Explicit references to these activities are rather few (though the story of the Mas and their rich creditor is one) and a more detailed discussion will have to wait until the following chapter. To cite only one example, Chang Ying's own father, Chang Ping-i (1593–1667), the owner of over 2,000 *mou* of land, definitely made loans to people in the late Ming. This fact is only known, however, from reference to his charitable act in cancelling the debts during the troubles of the 1630s and 40s.[79] At a later stage, as will be shown, it became common practice to loan out rent income, or the cash obtained for it, at interest, and to buy land with the proceeds.

As is shown by some of the cases discussed above, the agrarian prosperity and wealth in the county from the sixteenth century onwards were increasingly being translated into education, examination success and in some cases official posts. Greater interest in the official sponsorship of scholarly activities is unmistakable at this time. During the 1520s or 30s the magistrate, Shen Chiao, and the prefect of An-ch'ing, Hu Tsuan-tsung, between them founded the county's first academy, the T'ung-hsi *shu-yüan*, on the site of a former monastery in the north-west district. Another academy was started by a later magistrate in the Wan-li reign (1573–1620).[80] In 1530 and 1574 purchases of land were made, with tax funds, for the support of the Confucian school and the county's official students.[81] In 1606 an enthusiastic sub-director of studies donated some money to construct a building of which the rent of 23 taels per year was also used to aid poor scholars.[82]

Scholarly interests and literary accomplishments, particularly in and around the county city, were said to have flourished from the Chia-ching and Lung-ch'ing reigns onwards; this may be presumed to refer to the 1560s, though greater prowess in the examinations became noticeable fairly early in the sixteenth century.[83] Between 1500 and 1600 there were 71 *chü-jen* and 39 *chin-shih* (in contrast to 44 and 12 respectively for the previous century); from 1600 up to the end of the Ming in 1644 there were 52 *chü-jen* and no fewer than 34 *chin-shih*. This makes a total of 85 *chin-shih* and 167 *chü-jen* for the entire dynasty, not perhaps impressive when compared to the record of outstanding areas of the lower Yangtze and Fukien in this period but still remarkable for a hitherto obscure county in a province with a moderate academic showing.[84] Anhwei comes only ninth in the Ming provincial league table with 1,036 *chin-shih*, of which T'ung-ch'eng produced approximately 8.2%.[85] Its inhabitants might now boast with some justification that it 'produces human talent in abundance, in a way that is not to be compared with other places'.[86]

That many of these examination successes were turned into official positions is shown by the fact that T'ung-ch'eng came to occupy fifteenth place among all the counties of Nan-Chihli (i.e. Anhwei and Kiangsu) in terms of numbers of posts held by its natives during the Ming. Among the counties of Anhwei it was third, ranking only behind She-hsien and Wu-yüan, both in Hui-chou prefecture (a remarkable contrast to their respective showing in the Sung, noted earlier).[87] T'ung-ch'eng's officials by the end of the Ming included some men of national eminence, such as Ho Ju-ch'ung (*chin-shih* 1598, later president of the Board of Civil Office and a grand secretary early in the Ch'ung-chen reign); Yeh Ts'an (*chin-shih* 1613, president of the Board of Rites in the T'ien-ch'i reign, 1621–7); Tso Kuang-tou (*chin-shih* 1607, the censor who espoused the cause of the Tung-lin party and was imprisoned and tortured to death in 1625); Chang Ying's uncle, Chang Ping-wen (*chin-shih* 1610, Shantung administration commissioner, who died fighting the Manchus at Chi-nan in 1639); and Fang K'ung-chao (*chin-shih* 1616, governor of Hukwang in the late 1630s).

Such men as these were a source of intense pride to the county, and many were subsequently honoured with a place in its shrine to the memory of eminent local men. Yet it should be pointed out that official position was apparently not an automatic, nor even the only, criterion for local esteem here in the late

Ming, for some of those enshrined among the local worthies were not distinguished by any higher degree or official post. The most notable of these was Fang Hsüeh-chien (1540–1616), a great-grandson of Fang Yin (see above) and grandfather of Fang K'ung-chao. He was an important local scholar who in his youth had avoided taking any examinations and more than once in his life declined appointment to office. He had been inspired with enthusiasm for the Neo-Confucian school of Wang Yang-ming by the county director of schools, Chang Hsü, and spent the later years of his life propagating these ideas and discussing morality with friends and disciples. (He did not support himself entirely by teaching though, for on the death of his wife's father, the prefect Chao Jui, he inherited the latter's property, which proved ample for his needs.)[88]

Though the esteem in which a man like Fang Hsüeh-chien was held locally may have had something to do with the achievements of others in his family, he does also exemplify the tradition of pure scholarship and intellectual distinction that was being formed in the county at this time. A strong interest in Neo-Confucian learning, especially that of the Sung school, is continually apparent and was to bear remarkable fruit in the eighteenth century. A shared scholarly idealism may well be one of the reasons why several of the county's officials besides Tso Kuang-tou became disastrously involved in the Tung-lin fiasco at court in the 1620s, and also why so many of its notable scholars participated in its successor movement, the Fu-she. Not surprisingly, their works feature prominently on the list of those proscribed in the Ch'ing.[89]

More interesting than the tale of individual successes in T'ung-ch'eng at this time is the fact that certain names and certain families constantly recur among them.[90] In the *chü-jen* lists of the sixteenth and seventeenth centuries down to 1643 there are fourteen more Fangs, all with one possible exception directly descended from those described earlier; nine of them became *chin-shih*. This is the largest single group of any one surname to figure in the lists. One of the next largest is that of Yao; seven Yaos became *chü-jen* in this period (mainly towards the end of it), all but one being the direct descendants of Yao Hsü (*chin-shih* 1451) and Yao Hsi-lien, and six of these became *chin-shih*. Other names that begin to feature with reasonable frequency in the lists are Ho (of whom the grand secretary Ho Ju-ch'ung was one), Wu, Ch'i and Tai, individuals of these names in most cases proving to be of the same families. Also to be noted, though they do not occur quite so often, are the names of Tso and Ma. Last but not least, four Changs rose to the heights of a *chin-shih* degree after the 1520s; three of them were relatives of Chang Ying, namely his great-grandfather, his uncle and his father's cousin.

What is more, investigation of these individuals of different families reveals frequently that they were further connected with each other, either by marriage or by scholarly and political association, occasionally by all three. Their inter-relationships were sometimes of such bewildering complexity that it would be tedious to enumerate them in detail; a few examples will have to suffice. The Fangs for instance can be shown to have had connections with the Yaos from the mid fifteenth century, ever since the Yaos' first *chin-shih*, Yao Hsü, formed a close friendship with Fang Lin, the real architect of the Fang family's success in this early period.[91] Fang Lin's great-great-grandson in the sixteenth century, Fang Hsüeh-chien, had as his closest disciple the *sheng-yüan* Yao Hsi-yen, a first cousin of Yao Hsi-lien (see above) and great-grandson of Yao Hsü. Yao Hsi-yen in his turn married his daughter to Fang Hsüeh-chien's son, Fang Ta-chen (*chin-shih* 1589).[92] The latter's son, Fang K'ung-chao (the governor of Hukwang in 1638, referred to above), had one elder sister married to Yao Sun-ch'i (1581–1602, a non degree-holder but a great-grandson of Yao Hsi-lien), and another to the heroic defender of Chi-nan, Chang Ying's uncle, Chang Ping-wen. Another female cousin was married to one of the Wu family.[93]

The Changs themselves, though emerging to prominence comparatively late, were not slow to form connections with others besides the Fangs. Chang Ying himself was at pains to emphasize that his mother was from the Wu family of Ma-hsi, noted for its scholastic and official traditions.[94] One of them, Wu I-chia (*chin-shih* 1556, provincial administration commissioner in Honan), had a grand-daughter who in the early seventeenth century married a Tai and thus became the grandmother of the scholar Tai Ming-shih (1653–1713, executed as a result of the first famous literary inquisition case of the Ch'ing dynasty). One of her daughters, Tai Ming-shih's aunt, in turn married into the Yao family in the mid seventeenth century.[95] The Yaos, as will be seen, from the early seventeenth century onwards were also beginning to make marriage connections with the Changs. Such instances could be multiplied almost ad infinitum, though at the risk of confusing the reader totally.

That these interlocking relationships might possibly be translated into an alliance in court politics even at this early stage is hinted by the fact that a sizeable group of T'ung-ch'eng officials joined together as Tung-lin partisans in the 1620s and suffered for it. Chief of them of course was Tso Kuang-tou, martyred in 1625.[96] Another was the censor Fang Ta-jen (*chin-shih* 1616, a member of the same Fang family discussed earlier, in the branch descended from Fang Yü and his son Fang Hsiang), who denounced the eunuch Wei Chung-hsien in 1623. He had long been associated in scholarly activities with Tso Kuang-tou and with Wu Ying-pin (*chin-shih* 1586, the son of Wu I-chia, mentioned above).[97] One of Wu Ying-pin's close relatives and friends, Wu Yung-hsien (*chin-shih* 1592), who had military responsibilities in the Liao-tung campaigns, also fell foul of Wei Chung-hsien at this time and was forced to retire, as was Wu Ying-pin's son-in-law, Fang K'ung-chao.[98] After Tso Kuang-tou's downfall it was a relative of Fang Ta-jen's, Fang Hsiang-ch'ien (*kung-sheng* in the 1620s), who arranged a collection of 1,000 taels to assist his family.[99] It is not surprising to find that many of the prominent leaders and sympathizers of the Fu-she were also related to these men. Among them were Fang Hsüeh-chien's great-grandson, Fang I-chih (died *c.* 1671), Tso Kuang-tou's youngest son, Tso Kuo-ts'ai, some of his nephews, and several others.[100]

One more fact that must be noted about these families (though discussion of its implications will have to wait until Chapter 4) is that some of them in the late Ming began for the first time to organize themselves systematically into lineage groups, that is, by listing all their members in genealogies, building temples for ancestral sacrifices and in some cases buying common land to finance them. Among the first to do so, perhaps not surprisingly, were the Fangs and the Yaos, the two families that had sprung to prominence earliest. Yao Hsü (*chin-shih* 1451) in the later part of the fifteenth century compiled a genealogy in which he attempted to include all the members of the family since their first appearance in T'ung-ch'eng in the Yüan dynasty.[101] In the sixteenth century Fang Hsüeh-chien, a member of what became the first branch of the Fang lineage, compiled its genealogy (possibly not for the first time), bought land to finance joint sacrifices and devised rules for the conduct of its members.[102] Fang Ta-mei (the official already referred to as being scrupulous over his acquisitions of land) in the early seventeenth century did much the same for its sixth branch by building a separate hall for it with ritual land attached.[103] Such activities, even if in rather rudimentary form, were undertaken by quite a few other families in the last fifty years or so of the Ming, including the Changs, Tais and Tsos.

From all this it is permissible to conclude that the society of T'ung-ch'eng by the end of the Ming dynasty was very different from what it had been at the beginning. Then it had probably consisted mainly of individual farm families, most of them very recent immigrants and differentiated from each other principally by the size of their landholdings and their relative affluence. In the course of two hundred years or so however there had arisen a distinctive local elite consisting of landowning families wealthy enough to finance protracted education and thus to gain academic and official success and the prestige that went with it. Though the above discussion is not exhaustive it is sufficient to demonstrate that one or two families became consistently rather good at this, and thus came in time to constitute the topmost layer of the elite. In all attempts to rank them, the Fangs and the Yaos come first, after them usually the Changs and the Tsos, and after them the important but slightly less distinguished ones such as the Wus, Mas, Hos and others.[104] There is also enough evidence to show that their social eminence began to be deliberately cemented by intermarriage over long periods. That members of such families could enjoy considerable local prestige without necessarily holding any higher degree or official post is suggested by the case of Fang Hsüeh-chien (and he is not the only example that could be cited).

With education and prestige came in some cases a change in style of life for these families. From the sixteenth century onwards it does appear that certain of them were no longer living on their original landholdings in the countryside but were moving instead to the county city, where literature and learning were beginning to flourish and presumably the amenities of urban life were to be found. The Yaos for example lived for generations at or around Ma-hsi in the east district where they had first settled, but in the tenth generation Yao Hsi-lien's grandson, the *chin-shih* of 1601, Yao Chih-lan, acquired a mansion in the city and went to live there. Many of the other educated and successful Yaos from this time onwards appear to have done likewise, and this particular house was still in the family's possession at the beginning of the nineteenth century.[105] Another example of this trend is afforded by a sixteenth-century ancestor of Tai Ming-shih, Tai Nan-chü (a wealthy man though not a degree-holder), who left his estates at Nan-wan and went to live in the east of the county city. Such moves did not mean the abandonment of interest in landowning, as is shown by the fact that Tai Nan-chü left his son at Nan-wan 'to take charge of the serfs and farming', and kept a close eye on him.[106] The Yaos likewise retained their ancestral property at Ma-hsi and many of them continued to live there.

The presence of increasing numbers of wealthy families in the county city at this time is probably one reason why the magistrate, Ch'en Yü-chieh (the second of that name, in office 1575–81), was able in 1576 to persuade the provincial governor and the resident elite to have the city fortified with walls. He was joined in his request by two well-connected members of local families, both *chin-shih* and officials, namely Wu I-chia (see above) and Sheng Ju-ch'ien. They subsequently helped to direct the work and may have raised contributions for it.[107] The need for defences was not apparent to everybody at the time, for T'ung-ch'eng had been peaceful since the beginning of the dynasty. When in 1616 an army passed through the county on its way north 'there had been peace for so long that the people were alarmed at the sight of the soldiers and many fled from them'.[108] Nonetheless, not many years later the situation in the county was such that city residents were to be glad of their walls.

Though it certainly cannot be shown that all members of important families took to urban life at the end of the Ming, those who did must have found it hard to retain their ancestral habits of peasant thrift and frugality, especially if they had large incomes from land (and in some cases office) to spend. It is not surprising, particularly in view of what is known of the behaviour of wealthy landowners elsewhere at this time, to read that urban families were becoming extravagant and overbearing and that this led repeatedly to social friction. The precise ways in which this arose are not very clear because the gazetteers, doubtless unwilling to offend powerful local interests, are deliberately vague in their references to it. The seventeenth-century edition, written when events were still recent enough to be painful, merely states in its description of customs in the county city that 'by the Ch'ung-chen period [1628–44] extravagance became excessive and distinctions were confused' and also intimates that in the prosperous central district affluence and extravagance resulted in habitual conflicts.[109] The 1827 edition, which reprints (without acknowledgement) Tai Ming-shih's account of T'ung-ch'eng's troubles, is however rather more explicit. 'Previously the scholar-officials and worthies of the county had all been noted for virtuous conduct in their localities while the common people stood universally in awe of the authorities and respected the scholar-officials. But by the T'ien-ch'i and Ch'ung-chen reigns many of the long-established families and powerful lineages had become accustomed to licence and extravagance; their young men and serfs made depredations everywhere which the common people resented.'[110]

The ruthless pursuit of wealth and the exploitation of social privilege by the elite soon led in T'ung-ch'eng as elsewhere in the Yangtze valley to violent antagonism and then resistance, as popular leadership emerged. According to one source the first move in 1634 was made by a serf, Chang Ju, in response to rebel movements in Kiangsi and Hupei. Though very little is known of the conditions of the tenant and serf population in the county it is likely that it would have borne the brunt of the arrogance of urban landowning families and would thus have been among the first to take reprisals. Chang Ju's adherents grew steadily in numbers and fairly soon leadership was taken over by two other local desperadoes, Wang Kuo-hua and Huang Wen-ting, who started to plan a rising. Though their band remained hidden, rumours of their ferocity and huge numbers (said to be 10,000 or more) reached the city, whose inhabitants trembled in hourly expectation of an attack. 'The great and important families were torn between doubt and confidence. Some wanted to defend the city walls, others the streets. They regarded all their family serfs as savage wolves, none of whom would protect them.' As for some time nothing happened they were lulled into a false sense of security and evidently relaxed precautions. Then one night the rebels launched a sudden raid on the city, started a fire that burned down hundreds of houses belonging to rich families, and escaped before dawn laden with their valuables.[111]

This event inaugurated ten years or so of violence, bloodshed and devastation in the county, aggravated by the fact that T'ung-ch'eng, in addition to suffering from local risings, lay directly in the path of the great rebel armies of the north-west, notably that of Chang Hsien-chung, the butcher of Szechwan. No effort will be made to relate in detail the miseries of these years, the succession of sieges and battles, the comings and goings of government and rebel troops (each as bad in their way as the other), the famines and the plagues. The most interesting thing about the revolts is the evidence they reveal of extreme hostility to the local elite and the role which the latter played in organizing T'ung-ch'eng's defence. It appears that during this period almost all the 'great gentry families had their property burned and plundered'. One of the only exceptions is said to have been Tai Chün-ts'ai (a retired county magistrate, one of Tai Ming-shih's relatives), whose fields and house were not attacked because his conduct had won the goodwill of the local populace.[112] Another popular figure who escaped attack was Fang K'ung-chao (on whom see above) who had been restored to office early in the Ch'ung-chen reign but at this point was living at home to observe mourning. He subsequently managed to inveigle a large number of the rebels into coming to him, and then had them all killed.[113]

Not all the local elite had the strong nerves of Fang K'ung-chao. As early as 1636 many of the great families in the county were reported to have fled south across the Yangtze, as did many of the people who lived along its banks. By 1642 'over half' of the gentry (*shen-chin*) were said to have gone.[114] Some, like members of the Fang, Hu and Chang families, simply went down the Yangtze to the Nanking area and stayed there for the duration of the troubles.[115] Others took members of their families to safety but returned themselves to look after their interests in T'ung-ch'eng as best they could. One such was Chang Ying's father, Chang Ping-i, who in 1635 took his children to Nanking but came back to T'ung-ch'eng with his wife the following year. Chang Ying was born two years later. Those rash enough to stay on their estates often did not survive long; one of Chang Ying's relatives who did this was massacred together with his four sons in 1637.[116]

Those of the elite who remained behind were forced to take refuge in the county city. They evidently played a leading role, along with two successive magistrates, in organizing its defence in the almost constant sieges that ensued. In this task they appear to have received little positive assistance from the various imperial armies in the area, whose troops did about as much damage as the rebels and were admitted by one commander, Tso Liang-yü, to take bribes from them. From the beginning the elite used all the influence they could muster in order to get help for the county. In 1635 messengers were sent to Soochow to ask for extra troops and the same request was made at court by one of their number, Sun Chin, who was then a supervising secretary in the Board of War.[117] Two at least of the gentry defenders of the city were members of the Yao family, Yao Sun-fei (*chin-shih* 1640, soon to hold office in the Board of War), and Yao Sun-sen (*sheng-yüan* and father of Chang Ying's later wife).[118] At a slightly later stage one of their relatives, Yao Sun-chü (*chin-shih* 1622), who held provincial office in Hukwang, was approached by the gentlemen of the county with the request that he get unruly Hukwang troops withdrawn from the area, which he did.

Whether the elite organized more active military measures on their own initiative is not clear. In general the imperial authorities were very anxious to prevent military power falling into local gentry hands, and the only local militia force described at this time was an ad hoc band led in 1641 by the county warden (*tien-shih*) who of course was not a local man.[119] It was soon dispersed, not by the rebels but by imperial troops. The local degree holders do appear to have led protests over attempts to squeeze extra taxation from the county's devastated land, and also to press for remissions, but whether this can have had any effect in the confusion of the times is doubtful.

By 1642, when Chang Hsien-chung and his army finally arrived and subjected the city to a siege worse than any that had gone before, the situation was desperate.[120] Food was in short supply and pestilence spreading; the water in the city's wells was polluted and the people reduced to eating the flesh of corpses. Those of the elite who had elected to stay behind must have regretted it, for at this time it was said that many 'who had had property worth tens of thousands of taels outside in the *hsien* were now dying of starvation within the city'. Towards the end of the year food was so short that the gentry were preparing to kill themselves and their wives if help did not arrive. Help eventually did arrive but brought little consolation, for imperial troops continued to prove as destructive as the rebels, and the people were 'as if caught between flood and fire'. In these circumstances it is not surprising that when in 1645 forces loyal to the Manchu conquerors appeared they were apparently welcomed with relief, and that in T'ung-ch'eng there was subsequently very little sign of local loyalist resistance on behalf of the vanquished dynasty. One or two sporadic risings did occur but were easily suppressed owing to complete lack of popular support.[121]

The scene in T'ung-ch'eng in 1645 after peace returned must have been one of desolation, for all the sources, though they vary as to the details, are agreed that there had been huge loss of life and laying waste of land. In one year alone it was claimed that 160,000 people had been killed, and by 1643 it was said that 70–80% of the cultivated land in the county had been devastated.[122] In addition many of the population had fled the area. In view of this, the county's subsequent recovery seems to have been remarkably rapid. It is hard to document it from the population records because these are so greatly underestimated, but they may nonetheless give some idea of orders of magnitude. It is worth noting therefore that the official figures for 1645, 25,530 persons and 5,010 households, are almost precisely half those for 1631. By 1672 they had recovered to something like their previous level, which may indicate a corresponding increase in the real population total, or at least that some administrator thought that things were more or less back to what they had been before the revolts.[123]

It looks as if the amount of land under cultivation also returned quite soon to the late Ming level (though again whether this actually corresponded to the real area under cultivation is something that will have to be discussed later). From 1645 to 1647 there were orders for tax remissions on just over 1,392 *ch'ing* of land that had apparently been totally devastated in the course of the revolts. This comprised roughly one-third of the total registered acreage. In the following fifteen years there were successive reports that varying amounts of this had been put back under cultivation, until in 1663 the total corresponded to the original figure.[124]

The decrease in population and the large-scale tax remissions probably provided good opportunities for those who survived the rebellions or who were able to return to their native area. In particular it looks as if members of the local elite families had no difficulty in taking possession of their former land-holdings on their return, and possibly even in extending them to include the property of deceased neighbours.[125] This was no doubt one reason why Chang Ying emphasized so strongly the safety of land as an investment that would survive war and rebellions. Those of his own family who had gone off to Nanking seem all to have recovered their land quite easily afterwards, and the same was certainly true of some of the Hu family, one of whom found that his holding had practically escaped the disasters.[126] The Yaos were perhaps even more fortunate, for their property was mainly in the highly fertile east district of the county which had suffered far less than any other part of it.[127]

By the 1660s the county's former prosperity was definitely reviving. In 1659 the great irrigation system to the south of the county city, which must have been extensively damaged during the prolonged fighting, was extended on the orders of the magistrate, and a few years later was further repaired and overhauled.[128] Recovery was aided by fairly favourable weather conditions and good harvests. Grain had been in short supply and therefore expensive in the 1640s but after 1647 there were no major droughts until 1671–2 and 1679, and supplies were so abundant that prices probably remained fairly low, as Chang Ying observed.[129]

As agricultural production got under way once more, trade seems also to have revived. The market town of K'ung-ch'eng in the north-east of the county had been severely damaged in the revolts, and commercial activity virtually ceased there. Some years afterwards however it was reported that 'the brokers and peddlers there were growing wealthy and prosperous; over five hundred trading households settled there and K'ung-ch'eng again became an important town'.[130] In the 1680s and 90s when the gazetteer was recompiled and revised, its descriptions attest that all economic activity had returned completely to normal, almost as if the revolts had never happened.

Not only did things return to normal, but this recovery paved the way towards another great spurt of agrarian prosperity in the county in the eighteenth.century. This is confirmed once more by expanding population and cultivated land acreage, as well as greater diversity of products and intensified commercial activity. The eighteenth-century population figures show a very rapid increase in numbers of persons after 1693, from 109,165 in the latter year to 850,168 in 1765. Registration procedures were considerably tightened up after 1775, so that the next figure, that of 1790, shows a great leap to 1,330,876 individuals. These later figures are very probably exaggerated, for few counties in this period, even in the Yangtze delta, had recorded populations of even half this total. The real increase must nonetheless have been considerable.[131]

These pressures were responsible for even more intensive efforts at land reclamation. Dyked fields or polder lands (*yü-t'ien*) were now to be found all over the county, wherever there was low-lying, inundated land to be reclaimed, and are described at some length in the 1827 gazetteer. At the same time the Yangtze islands or sandbars (*chou*) were further extended and new ones created. This process must have gone on at a great pace, for modern maps of the county now show few *chou* along the Yangtze; most have apparently become joined together as regular paddy land and only the occasional survival of the old names betrays their former separate state.[132]

A greater variety of crops was certainly being cultivated in this period.[133] The gazetteer now describes three types of rice that ripened at different times, early, 'delayed' and late. The statement that the same ground was used for the late as well as for the early variety may actually imply in some cases a double crop of rice (though this is generally held to have been rare in China outside the south-east provinces).[134] More kinds of wheat and barley are listed and also far more vegetables, some of which were apparently dried and sold in local urban markets. Certain items of food were now being imported from other provinces, namely comparative luxuries like apples, pears and grapes from the north, oranges from Kiangsi and sugar cane from south of the Yangtze. Another import from Kiangsi was the sweet potato, which soon began to be cultivated everywhere in the county.

More commercial goods were now said to be produced locally, though some of the additions were such things as boats, carts, wheelbarrows, pottery and tiles, which surely must have been made at earlier periods, though very likely not for sale. Cotton thread and cloth were made and also some silk, though these were still clearly home industries. Several types of paper were manufactured from cotton and from mulberry bark, and also all the earlier products like writing brushes and umbrellas. Local comestibles processed for sale in addition to tea included all kinds of alcoholic liquor, pickles and preserves. Even if these things did not travel far, local demand for them must have helped swell the volume of trade in rural and urban markets. Its growth can be illustrated by the fact that the number of market towns in the county between the late seventeenth and early nineteenth centuries jumped from five to twenty-nine, fairly evenly distributed. There were also four major annual fairs (one of them for the sale of livestock, that is, cattle, horses, donkeys and mules) that followed one after the other in the second month. Merchants from 'all provinces' congregated at these, and outside merchants from places like Hui-chou and Ning-po, shopkeepers from Shansi and Hupei, and artisans from Kiangsi were to be found in major towns like Ts'ung-yang and K'ung-ch'eng.[135]

This thriving and expanding commerce does not however constitute proof that the economy of the area was undergoing fundamental changes after the seventeenth century. It is apparent that much of the increase in the volume of trade was a consequence of the greatly enlarged population; its content, though rather more diversified and giving evidence of greater local purchasing power, was not dramatically different, and there is no evidence that local manufacturing even now was becoming highly sophisticated. The most important item of local trade, as in earlier times, was probably still grain. The continuing predominance of agrarian occupations is illustrated by the timing of the four great fairs mentioned above, which were arranged to end just as the busy season for farming started. It is also confirmed by what is known of all the surrounding counties at this time and later.[136]

It is particularly noticeable that the county city, despite the presence of numerous merchants, was never dominated by commercial activity. There were no pawnshops there until quite a late stage, possibly as late as the early nineteenth century, and shops and markets existed only in the eastern and southern quarters. The rest was still occupied by the residences of old-established families, whom the revolts had obviously failed to dislodge.[137] Their economic foundations and way of life, as far as can be seen, were still basically very much as they had been in the Ming. Trade, though in most cases a permissible profession, was even now regarded mainly as a recourse for those who could not make ends meet by farming or who could not afford a proper education and the life of leisured scholarship.[138] It is therefore quite possible that in this era of steadily rising grain prices and land values, and increasing demand from densely populated regions like the Yangtze delta, land-ownership was still of fundamental importance to them.[139]

Desire for learning and scholastic success obviously continued unabated.

The 1827 gazetteer takes pains to emphasize just how intense was devotion to scholarship in the county city. 'The young men, no matter whether rich or poor, are all taught to study. In the thoroughfares and lanes the sound of recitation continues past midnight . . . The scholars spend day and night in literary discussion and in correcting each other's faults.' Even more remarkable, it was customary to educate girls. Manners were polite and dress unostentatious, both in the towns and in the county as a whole. 'The customs of the four districts are plain and simple and they do not have elaborate ceremonies on festive occasions. Even going round the streets and market places they all wear long gowns and small caps. They are equally good at the professions of agriculture and study, esteem integrity and are meticulous about paying rent.'[140] There is no mention here of the arrogance and extravagance that had brought about such calamities at the end of the Ming, and one can only assume that in this respect at least the elite had learned from bitter experience to moderate their behaviour. Just how this transformation (which must have entailed a remarkable compromise of interests) was achieved is one of the more important questions in the social history of the area. It will be raised again in later chapters, though it cannot be pretended that answers to it are complete.

Local wealth and ambition brought about an even greater flowering of talent in the late seventeenth and eighteenth centuries than had occurred in the Ming, an achievement that is all the more startling when it is remembered that examination quotas remained very restricted and that population was expanding rapidly. Throughout the Ch'ing dynasty T'ung-ch'eng produced 150 *chin-shih* and very probably 500 or so *chü-jen*.[141] Though it was only one of sixty counties in Anhwei province its *chin-shih* comprised no less than 12.6% of the provincial total and compare quite favourably in numbers with some of the outstanding localities in the lower Yangtze region and eastern seaboard.[142] Anhwei quotas were particularly low and most restricted of all in the eighteenth century; from 1744 the province's annual *chü-jen* allowance was only 45. In addition one would expect a county like T'ung-ch'eng to be hard hit by the rule introduced after 1700 that severely restricted the numbers of new *chü-jen* from the families of central government officials of rank 4 and up, and of all Han-lin and imperial tutorial officials.[143] Yet T'ung-ch'eng in the eighteenth century regularly produced five or six *chü-jen* per examination and frequently far more; in 1736 for instance there were thirteen and in 1774 the number was sixteen. Its *chin-shih* performance likewise was not affected by the freezing of quotas after 1700. In the Yung-cheng reign alone (1723−35) it had fifteen, fully one-third of the total for the entire province of Anhwei in that period.

It is hardly surprising to find that the names of families already distinguished

in the Ming figure prominently among these successes, especially those of
Fang, Yao, Chang, Wu, Ma and Yeh. Twenty-four Changs became *chin-shih*
in the Ch'ing, of whom at least sixteen were members of Chang Ying's family,
the last being in 1874. There were fourteen Yaos, eleven of them descendants of Yao Hsi-lien; twenty-one Fangs, most of whom appear to be from
the same kin group, and eight Mas, also all related to each other and very
likely all descendants of Ma Meng-chen. Their representation among the
chü-jen is even more noticeable. To take the most outstanding example, in
1774, the annus mirabilis in which the county had sixteen *chü-jen*, a third
of the whole provincial quota, at least six of them and possibly another two
were from the prominent Chang and Yao families.

It was in this period likewise that the county reached the pinnacle of
success in terms of government office. The most dazzling examples are of
course from the Chang family, Chang Ying himself and his second son, the
grand secretary Chang T'ing-yü (1672–1755), the trusted confidant of
three successive emperors and one of the most powerful Chinese ministers
of the entire Ch'ing period. It was he who attained the unique honour of
having his name posthumously entered in the imperial ancestral temple. The
Changs in addition were one of only six families in the whole dynasty to
have four consecutive generations admitted to the Han-lin Academy.[144]
Though no others attained quite this degree of eminence there were still
many central and provincial officials of distinction from other families,
like Yao Fen (1726–1801), who rose to be governor of Yunnan and then of
Fukien at the end of the eighteenth century, and Fang Kuan-ch'eng (1698–
1768), who became governor-general of Chihli and later senior guardian of
the heir apparent. Distinguished scholars in these centuries included Tai
Ming-shih, executed for treasonable writings in 1713; Fang Pao (1668–1749),
like Fang Kuan-ch'eng a member of the sixth branch of the Fang lineage,
who spent most of his life in Nanking; Liu Ta-k'uei (1697–1779), and Yao
Nai (1732–1815), both great *ku-wen* writers.[145]

The continuing closeness of the connections among the county's leading
families can be appreciated from the fact that Tai Ming-shih was closely
involved with more than one of the Fangs, including Fang Kuan-ch'eng's
great-grandfather, Fang Hsiao-piao (*chin-shih* 1649), and his relative Fang
Pao; many of them were imprisoned and then exiled as a result of the inquisition case in 1713.[146] Fang Pao, his protégé Liu Ta-k'uei and Yao Nai
shared a common devotion to Sung Neo-Confucianism and were regarded as
the founders of the so-called T'ung-ch'eng school that proved a major stimulus
to the revival of 'statecraft' learning in the nineteenth century.[147] The Tais
and the Fangs had long been connected in marriage, as is attested by a preface
by one of the Fang family found in Tai Ming-shih's collected works.[148] The

Fangs continued to marry extensively with the Yaos at least to the nineteenth century (Yao Fen, governor of Fukien, was for instance married to a daughter of Fang Hao, *chin-shih* 1730, also of the sixth branch) and with some of Chang Ying's descendants.[149] As will be seen, the Changs in the seventeenth and eighteenth centuries became so intermarried with the Yaos that in 1742 a censor could claim that the two families between them accounted for almost half the gentry (*chin-shen*) of all China.[150]

Those active in the public life of the county during this era of greatness naturally included many members of these prominent families. One of Chang Ying's descendants, Chang Tseng-ch'ang (*chin-shih* 1751), in 1758 took the lead in founding a charitable granary. In 1767 a member of the Fang family donated to the county some charitable land to provide the examination expenses of poor scholars and in 1797 Yao Fen made a similar donation.[151] More examples of their role on the local scene will be discussed in later chapters. It should be noted though that not all local benefactors were necessarily higher degree holders (the Fang who gave the land in 1767 apparently was not). nor were all of them even from great official families. When the T'ien-ch'eng academy was founded in 1826 its major sponsors were two members of the P'an and Liu families (not among the most outstanding), neither of whom was a *chü-jen* nor a *chin-shih*. It is also extremely interesting that many of the substantial contributions to it of land and cash were made not by individuals but collectively by lineage halls, a hint of the importance which lineage organization must have assumed in T'ung-ch'eng by this time.[152]

The continuous record of T'ung-ch'eng's history comes to an end in 1827 with the compilation of the last edition of the gazetteer, and disappointingly little is known of events for most of the nineteenth and twentieth centuries.[153] What information there is has had to be pieced together from the other sources, especially individual biographies, and is still very fragmentary. One thing that can be stated with confidence is that the county must inevitably have suffered from increasing pressure of population. The recorded population in 1825 was almost two-and-a-half million, again an almost certain exaggeration but indicating persistent increase nonetheless.[154] An indirect indication of this is afforded by the fact that by 1827 the sweet potato was being grown all over the county. Much hitherto uncultivated mountain land was in addition being opened up to grow maize, which was widely relied on as a standby in case of shortages and crop failure. The third of the New World food plants, the peanut, was known in the county as a crop that would thrive in sandy soil but was still not much cultivated at this point.[155] If the population went on growing, even at a lower rate, it must have entailed some decline in standards of living.[156] Hardship is certainly suggested by the number of lineage rules in the nineteenth century that contain injunctions against drowning daughters.

It may be that population pressure and greater economic competition resulted in a change in the hitherto sober and scholarly customs of T'ung-ch'eng. This is hinted in one exasperatingly brief statement by Ma Ch'i-ch'ang, discussing the father and another relative of the late-nineteenth-century official Wu Ju-lun (on whom see below). He observes that customs were at their finest in the Ch'ien-lung and Chia-ch'ing reigns (1736—1820) when the 'old-established lineages' lived in great numbers in the county city, study was incessant and the behaviour of gentry and scholars extremely courteous, yet implies that by the end of the Tao-kuang reign (1821—50) there were not so many who like the Wus still meticulously preserved the old ways.[157] Even if the strict behaviour patterns of the local elite were somewhat weakened, interest in education must nonetheless have remained strong in some quarters to account for the county's very respectable, even if not quite so startling, *chin-shih* and *chü-jen* production right down to the end of the dynasty.

In the middle of the nineteenth century the whole area was devastated again, perhaps even more disastrously than it had been in the seventeenth, by rebellion and warfare. In 1853 the county city fell to the forces of the Taiping rebels, who held it almost continuously thereafter until 1861, when Tseng Kuo-fan captured An-ch'ing and brought an effective end to Taiping dominance in the Yangtze valley. It would be of enormous interest to know how the county fared during this period of 'alien' rule but little information has yet come to light. As was common in many other localities at this time, some of the local elite did step into the vacuum left by the failure of imperial authority and train *t'uan-lien* forces to combat the rebels. Chief among them was one of Ma Ch'i-ch'ang's immediate forebears, the *kung-sheng* and scholar Ma San-chün, aided by a *sheng-yüan*, Chang Hsün (from which Chang family is not known). Ma attempted to pressure the governor of Anhwei into co-operating in a joint campaign, and then to get help from Lü Hsien-chi who had been sent from Peking to organize local militia forces, but to no avail. In 1854 Ma was killed in a surprise attack, and Chang Hsün not long after-wards.[158] Another of the local elite who took part in the military campaigns at this time was the *sheng-yüan* Hu K'o (a friend of Wu Ju-lun's father) whose own forebears had distinguished themselves in the defence of the city at the end of the Ming.[159]

There is no telling just how much destruction and loss of life resulted from the Taiping occupation. It cannot have been slight, for lineage records of the period speak almost unanimously of the ruin of ancestral halls and the flight or death of many of their members, much as had happened two centuries earlier. Even so it seems not to have brought about any drastic changes in economy or social structure and quite probably provided a much needed respite from relentless population growth. Most of the lineages seem to have hung on to or recovered their joint landholdings, and began to rebuild their halls and re-compile their genealogies rather quickly, in some cases in the late 1860s. It would thus appear that there was a fairly rapid return to normal on this occasion also.

Though T'ung-ch'eng did not shine as brightly in national life in the nine-teenth and twentieth centuries as it had done before it still produced several respected officials, in particular Wu Ju-lun (1840–1903), who was a member of one of the lesser Wu lineages, a devotee of the T'ung-ch'eng philosophical school and a distinguished *ku-wen* writer. He was introduced to Tseng Kuo-fan through Fang Tsung-ch'eng, another eminent local scholar (from a dif-ferent Fang family this time), whose relatives had been closely connected with Yao Nai and the T'ung-ch'eng school for several generations. Wu Ju-lun thus entered Tseng Kuo-fan's *mu-fu* and later in the nineteenth century became a prominent educational reformer, head of the Pao-ting Academy in Chihli and eventually in 1902 head of the faculty of Peking Imperial University. One of his last acts was to establish a modern primary school in T'ung-ch'eng, a sign that the local elite's traditional sponsorship of education was capable of moving with the times.[160]

It is gratifying finally to note that among Wu Ju-lun's closest disciples were the brothers Yao Yung-kai (1866–1923), and Yao Yung-p'u (*chin-shih* 1879), both grandsons of Yao Ying (1785–1853), one-time provincial judge in Taiwan and an important scholar.[161] These three Yaos were of course direct descend-ants of Yao Hsi-lien and thus of the *chin-shih* of 1451, Yao Hsü. Another of Wu Ju-lun's disciples was the scholar and biographer Ma Ch'i-ch'ang (1855–1929), to whom we owe the most complete record available of T'ung-ch'eng's notable men, and who was descended, as has already been noted, from the sixteenth-century official Ma Meng-chen.[162] Ma Ch'i-ch'ang had been betrothed to a daughter of the magistrate Chang Shao-wen (b. 1829), a sixth-generation descendant of none other than Chang Ying himself, and on her death married instead a sister of Yao Yung-p'u and Yao Yung-kai, who were both notable scholars in their own right. Seven of his eight daughters in their turn married Yaos, Changs and Fangs.[163] What could be a more fitting epilogue than this to the social history of the county, demonstrating its unbroken continuity of eminent families and the connections and marriage ties among them?

The above discussion is admittedly not exhaustive but it is certainly sufficient to show that T'ung-ch'eng, despite its favourable geographical loca-tion, prosperity and national eminence, was still throughout its history a predominantly agrarian area in which the basic occupation for the majority of the population was farming and in which landownership thus inevitably played a major role in the fortunes of the local elite. It is clear also that there was a definite continuity in the composition of at least part of this elite over a very long period. Chang Ying himself once remarked, when speaking of T'ung-ch'eng's academic distinction: 'In my district there are many eminent families that have maintained themselves continuously for ten or more generations or for several hundred years without declining', something that could still have been said, as we have seen, long after his own time.[164] All this is hardly consistent with the picture painted by some scholars of an impermanent and insecure upper class that was constantly changing in composition as families were levelled by the effects of the inheritance system and the increasingly competitive nature of the examinations. It therefore looks at first sight as if Chang Ying's assertions in *Heng-ch'an so-yen* of the importance of agriculture and study to continuing social prominence may have been well founded, at least in terms of the history of his native area.

It is essential now to investigate in more detail by what means and to what extent this social prominence was maintained, and first of all to discover how the landed interests of the elite were safeguarded. An examination will therefore be made in the following chapter of the changing role which its members played in the public affairs of the county, especially in fiscal matters, and of conditions of landownership there.

3

LAND AND TAXATION

An attempt is made in this chapter to assess the nature and weight of the fiscal burden in T'ung-ch'eng from the early Ming onwards and to discover how adversely it may have affected the returns to be had from landowning. It is clear that fiscal matters were of immense concern to the local elite, and a detailed investigation is made of the ways in which they were apt to intervene in order to protect their own interests in different periods. Two appendices are added. The first gives the official figures of the county's population, acreage and tax quotas for the whole period under discussion. The second describes briefly some of the other conditions affecting landowning in T'ung-ch'eng aside from taxation. From all this it should be possible to obtain a more accurate picture of the economic background to Chang Ying's theories on investment in land.

It must be stressed at the outset that the material for this section is fragmentary and often difficult to interpret, especially when it comes to assessing the complex interplay of interests involved. Numerous deeds of land transactions have been found in the lineage genealogies but are complicated by special local conditions and terminology, so that they cannot be used with confidence as a source of statistical information. The following conclusions must therefore be regarded as tentative and provisional.

One of the most striking of the findings in the preceding chapter is that throughout the Ming and Ch'ing, especially from the sixteenth century onwards, the economy of T'ung-ch'eng underwent continual expansion in terms of population, acreage under cultivation, diversity of crops and intensity of cropping patterns, agricultural output, trade and local prosperity. It must therefore be asked to what extent the state administration may have attempted to tap this increasing wealth by raising or altering the nature of taxation in the course of this period. In other words, how much truth is there, as regards this one county, in the rather widely held view that the growing pressures of taxation and unofficial extortion between them steadily reduced the profits to be made from landowning and worsened the condition of the rural population?[1] If the administration did attempt to improve tax collection techniques

or to expand their scope, were such efforts resisted, either by illicit evasion
or open action, by whom, in whose interests and with what success? The
evidence available does not always permit certain answers to these questions
but they should be constantly borne in mind.

As was shown in Chapter 2, T'ung-ch'eng in the early Ming was still very
much a backwater, an almost completely agrarian and underdeveloped area
whose resources were only gradually beginning to be exploited more effectively in the course of the fifteenth century. Information on fiscal matters
for this period is extremely slight. The first edition of the gazetteer presents
a very summary account of local taxation for the years 1391 and 1481
which shows it to have been pretty much the same as in other parts of central
China at this time.

The most important item was the land tax, levied as usual in two instal-
ments, in summer and autumn, on both official (*kuan-t'ien*) and private land
(*min-t'ien*). No rates of taxation per *mou* are given, however. The usual
miscellaneous impositions such as farmland silk (*nung-sang*), business tax
(*shang-shui*) and excise on wine and vinegar (*chiu-ts'u k'o*) are also listed, to
be paid in kind or in paper currency, but the amounts appear insignificant.
The only extra items of importance, understandable in an area of lakes and
rivers, were the fish tax (*yü-k'o*), levied in paper currency and fish by-products,
such as oil and glue, at six different places in the county, and also the reed tax
(*lu-k'o*), which was originally paid in bundles of reeds by the inhabitants of
marshy areas, mainly along the Yangtze.[2]

Of the labour services (*i*, consisting of miscellaneous duties, contributions
and cash payments) which together with the land tax constituted the most
important burden on the rural population in the first half of the Ming, there
is no mention at all. This is perhaps because in the early years, when government requisitions were fewer, the system worked fairly informally and easily
through the village *li-chia* organization, whereby groups of ten households
led by one wealthy family took it in turns to render services once every ten
years. It may have been so taken for granted as not to require explicit description in the gazetteer.[3]

Both land taxes and labour services were in theory assessed progressively,
the former on the basis of the household's cultivated acreage, the latter on
property and the number of adult males (*ting*) combined. The accurate registration of both land and population was supposed to be effected throughout
the dynasty by the decennial compilation of the yellow registers (*huang-ts'e*),
mainly a record of population to which details of property were also attached.
It was on this registration that the government's tax collection capacity in
the last resort depended.[4]

It is obviously, therefore, of great importance to determine how effectively the authorities managed to record cultivated acreage and to register any increases in it.[5] In T'ung-ch'eng it is impossible to say whether the first Ming figure of 1391 represents accurately the area being farmed at that time. The total registered acreage in the Yüan, presumably based on that of the southern Sung, was 201,383 *mou*. The 1391 figure of 392,702 *mou*, nearly double this, is by no means implausible considering the large numbers of settlers who arrived and occupied land at the end of the Yüan. Of this total only 9,502 *mou*, approximately 2.4%, were government land, a very insignificant amount compared with the scale of *kuan-t'ien* in the Yangtze delta.[6] Whether or not the acreage was at this stage measured in standard *mou* or in converted *mou* that made allowance for differences in the fertility of the land is unknown. It is quite possible, as was shown in Chapter 2, that during the fifteenth century the area under cultivation was already beginning to expand somewhat, and the figures for 1481 do in fact show an increase of 17,000-odd *mou*, to make a total of 410,388.[7]

For the performance of labour service, registration of population was just as important as that of land. There is a reasonable likelihood, as has already been mentioned, that the 1383 population figures of 58,560 persons and 10,427 households may in fact represent something like the real situation.[8] They must be based on the registration certificates of 1370, surviving examples of which give evidence of an attempt to register all household members, old and young, male and female alike. To cite an example, that of the 'first ancestor' of the Chao lineage of T'ung-pei comprised 4 males between the ages of 37 *sui* and 1 *sui*, and 4 females between 70 *sui* and 5 *sui*.[9] An additional reason for the plausibility of these figures is that they give a ratio of 5.6 persons to a household, which is consistent with the generally accepted ratio for all periods of Chinese history of an average of 5 persons per household.[10]

The next available population figures, for 1481, give a total of 109,650 individuals. This, as was explained in Chapter 2, may possibly represent something like the actual rate of increase during the century.[11] The household figure for that year, on the other hand, is only 9,601, which is smaller than that of a hundred years earlier, and results in a dubiously high ratio of 11.4 persons to a household. It would be wrong to jump to the conclusion that the people of the county had all by this time taken to living in large, joint family compounds. These did exist (witness the case of Fang Lin, described in Chapter 2) but are unlikely to have been prevalent among the mass of the peasant population. A more likely explanation is some attempt to evade labour services.

These had in general become more complicated and more onerous in the course of the fifteenth century, as the government expenses to be borne by the *li-chia* system proliferated and richer families tried to avoid performing the services in person. The T'ung-ch'eng magistrate Yen I in the Cheng-t'ung reign (1436—49) was reported to have 'equalized labour services (*chün yao-i*) and removed selfish desires, encouraged the good and punished the bad'.[12] This of course must refer to the implementation in T'ung-ch'eng of the first major revision of the service system, the *chün-yao* reform, whereby the previous ten-year service cycle was split into two five-year cycles for the separate performance of labour service and tax delivery by the *li-chia* organization, and services were in theory graded according to the capacity of the tax-paying household.[13]

It also indicates the existence of a certain degree of malpractice. One way for a large but not particularly affluent family to reduce its labour service burden was to split up into smaller units so as to make its tax-paying and service capacity appear minimal. This practice was certainly known in T'ung-ch'eng. The family of the first ancestor of the Chaos of T'ung-pei were registered as being the head of their ward in the *hsien* city but 'because their descendants were numerous and their labour services multiplied they split off one household' as head of a different ward of the city, and another to be a *li* head in the east district.[14]

Such action on a large scale would, however, result in an increase in the total number of households rather than a decrease. A rather more common method of evasion, especially among the wealthy, was to have many households registered as one so that they might count as one for the performance of labour service. Ho Ping-ti describes this as being done extensively by large clans in Szechwan and some northern provinces, accounting for their very high ratios of persons to households, but there is no reason why it should not have happened in the Yangtze valley also.[15] Its occurrence in T'ung-ch'eng is shown by Wu Ju-lun's account of one of the Huang families in the early Ming. At this time 'labour services increased; they were troublesome if undertaken alone but easy to evade if undertaken jointly. The Wus and the Huangs continued to perform them however.'[16] This would appear to be the explanation for the remarkably low household figures of 1481. The fact that evasion of labour service often apparently took the form of deliberate, large-scale household amalgamation may perhaps indicate considerable kinship solidarity in the face of demands from the local administration, a point that will be taken up again later.

It cannot be directly proved that the newly forming local elite were among the chief offenders, but it seems rather likely, at least to judge from the information that Ch'en Mien, the outstanding magistrate of the late fifteenth century, was very sympathetic towards the common people, something that inconvenienced 'powerful persons'.[17] So far not much evidence has emerged to show whether they attempted yet to intervene in fiscal matters more openly. The only instance found in the fifteenth century shows one of their number in a highly favourable light, acting as a spokesman in the interests of the locality.

This was the case of the well-to-do landowner Tso Lin (ancestor of Tso Kuang-tou), that occurred in the Ch'eng-hua reign (1465–87). The reed tax at this time is said to have been particularly heavy; many of the poorer people subject to it were in perpetual arrears and were flogged and imprisoned as a result. Though Tso Lin and his wife at first planned to sell land and raise a loan in order to get them released he realized that this was hardly a permanent solution to the problem. He therefore, so it is claimed, travelled to the capital and memorialized in person, ready to suffer death if need be, requesting a reduction of the tax. This heroism was in due course rewarded by the grant of a 30% reduction.[18]

As the precise date of this episode is unknown it would be difficult to substantiate it from the *Ming shih-lu*. In the account of the reed tax given in the 1490 edition of the T'ung-ch'eng gazetteer there is however a note to the effect that 40% of the total amount was by then regularly remitted, which may conceivably have had something to do with Tso's action.[19] On his return to acclamation in T'ung-ch'eng another wealthy individual by the name of Ch'ien, wishing to share in the kudos and knowing that he had had to spend 1,000 taels over the matter, presented him with 300 to help make up the cost. Tso accepted the money but insisted on using it to build a stone bridge for the further benefit of the community.[20] Tso Lin, though certainly a rich and presumably educated man, was neither a *chü-jen* nor a *chin-shih* and held no official post at any time.[21] Whether or not the precise details are true, the story does show that it was the county's wealthy landowners who were assuming local leadership and the right to negotiate with the authorities at this time, even before there was much of a 'gentry' elite in the strict, formal sense.

It appears that it was in the sixteenth century that T'ung-ch'eng's prosperity began to rise rapidly, consequent on increasingly effective exploitation of its agrarian resources and its participation in the commercial development of the Yangtze valley. The county's tax-paying capacity must have become considerably greater than at the beginning of the Ming, and it is of great importance to discover whether this actually was reflected in higher payments. As far as is known basic land-tax rates were not effectively increased before the seventeenth century, and the fact that most of the available evidence relates in one way or another to labour service suggests that it was this that still constituted the major burden on taxpayers.[22]

By now the county's educational standards were also rising, and with them the number of degree-holders who enjoyed some exemption from service liabilities. In particular the *sheng-yüan*, who were entitled to the exemption of two family members (*ting*) from service, must have proliferated in the sixteenth century. It evidently became common here as elsewhere for them to evade more of their obligations than they were entitled to and also to extend their privileges to their kinsmen.[23]

That this was the accepted and even socially respected practice in T'ung-ch'eng is shown by a very revealing episode involving Yao Hsi-lien (1514—62), the landowner described earlier as the founder of the Yao family's later fortunes. It is stated in his biography that labour services at this time were troublesome but that the families of those with the *sheng-yüan* degree managed to be excused them. Yao Hsi-lien did not himself have any degree but there were indeed *sheng-yüan* among his relatives. Some of them, however, on account of some private grudge, so far from protecting him, actually managed to transfer extra services to him. In his distress he composed a poem for the benefit of his descendants, warning that in future those of the family who rose in the world must be more generous to their kinsmen.[24]

When in 1566, after his death, four of his sons became *sheng-yüan*, they summoned those of their kin who were in difficulty with their labour services and solemnly undertook from then on to use all their own service exemptions to exempt their relatives, in deference to their father's wishes.[25] It is said that one of their sons, Yao Chih-lan (1562—1624), who later became a *chin-shih* and a prefect, continued to behave respectfully to the *sheng-yüan* who had so annoyed his grandfather, and was generous to their sons and to his kinsmen as a whole.[26]

These incidents suggest not only that it was common for members of the group that was coming to constitute the social elite in T'ung-ch'eng to evade service on their own account, but also that they were automatically expected to use the privileges of their newly acquired status to protect their humbler relatives, regardless of the latter's social position. They provide another scrap of evidence pointing to considerable kinship solidarity in the face of administrative demands. It appears in the above case that such attitudes might be carried further and action undertaken on behalf of a wider community. Yao Chih-lan in addition to being helpful to his relatives was claimed to have spoken out on all matters affecting the welfare of the district as a whole, and in his letters to the authorities never once took account of his private interests.[27] A tradition of spokesmanship was apparently cultivated in his family, as will be seen from the actions of other Yaos later in the seventeenth century.

By the mid sixteenth century the problems caused by complicated labour services and their evasion were evidently so acute as to justify the drastic

remedy being tried by other local authorities around this time. During the
term of office of the magistrate Ch'en Yü-chieh, 1563—6, at the very end of
the Chia-ching reign, because 'the labour services were a dozen or more and
exacting them was very complicated and troublesome' he 'combined them
in one, calling them *i-t'iao pien*, at which the clerks no longer annoyed the
people; the authorities found it a good method . . .'.[28] This clearly refers to
the implementation of the so-called Single Whip reform in the county.[29]
The gazetteer gives no details of exactly how it was carried out but one can
say, on the analogy of other places, that it must at the very least have entailed a drastic reduction and simplification of labour services which would
henceforth be financed with the proceeds of an extra levy, assessed on land
acreage and paid in silver.[30]

The Single Whip reform was almost certainly a benefit to the county in
that it must have eased the difficulties connected with the personal performance or evasion of labour services and spread the burden more fairly. It did
of course mean the addition of an extra item (the exact amount of which is
unknown) to the land tax. Whether this was really a hardship is doubtful, in
view of the apparent local prosperity and the growing use of money as more
agricultural produce found its way on to the market. Direct evidence is slight,
and any attempt to evaluate the real effects of the reform and the interests
it may have prejudiced has to be made on the basis of what is known of two
land surveys carried out in the county in the 1580s.

The first of these was part of the national land survey ordered by grand
secretary Chang Chü-cheng in Wan-li 9 (1581), the main aim of which was to
discover the land deliberately kept off the registers by wealthy households
and to reallocate local tax quotas more fairly.[31] The survey was supposed to
be made in standard *mou*, though it appears that in many areas measurements
were not very accurate and the undertaking as a whole was not a success.[32]

In T'ung-ch'eng, which provides an interesting case study of the way in
which the survey was made, and its repercussions, it evidently caused some
commotion. It appears from the complaints made that prior to 1581 the
land in the county had not been measured in standard *mou*. The system in
use was said to date from the Chia-ching reign, which may imply that it was
introduced in the course of the Single Whip reform. In this way, instead of
taxing each grade of land differently, tax collection could be simplified by
measuring fertile land in small-sized *mou* and poor land in large *mou*. The
1581 survey however 'made no distinction between different grades of land
but in all cases simply assessed three [standard] *mou* as one [fiscal] *mou*'.
As a result people with poor land had their taxes greatly increased and were
in constant arrears. After continued vociferous protests (led, one might suspect, by the landowning elite) permission was given in 1585 for a new survey
that would take differences in fertility into account.[33]

The fact that the 1581 survey, for all its 'injustice', still used a 3:1 ratio for conversion of actual to fiscal acreage, gives rise to the suspicion that somehow in the course of the previous century or two the registration of land had not kept up with the undoubted increase in cultivated acreage. This suspicion is startlingly confirmed in the report on the subsequent resurvey carried out in 1585–8, where it is casually stated at one point that the original estimate of acreage in 1581 had been no less than 1,302,444 *mou* (more than three times the previous figure of 410,063 *mou*).[34] This total had then been simply divided by three to give a universal rate of *mou* conversion that still resulted in a total fiscal acreage of around 434,000 *mou*, not really a great deal more than before.

The magistrate in charge of the later survey stated quite unequivocally his intention to return to the old system of *mou* conversion whereby there had been 'fixed quotas' for acreage and tax, and no unauthorized increases and decreases were possible. His ostensible reason was that while public opinion considered the land tax as something immutable and was not particularly worried about it, there were considerable anxieties over the labour service levy, now assessed on land. It was admitted not to be heavy at that particular time, but in the event of any military emergency it was bound to be increased. If the change in the method of assessment and increase in acreage brought about by the 1581 survey were to be permitted this would mean potentially a far heavier weight of service levy and an intolerable burden for the common people.[35]

Whether or not he was also bowing to the pressure of local elite opinion in voicing these sentiments is impossible to prove but by no means improbable, for affluent landowners would not be the last to benefit from a continued freeze on the county's taxable acreage. The new survey was firmly and deliberately based on the original land quota which, after some adjustments to take into account land that had escaped registration or had been registered twice in 1581, was deemed to have been 419,705 *mou*.[36]

The actual *mou* conversion system adopted was virtually the same as the earlier one. Irrigated land (*t'ien*) was divided into three major categories, upper, medium and lower, each of which was further subdivided into three grades. The basis for the conversion was taken as grade two of the medium category (*chung-chung*) which was assessed in standard fiscal *mou*.[37] It must be emphasized however that in T'ung-ch'eng, in contrast to all the other cases discussed by Ho Ping-ti in Chapter VI of *Studies on the Population of China*, there was no category of fiscal *mou* that actually corresponded to one standard *mou*.[38] On the contrary, the basic fiscal *mou* still consisted of three standard *mou*, so that three actual *mou* of medium-grade land would pay the tax of one standard *mou*. The *mou* size for upper and lower grades of land was respectively decreased and increased by an average of 30% either way, so that three actual *mou* of good land would pay the tax of 1.3 standard *mou*, and three actual *mou* of poor land paid the tax of 0.7 standard *mou*. Even more generous conversion rates were allowed for unirrigated land (*ti*, with the exception of some city sites which counted as top grade), for ponds (*t'ang*, which were also exempted from the payment of the Single Whip surcharge in silver), and for marshy land along the rivers. After all the land had been classified and converted to fiscal acreage under this system the total was once more brought down to almost exactly what it had been before the 1581 survey, namely 410,061 *mou*. As this was only approximately 30% of the real total in standard *mou* it is clear that under-registration of land acreage in this part of Anhwei was even more severe than Ho Ping-ti suspects it to have been in the province as a whole.[39]

Malpractice in land registration and land transactions was always common in Ming China, but the fact that in T'ung-ch'eng the taxable fiscal *mou* was not firmly tied to the standard *mou* evidently made it particularly easy. Changes of land ownership were registered only at ten-yearly intervals on the compilation of the yellow registers, to which the people themselves in any case had no access.[40] When land changed hands it was fairly simple for unscrupulous dealers to alter the amount of fiscal acreage with which it was rated. As the T'ung-ch'eng magistrate put it in 1588: 'When land is sold its extent is arbitrarily assessed and there is confusion over the weight of its tax liability.' If the seller were the stronger party his advantage lay in transferring much of his property's tax liability on to the land he was selling, so that the remaining unsold acreage was lightly assessed. If the buyer were the stronger he would endeavour to accept as little of the tax as possible so that the unsold land was heavily assessed. In some cases this was done with the connivance of both parties. When a man was selling rich land he could get away with deliberately 'increasing' its acreage, and thereby its tax assessment, knowing that prospective purchasers would still find it attractive. If the land were poor and he wanted to get rid of it he would 'reduce' the acreage, and thus the tax liability, in order to make a sale. Some people actually pursued this kind of strategy so systematically that even when a man's land had been completely sold off the luckless vendor still had some *mou* 'left over', that is, he was still credited with land on the registers on which he would have to pay tax.[41]

Such practices were certainly not unique to T'ung-ch'eng but it is interesting that in most cases they consisted in an affluent or influential man or family shuffling off his tax liabilities in one way or another on to other people. There is never any mention of the expedient of *t'ou-hsien* or *t'ou-k'ao*, so common in the more heavily taxed Yangtze delta, whereby poorer individuals in order to evade tax payments put their land under the protection of great, tax-exempt families.[42] It is very probable that, with the highly favourable acreage con-

version referred to above, taxes in T'ung-ch'eng were never so onerous as to
drive people to this.

The magistrate proposed to end these long-standing abuses by decreeing
that henceforth every transfer of land should be accompanied by an officially
stamped certificate of ownership. On this there were to be entered the boundaries of the plot, its acreage as 'originally measured' (i.e. in standard *mou*)
and the converted fiscal acreage (in effect its tax liability).[43] Whether this
measure was really carried out or can have had much long-term effect is
extremely doubtful. Surviving T'ung-ch'eng land deeds of the Ming period do
in almost all cases contain a clause to specify that the tax and service liabilities
attaching to the land were to be assumed by the purchaser at the time of the
'major registration' (*ta-tsao*, i.e. the decennial compilation of the yellow registers) without further interference of any kind from the vendor. Many also
contain a provision to the effect that the sale is made voluntarily, without
any coercion or 'discount' (*chun-che*, evidently referring to illicit adjustment
of acreage).[44]

On the other hand no deed for any period ever gives more than one set
of acreage figures, which are almost certainly always the fiscal rather than the
actual acreage. This is confirmed by a deed relating to an acquisition of ritual
land by the Chou lineage of Yao-shih in 1598, in which the acreage is stated
explicitly to be the converted acreage of the 'new survey', in other words that
of ten years before.[45] If the real amount of land were never stated in the
contract then the opportunities for malpractice would continue as before.

It appears from the evidence of these surveys that the Single Whip reform,
despite the extra levies on land that it entailed, cannot have caused any enormous economic hardship to landowners as a whole if they were able with
the help of the magistrate to keep the county's quota of taxable acreage fixed
at a figure approximately 30% of the real amount. Degree-holders and their
families did enjoy considerable exemptions from it, however, and it is clear
from one interesting episode in the early seventeenth century that they
attempted to guard their privileges jealously.

The evidence on this is preserved only in Ma Ch'i-ch'ang's biographical
account of a certain Hu Tsan, *chin-shih* in 1595 and a member of a respected
local family, who held office in the Board of Works and later became senior
administrative vice-commissioner (*tso-ts'an-cheng*) in Kiangsi.[46] Sometime
after 1602 he returned home to a lengthy retirement, during which he became
involved in what was evidently a heated controversy over a recent change in
the registration system. The Single Whip method of assessing service liabilities
on the basis of land had evidently in T'ung-ch'eng been extended to cover
the *ting*, the individual adult male who was earlier liable to service in person.
As a result, according to Hu Tsan, the traditional *li-chia* registration of the

actual number of *ting* in each household was abandoned. Their number was instead determined by the amount of land the family owned. Thus 800 *mou* were to be the equivalent of one unit of tax and labour service (i.e. a *chia*) and a family with 8,000 *mou* would thereby constitute a *li* on its own. Every 50 *mou* were to be counted as one *ting* and those with less than 50 *mou* were to be exempted from the *ting* charge entirely.[47]

Hu Tsan declared that these changes were introduced at the behest of a certain unnamed 'flatterer' who considered it a good way to check the continued evasion of service duties and charges and had managed to get his ideas accepted by the local authorities. Hu objected ostensibly on the grounds that it would mean a complete change in the ancestral *li-chia* regulations and cause considerable disturbance. If actual *ting* moreover were no longer registered, in the event of any military emergency it would be impossible to recruit militia. He felt that the measure was in any case unnecessary because the tax and service burden in T'ung-ch'eng was not nearly as heavy as in those areas 'south of the Yangtze' where it had already been put into effect.

His other objections, however, betray his real interest in the reform, which had been introduced, he asserted, merely in order to 'please the common people by equalizing labour services'. Its most iniquitous feature in his eyes was that, in contrast to the south, where under this scheme exemptions were still to be allowed on up to 1,000 *mou* of land, in T'ung-ch'eng no exemptions from the *ting* charge were to be allowed at all. 'Thus the gentlemen (*i-kuan*) will be in the same category as the commoners and their exemptions will be merely an empty favour, which is extremely improper.'[48] The great households with few adult males proportionate to their landholdings would be 'unfairly' burdened while the poorer people with large families would escape their proper liabilities.

It is clear that Hu Tsan's impassioned appeal, addressed to the rest of the local elite, did not achieve all its objectives. The continuance of the new method of *ting* assessment is proved by the fact that the registered *ting* total for the late Ming was only 8,719, quite impossible as the real number of adult males, but in fact approximately one fiftieth of the county's total registered acreage. This would also explain why the population figures for 1631, 10,417 households and 58,560 persons, simply repeat those for 1383; the registration of real individuals was presumably now of little fiscal importance.[49]

His protest was not completely without effect, however. Ma Ch'i-ch'ang notes that while 'those in charge of the matter resented it as loose talk', when his complaint reached a higher level 'there was a return to the old system'.[50] By this he meant, as is proved by the early Ch'ing regulations on *ting* assessment, that some of the elite's accustomed privileges of exemption were hastily restored.[51]

It is nonetheless interesting to find that all mention of Hu Tsan's conservative arguments, made purely in the selfish interests of his own class,
appears subsequently to have been suppressed.[52] The text of his appeal was
cut out of his collected works and Ma Ch'i-ch'ang was able to find it only by
searching his lineage's genealogy. The reason was probably a desire on the
part of later generations to eliminate all reference to the short-sighted self-
aggrandizement of the local elite towards the end of the Ming. This is no
doubt why both later editions of the gazetteer are so reticent on the subject of the unrest and social antagonism that arose in the county at this time.

The only contemporary evidence of it so far is that found in the earliest
set of rules of the Tso lineage, drawn up in 1634. These contain a section
headed 'Forbidding what should not be done' which condemns those members
who embezzle taxes and swindle others, counterfeit currency, 'intimidate
the officials and assume illicit authority', and commit other similar offences.
Another section castigates those who stir up litigation with the express aim of
enriching themselves and buying landed estates with the proceeds. The tone
of anxiety in which these prohibitions are couched may testify to the preva-
lence of such behaviour at the time.[53]

To sum up, on the balance of all the evidence available so far, it seems
reasonable to conclude that in T'ung-ch'eng the land-tax burden was not
especially heavy throughout most of the Ming dynasty. In fact, it became
progressively less so, since it was levied at a moderate rate on a decreasing
fraction of the county's cultivated acreage. The major problem seems always
to have been the imposition of labour services (which almost certainly did not
disappear entirely, even after the Single Whip) and then the unprecedented
item of the service levy, raised in silver on the basis of land acreage. This,
even if not heavy, was apparently feared as being something capable of ex-
tension.

The local elite families with any degree-holding members at all did however
enjoy exemptions from both of these items, sometimes on quite a considerable scale, which they could also use to protect most of their relatives. If
Hu Tsan is any guide, they resented any attempt to make them pay more than
they were accustomed to, even if this were well within their financial capabilities. As time went on they very probably exploited their privileges even
more unscrupulously to evade what remained of their fiscal obligations. The
fact that this problem apparently worsened sharply in the 1620s could be
due to the imposition of the seven successive surcharges on the land tax
itself from 1619 onwards, which are likely to have aroused the same resentment among the elite as did the service levy.[54] Any previous concern for the
wider interests of the locality as a whole seems to have become submerged in
narrow self- and kin-interest. This, coupled with an increasingly arrogant
attitude towards the general population, was probably sufficient to set the

elite families and their relatives apart and to create a gulf of dangerous antagonism between them and the rest of society.

It is only by postulating some developments such as these that one can explain the violence of the revolts that occurred in the 1630s and 40s and the savagery of the reprisals directed against the local elite. The rebellions must have come as a traumatic shock to them, and seem in themselves to have brought about a fairly rapid change of heart. There was a sharp reawakening to the fact that it was in their own interest to show some concern for the welfare of the county and its people and to use their influence to this end. This is no doubt one reason why Chang Ying's father during the rebellions was so quick to cancel all the debts owed to him.[55] It also accounts for the assiduity of the elite in organizing relief measures of all kinds. Chang Ying's father's cousin, Chang Ping-chen (1608–55, who eventually became president of the Board of Punishments) in addition to helping in the city's defence got together with Fang K'ung-chao to provide grain rations for the population and issued gruel to countless refugees.[56]

When protests arose over the weight of taxation still levied on the county's devastated land it is not surprising to find that the local degree-holders were in the forefront of them, though obviously their motives cannot have been entirely disinterested. The efforts of the military authorities from 1640 onwards to raise extra levies in order to supply nearby troops were said to have caused particular distress. They led to a riot outside the headquarters of the local military commander, who was inclined to put the blame on the *sheng-yüan* for inciting it. In 1643 the situation was so bad that all the county's taxes were being paid by the east district, which alone had escaped severe damage. The degree-holders pressed for a 70% tax remission but in the chaos of the times it seems unlikely that their request can have reached the central government.[57]

As was described in Chapter 2, the initial scene after the revolts was one of chaos and destruction. The fact that much land had gone out of cultivation evidently resulted for a time in considerable injustice with regard to tax collection. Some of Chang Ying's relatives who had returned to their holdings from Nanking were dismayed to find 'the registers in confusion and the taxes and labour services particularly troublesome for, quite apart from the regular taxes, the wastage fees were increased several times over'.[58]

It looks nonetheless as if all these hardships cannot have persisted for very many years. Extensive tax remissions were granted on devastated land, which was rapidly brought back under cultivation. In one or two cases the grading of the land was altered because of the damage it had suffered, but by and large the Ming system of land classification and *mou* conversion was adhered to almost unchanged.[59] Once the total acreage in 1663 reached exactly the late Ming figure of 410,061 *mou*, no further increases were registered. The land-tax rates of 0.083 taels of silver and 0.05 *shih* of grain per *mou* were probably very close to, if not identical with, the Ming rates of service levy and land tax before the surcharges of the dynasty's last twenty years were imposed. They were increased only once, but very slightly, in 1672, as a contribution to the costs of the military campaigns against the three rebellious feudatories.[60]

Remissions were also made with regard to the item of *ting*, since this was evidently still levied on the basis of land under cultivation rather than on actual individuals. In 1645 their number was reduced from the late Ming total of 8,719 to 6,935. Though it was gradually increased again in the following years it never, throughout the rest of the seventeenth century, rose very much higher than the late-Ming figure.[61]

As far as can be discovered, the only item of taxation in T'ung-ch'eng that did increase substantially in the seventeenth century was the reed tax. There was good reason for this, for in the course of the Ming much reedy land had been steadily converted to arable and its tax quota was therefore unreasonably low. The Wan-li emperor had ordered a sharp increase in the national quota of reed tax, which in T'ung-ch'eng resulted in a rise of approximately one-third, from 2,706 taels to 3,611 taels.[62] This was gradually raised in the early Ch'ing, probably not unreasonably in view of the large tracts of land involved and the fact that it did not pay the other regular taxes, until by 1697 it stood at 5,837 taels.[63] In the Shun-chih reign (1644–61), however, an attempt was made to minimize any resentment this might cause, and to ensure fairer allocation of the increase, by having the people of the 'sandbar' areas registered in *chia* and *li* in the same way as the rest of the population. This reform was first proposed by three *sheng-yüan*, among whom was Tso Kuo-ch'u, a younger relative of Tso Kuang-tou (perhaps consciously emulating the benevolent act of his forebear Tso Lin).[64]

With this one exception it therefore looks as if, on paper, the county's tax load in the early Ch'ing remained static at very much the same level as in the Ming. In view of the continuing economic growth in the seventeenth and eighteenth centuries described in Chapter 2 it is hardly likely to have caused immense distress.[65] This continuing failure to exploit the district's tax-paying potential may of course be largely explicable by the fact that the new government was anxious to win the support of the population and reluctant to make them pay a higher rate of tax than they were accustomed to. One may suspect however that it is also connected with the attitudes and activities of the local elite, and it is the changes in these that are crucial to our understanding of the fiscal and social history of the early Ch'ing.

There is certainly some evidence to show that at least in the very early period after the revolts the eminent families of T'ung-ch'eng did continue to exert their influence in their own narrow, financial self-interest. A case in point is that of Chang Ying's relatives, mentioned above, who were so dismayed by their tax liabilities on their return. Their property was all in the same area, and one of their number, Chang Ping-ch'ien (1618–75, in the same generation as Chang Ying's father) apparently undertook to negotiate with the authorities (or the clerks) on their common behalf. Though he was not a degree-holder himself he still managed to get their land classification sorted out and their taxes 'somewhat reduced', which makes one suspect that he must have relied heavily on his family's position and prestige to do it.[66] Despite this kind of activity there seems, as was earlier pointed out, to have been no revival of the short-sighted and arrogant behaviour of the late Ming. There can be no doubt that T'ung-ch'eng's elite in the Ch'ing in general adopted much more cautious attitudes, and were much less blatant in their assertion of social privilege.

It cannot be pretended that all the reasons for this change are as yet fully understood. Two outstanding causes can however be discerned. One was quite obviously the fear that any repetition of former excesses might once again bring about violent reactions. The other, though its crucial importance seems not to have been generally recognized, was the Ch'ing government's abrupt change in the laws of tax exemption. In 1657 the former generous scale of exemption allowed to officials and degree-holders was abolished. Henceforward no exemptions whatever were to be allowed from the service levy on land, and when it came to personal service (for instance as a *li-chia* head with tax collection responsibilities) only the holder of the degree or office himself was to be immune; his relatives were no longer to share the benefits. This limitation applied also in the case of exemption from *ting* assessed on land.[67]

This drastic move must surely have been aimed not merely at reducing mounting tax arrears but also at ending the selfish and disruptive exploitation of excessive privilege that had helped to bring about such social chaos at the end of the Ming. Its enforcement, though initially difficult, was crucial to the stability and long-term survival of the new government, which may in part explain the severity of Ch'ing measures against continued tax evasion and malpractice by the upper classes. The most famous showdown was of course the so-called Chiangnan tax clearance case, which took place in 1661 in the heartland of 'gentry' tax resistance.[68] It was not unique, however, and it may be that, even if such harsh measures were not used in T'ung-ch'eng itself, warning rumours still reached the ears of its elite.

A similar case did in fact occur at about the same time in Feng-yang prefecture, north Anhwei, where over a hundred 'gentry' were arrested and imprisoned for tax default. One of the local judicial personnel, Huang Chen-lin, had them released, however, and it was eventually decided not to press the charges. This cautionary tale was certainly known to some of the T'ung-ch'eng elite because Huang was a friend of Chang Ying, who preserved the story.[69]

Unfortunately there appears to be only one surviving piece of evidence to indicate that the authorities in T'ung-ch'eng itself may have been forced to adopt similar methods. Rather appropriately it concerns both the Chang and Yao families, and seems to suggest that Chang Ying's enterprising relative Chang Ping-ch'ien, who so cleverly managed to get his kinsmen's tax liabilities reduced, may subsequently have come to grief in the course of his activities. In the Yao genealogy in the biography of Yao Wen-ao (1629–88, a grandson of Yao Chih-lan) it is stated that 'when his relative by marriage Chang Liu-chi was seized and imprisoned for being in arrears with his taxes he [Yao Wen-ao] sold some property in order to pay them for him'. Yao Wen-ao was definitely married to one of Chang Ying's relatives and Liu-chi appears to be a mistake for or a variant of Liu-chieh, the *hao* of Chang Ping-ch'ien.[70] Perhaps he had presumed too long on his family's influence to protect him from paying his proper dues. No other mention of this kind of thing has yet come to light but it is hard to believe that it can have been a unique case.

Such events, following the shock of the rebellion and the change in the exemption laws, may well have induced a somewhat chastened mood in the elite of T'ung-ch'eng and have reinforced the change of heart that appears to have begun in the course of the revolts. If they henceforward enjoyed no enormous legal privileges, other than personal exemption for degree-holders from actual performance of labour service and one unit of *ting*, then it would be much more difficult and dangerous for them to attempt to protect large numbers of their relatives as they had been able to do before, and to set themselves apart too obviously from the mass of the population.

They therefore had to find more subtle and more altruistic-seeming ways of protecting their own interests that would at all costs avert any further social unrest and antagonism. The solution, it appears, was to return firmly to the earlier tradition of intervening directly with the authorities in fiscal matters, ostensibly for the benefit of the whole county. If their action also benefited themselves and their families it was no coincidence. It can be demonstrated that this happened over and over again in the second half of the seventeenth century and was strongly instrumental in preserving the fiscal status quo in the county.

It looks from the surviving evidence as if it was usually the member of the local elite who currently held the highest office and enjoyed the greatest prestige who took it upon himself to negotiate with the authorities on the county's behalf. His action may very well have been initiated by the promptings of friends and kinsmen, though it is often impossible to prove this. It comes as no surprise to find that the most frequent local spokesman in the very early Ch'ing, up to the 1670s, was a member of the Yao family, namely Yao Wen-jan (1621–78). He was a grandson of Yao Chih-lan (the prefect mentioned above, who had also attempted to defend local interests in the Ming) and elder brother of Yao Wen-ao. He was also the friend, mentor and relative by marriage of Chang Ying, and was to become the father-in-law of Chang Ying's second and most famous son, Chang T'ing-yü. He had become a *chin-shih* at the end of the Ming but evidently had no objections to serving under the new dynasty for by 1656 he had risen to the post of junior metropolitan censor at the capital. In that year he returned home to T'ung-ch'eng, partly it is said to look after his father but also probably because of a recurring illness.[71]

A large part of his ten-year retirement seems to have been spent interfering in matters of local administration. Though his family biographer insists that he never acted in his own private interests, it is admitted that 'whenever there occurred anything that would be of benefit or harm to the locality he would send letters back and forth until he got what he requested'.[72] By great good fortune many of his letters and proposals are preserved in the seventeenth-century edition of the gazetteer and elsewhere, so that it is possible to document in some detail the kinds of changes in fiscal arrangements he was anxious to prevent and the impositions he wished to remove. Not surprisingly most of them were concerned with the registration of land and above all with service liabilities in one form or another.

His first intervention occurred most likely in 1656, either when he was still at the capital or just after his return home. It amounted to an attempt to avert what he considered an unfair increase in the county's *ting* quota.[73] The authorities had allowed large remissions in this after the rebellions but were now anxious to get the quotas up to their earlier levels, if not above them.[74] In An-ch'ing prefecture, in order to hasten this, it was decreed that each county simply add 1,000 *ting* to its existing total. Yao Wen-jan argued cogently against this on the very rational-seeming grounds that as each county's original *ting* quota was different a blanket increase was improper. T'ung-ch'eng in particular had suffered heavily in the rebellions and some of its remitted *ting* had already been restored in 1655; a further increase of 1,000 would mean bringing the quota up to slightly more than the late-Ming figure of 8,719. It was also unfair, he claimed, because the rate per *ting* in T'ung-ch'eng of 0.358 taels was higher than elsewhere; in Huai-ning county (An-ch'ing itself) the rate was only 0.168 taels, though the original *ting* quota of 11,261 was larger. Any increase in the number of *ting* in T'ung-ch'eng should therefore be proportionately scaled down. In the following year, 1657, perhaps as a direct result of his protest, the number of *ting* registered in T'ung-ch'eng rose only by 399. There was nonetheless a further increase in 1662, bringing the figure to 8,796, rather more than the late Ming total.[75]

It is somewhat difficult to discern precisely why Yao Wen-jan was so anxious over this matter. The rate of 0.358 taels per *ting* was not heavy considering that it was imposed on approximately 50 *mou* of land, and the total annual quota, never as much as 3000 taels, was a mere fraction of the regular surcharge in silver levied with the land tax (the total of which amounted to over 33,000 taels in 1672).[76] It could be that the *ting* charge was particularly subject to malpractice and became the vehicle for all kinds of extra, unscheduled impositions, but this would be difficult to prove. On the other hand it may well be that this item fell most heavily on medium and large landowners if, as seems possible, the Ming regulation that those with less than 50 *mou* of land should be spared it, were still in force. It was just at this time moreover that the changes in the exemption system were about to come into effect. They could have been rumoured at the capital before the cuts were actually made and aroused widespread fears that elite liabilities to charges such as *ting* might be greatly increased.

In T'ung-ch'eng fairly generous exemption from *ting* payments was in fact allowed, very possibly as a result of Hu Tsan's protest in the late Ming. Before 1672 no fewer than 1,597 of the total quota were always exempted, a benefit that would go entirely to degree-holders and their families. Only in 1672 was it finally decided, in view of the revised regulation that officials and degree-holders should be excused only one *ting* each, to cut this figure to 789. Tax was collected thereafter on 8,007 *ting*.[77] The delay in the enforcement of the new rule may in itself testify to the strength of elite opposition to it. The amounts at stake cannot be considered large, however, and one is inclined to conclude that intervention in a matter of this sort was undertaken more on principle, out of a general dislike of seeing elite liabilities increased in any way at all, rather than from a rational fear of any real economic hardship that might result.

Because virtually all taxes and services in T'ung-ch'eng were by this stage exacted on the basis of landownership, accurate registration of fiscal acreage continued to be of crucial importance. The Ch'ing government in a nationwide attempt to tighten up the system at first ordered that registration of households and their property should take place every three years instead of every ten, but from 1647 made the compilation of registers quinquennial.[78] This in itself was apparently not enough to sort out the confusion in landownership and tax liabilities that flourished immediately after the rebellions.

The Board of Revenue was convinced that inaccurate registration of land and *ting*, combined with deliberate perversion of the registers by 'gentry' (*shen-chin*), rich households and clerks was largely responsible for continuing tax arrears. In 1663 therefore orders were issued for yet another national land survey.[79]

It was just at this time that the T'ung-ch'eng magistrate, Wu Ju-chi (in office 1660–7) reported that the amount of taxable acreage in the county had finally returned to the late-Ming figure.[80] The ordinary registers of households to which information on property was attached (i.e. the 'complete book of taxes and labour services', *fu-i ch'üan-shu*, corresponding to the Ming yellow registers) had by this time already been compiled more than once. The prospect of making out proper land registers, along the lines of the Ming fish-scale registers, must have threatened to expose many existing malpractices and aroused considerable alarm among local landowners.

Yao Wen-jan therefore stepped in swiftly to avert it, arguing once again in very practical terms over the unnecessary trouble and expense of a thorough land survey. According to him a single *mou* of land in T'ung-ch'eng might comprise as many as five or six individual plots (*ch'iu*). 'As there are over 390,000 *mou* in the county this is the equivalent of nearly two million plots. One page of the fish-scale register contains over 200,000 sheets of paper. The cost of making each page, including the cost of paper, printing forms, brush and ink, and copying, amounts to over 0.01 tael. The total cost of one register is over 2,000 taels. In addition heavy expenses are incurred in sending copies of the register to the provincial treasurer . . . The cost of making the registers for one prefecture and for the whole province is proportionately heavier . . .'[81]

He therefore 'discussed the matter [of the survey] with the magistrate, Mr Wu, and they decided to adhere to the system of the Wan-li reign [i.e. 1588] whereby the fields were divided into nine grades . . . There were no deficits in the taxes and no shortage or excess in the acreage [quota], and the local people praised him.'[82] In other words, he apparently succeeded in ensuring that the survey that was carried out retained the late Ming land classification and tax quota without change. No increases in acreage were registered in the county thereafter (with one very minor exception in 1729) and no further attempts were made to revise the grading of land to correspond to changes in its fertility.[83] This implies particular advantages for the owners of lower-grade and therefore lightly taxed land who were able to improve it, which may well be one reason why Chang Ying in *Heng-ch'an so-yen* insists on the wisdom of buying poor land cheaply and working hard to increase its yields.[84]

It was this kind of opposition from locally influential persons that eventually forced the government to abandon its plans for a national land survey as

impractical.[85] In 1665 the governor of Anhwei, Chang Ch'ao-chen, memorialized to this effect in terms too similar to Yao Wen-jan's to be entirely
coincidental. 'All the expenses of making registers and maps have to come
from the local people and in a large county amount to approximately 1,000
taels or more. According to the calculations of myself and my staff the total
expenses [for the province] will be at least several tens of thousands. Our
tax and labour service quotas are met in full every year . . . If, as in the case
of Su-chou and Sung-chiang, tax revenues are complete, even before the land
survey is carried out, this shows that surveying really bears no relation to
national revenues. If we are given permission to stop the survey we can thus
save a million taels in the empire as a whole.'[86] In other words the authorities
were more or less resigned to injustice as long as local tax quotas could be
met, and were unwilling to upset landowners by really determined efforts to
allocate them more accurately.

In the light of all these developments it is hard to believe that T'ung-ch'eng's
landowners in the early Ch'ing can have been troubled by excessively heavy
taxation. There was however one major grievance left, namely the fact that
personal labour service was still required in the matter of tax delivery. The *li-
chia* method that had proved so onerous and unpopular during the Ming was
something that the Ch'ing government became anxious to abolish. Instead,
taxpayers were to take their dues in person to the county offices, and delivery
of the taxes to higher administrative levels was to be undertaken by the county
authorities themselves, rather than by the *li* heads in decennial rotation.[87]

In T'ung-ch'eng, as in many other places, the older system seems to have
continued in operation for quite some time after the change of dynasty. It
was probably much too convenient for the county government ever to abandon it lightly, especially in the difficult years after the rebellions when administrative resources must have been strained to the utmost. The hardship
and financial burden of the service were considerable, for those chosen as
the head of their *li* for the year were responsible for all the expenses of tax
prompting and collection, and for making up any arrears out of their own
pockets. In T'ung-ch'eng several *li* constituted a *ch'ü* or section. From every
ten of these was chosen one household as *ch'ü-t'ou* or section head to undertake the even greater responsibility of organizing the delivery of taxes to
higher authorities. It was claimed that 'they were at the mercy of the yamen
clerks who exploited them ruthlessly . . . so that those chosen for this duty
immediately found their families ruined'.[88] These evils were clearly not unique
to the Ch'ing dynasty and seem never to have aroused any concerted protests
from the elite until the term of office of the magistrate Shih Lang, from 1653
to 1657. 'He followed the local gentry (*shen*) in advocating the abolition of
ch'ü-t'ou and the removal of *li-chang*.'[89] The timing is significant, for it was

in 1657 that the change in the laws of tax and service exemption was prom-
ulgated. Henceforward many members of elite families who had hitherto
relied on their degree- or office-holding relatives for protection from the
disagreeable duty of *li-chang* would now find themselves subject to it. As
affluent landowners they would in fact be among the first to be chosen for
the task; any attempt to avoid it would doubtless require enormous bribery
of the clerks. It is impossible to believe that this was not the real reason for
the sudden, intense efforts of the elite from this time onwards to get the
duty abolished.

Not surprisingly it was Yao Wen-jan who again played the leading role in
the struggle that ensued. He was backed up by his elder brother, Yao Wen-
lieh (1616–65), a *chü-jen* and prefectural judge who was also living at home
at this time. Between them 'they exposed this evil to the authorities, where-
upon collection and delivery were once more made the responsibility of the
officials and the people did not take part in it. The abuses were thus removed.'[90]
This must have taken place during the term of office of Shih Lang's successor,
Yeh Kuei-tsu (1657–60), who was said to have been the first magistrate to
abolish the *li* services.[91]

Yao Wen-jan's major concern was in fact the ending of the worst duty,
that of *ch'ü-t'ou*, as can be seen from a closely argued letter which he sent
direct to the provincial director of grain transport in 1657 or soon after.[92]
It was the *ch'ü-t'ou* who had the task of delivering the 'southern rice' (*nan-mi*),
a special item of the grain tribute that still, as under the Ming system, had in
theory to be sent to Nanking. His difficulties were compounded by the fact
that the clerks in the provincial government would arbitrarily change the
precise destination of the southern rice and exact heavy bribes into the bar-
gain. At this time the *li* representatives of the entire county held a meeting
in the temple of the local deity to discuss the problem. They argued about it
for three days without coming to any decision, for all were afraid to take on
the duty of *ch'ü-t'ou*. Yao Wen-jan, in a cleverly calculated gesture, intervened
to offer to take on the task himself for a year, but this was turned down as
being unseemly for a man of his high status and ill-health. He was then able
to write his indignant appeal, citing this impressive backing from public
opinion, in which he requested that the southern rice henceforth be simply
sent by the county authorities to the provincial capital at An-ch'ing to be
used as troop rations. Evidently he met with some success, for nothing more
was heard of the *ch'ü-t'ou* thereafter.[93]

Some of the *li-chang*'s duties evidently did continue, for at a slightly later
date, around the time of the projected land survey in 1663–4, Yao Wen-jan
made another protest on their behalf. This time he wrote directly to the
provincial treasurer who had recently circulated instructions that all counties'

complete registration and survey records (that is, the 'complete book of taxes and labour services', *fu-i ch'üan-shu*) be forwarded to the prefecture where a bureau was to be opened to compile them into comprehensive registers. Yao argued, with apparent success, that this would be an immense extra burden for the *li* heads who would have to go to the prefectural capital in person and finance the compilation there themselves, in addition to their tax-prompting responsibilities. His statement that these *li* heads all had land in the range of 500–700 *mou* (by which he almost certainly meant fiscal *mou*, so in practice more) shows them to have been fairly substantial property owners.[94]

There was thus continuing pressure on the provincial and local authorities to cut down the burden of *li-chia* service as far as possible. This was no doubt why magistrate Wu Ju-chi (1660–7), whom Yao Wen-jan had influenced so strongly in the matter of the land survey, was said to have determinedly continued the policy of ending *li* services 'in order to benefit the people'.[95] In addition to ensuring that delivery of taxes from the county to higher levels was undertaken by the authorities, there were probably also attempts to end the *li-chang*'s tax-prompting responsibilities. This is suggested by the orders received some time in the early 1670s from the governor of Anhwei, Chin Fu (in office 1671–7), that the method of 'official collection and delivery' of taxes be stringently enforced.[96]

The duty of *li-chang* nonetheless proved extremely difficult to eradicate. It was still in operation in the late 1670s, to the mounting exasperation of the county's elite. By this time unfortunately they had lost their most influential spokesman, Yao Wen-jan, who had died in 1678 in the exalted office of president of the Board of Punishments. They were therefore forced to look around for a new advocate to plead their cause and found one in the person of Chang Ying himself. He was closely related to Yao Wen-jan by marriage and was just then experiencing a meteoric rise at court. He had in 1677 been made head of the newly established and high influential secretarial office of the emperor, the *Nan-shu-fang*, and in addition became a reader of the Han-lin Academy in 1679. The following year he was given the concurrent ranks of Han-lin chancellor and vice-president of the Board of Rites, along with many other personal favours of the emperor, whose friend and confidant he was fast becoming.[97] Since Yao's death he must have had the greatest prestige of any of the T'ung-ch'eng elite. He was moreover, very usefully, a close personal friend of the governor of Anhwei, Hsü Kuo-hsiang, in office there from 1677 to 1684.[98]

Chang Ying while at the capital almost certainly received complaints and requests from relatives and friends at home about the continuance of the irksome rotating duty of tax-prompting because in 1680 'he sent letters repeatedly to Mr Hsü, who for the first time enforced its permanent abolition; a notice to this effect was engraved and set up in front of the county yamen'.[99] The notice in question, giving the text of Hsü's orders which are dated K'ang-hsi 19, third month, sixteenth day (14 April 1680), is preserved in the gazetteer. It states clearly that henceforth tax heads were not to be appointed but that instead each household was to bring the full amount of tax owed to the government granary, there to be checked by appointed tax officers.[100]

These orders were restated and reinforced in a subsequent decree issued in late 1683 in the names of Hsü Kuo-hsiang and Yü Ch'eng-lung, the governor-general of Anhwei, Kiangsu and Kiangsi. This was also engraved on stone.[101] It described the abuses to which the *li-chang* system had been subject at some length and also required that all land sales henceforth be registered at the time the transaction was made, so as to facilitate the accurate levying of taxes from individual households.[102] Yü Ch'eng-lung's decree was to be enforced throughout the area of his jurisdiction, so it appears that Chang Ying's intervention may have had wider repercussions than he anticipated.[103]

Only a few years later he intervened once again, presumably at the request of other members of the elite, to avert an unpopular measure. This was a change in the fish tax, a duty originally imposed on fishermen but by this time paid in silver by owners of property in six areas of the county where there were many lakes and ponds.[104] There was a growing tendency for miscellaneous levies of this kind to be assessed as a uniform surcharge on the land tax.[105] At some time in the 1680s there suddenly arose demands, very likely from those households subject to the fish tax, that it be incorporated with the land and *ting* tax. This meant that it would be levied as an extra surcharge on the registered acreage of the whole county, and was unlikely to be popular with other landowners who were disposed to object to even a slight increase in their tax rates. Chang Ying therefore, on the grounds that it was 'an irregular, extra levy that would cause the people great hardship, made strenuous representations over the matter to the governor, Yang Su-yün (in office 1687–8), and managed to get it stopped'.[106] The memory of his imposing opposition perhaps lingered on, because even after 1728 when all the major items of taxation were finally incorporated in the land tax, this one was not among them.[107]

It certainly appears from the evidence available so far that the T'ung-ch'eng elite in the first forty years or so of the Ch'ing dynasty were still far from helpless when it came to protecting their own financial interests against unwelcome government measures. They were successful in ensuring the abolition of personal labour services by the wealthy, in holding down land and tax quotas at their accustomed level and in avoiding the embarrassment of a detailed land survey. All of this may have compensated in some degree for the sharp reduction in their greatest privilege, that of large-scale tax exemption, one change which they really were powerless to reverse.

The successful defence of local vested interests did however make it virtually impossible for the authorities, handicapped in any case by inadequate staff, to ensure fairness in fiscal administration. Most magistrates were probably resigned to malpractice and to deferring to the implacable force of elite opinion, but T'ung-ch'eng at the end of the seventeenth century was for eight years under the rule of an energetic and idealistic administrator, Kao P'an-kuei, who between the years 1689 and 1697 attempted to carry out an extensive reform programme.[108] Many of his proposals are preserved in the gazetteer and afford a revealing glimpse of the intractable administrative problems the authorities were up against and the extent to which their actions were circumscribed.

Kao P'an-kuei's main concern was with the effective implementation of the quinquennial registration (*pien-shen*) of households and property, on the basis of which the 'complete book of taxes and labour services' was compiled. This was the key to all the government's tax collection procedures and afforded more varied opportunities for malpractice in all its aspects than any other measure.[109] One of Kao's first acts was to order the abolition of the numerous 'customary fees' (*lou-kuei*) hitherto collected on the occasion of every registration. These had officially amounted to nearly 2,000 taels in all, and were apt to be doubled by the unofficial exactions of the clerks and runners.[110] He then turned his attention to the problem of tightening up the registration procedures themselves, and set out his analysis of the difficulties and proposals for their solution in a closely argued memorandum to the provincial authorities.[111]

The crux of the problem was still the accurate registration of land and of the *ting* liabilities attaching to it. The quinquennial registers were supposed to take account of interim changes in each household's property but in T'ung-ch'eng they were simplified for the sake of convenience and did not correspond closely to the somewhat more accurate but less official 'registers of actual tax collection' (*shih-cheng-ts'e*) which were used, as the name implies, in the annual collection of taxes. The discrepancies naturally enough provided considerable opportunities for 'adjustments' by the clerks, and led to continual complaints of injustice. Kao therefore ordered that henceforth the quinquennial registration would be based closely on the 'actual collection registers'.[112]

This in itself would not have had much effect unless more precise records could have been kept of changes in land ownership. All the records in use were based on the registers compiled in 1664, which were said to have noted correctly the ownership and location of the various individual plots of land in the county. This, it will be remembered, was precisely the occasion of Yao Wen-jan's intervention over the land survey, whereby he ensured that no really thorough reassessment of taxable acreage was undertaken, so it is open to question whether even these registers were in fact accurate to begin with. No careful checks had been made in the following thirty years, moreover, which led to 'a constant stream of complaints about people collecting rent without paying tax and people paying tax without owning land'. In other words, exactly the same kinds of abuses that the Ming magistrate had attempted to deal with in 1588, a hundred years earlier, were still flourishing.[113]

Kao P'an-kuei could do little about this other than insist that all property transactions be registered annually and that the exact number and location of a household's individual plots be noted in the quinquennial registers. It is most improbable that this can have had any permanent effect. It is true that practically all land deeds in T'ung-ch'eng of Ch'ing date do contain the provision that tax on the land should be paid by the purchaser from the moment of transfer, but fraudulent manipulation of tax liabilities must in practice have proved impossible to eradicate. This is confirmed by some lineage rules. For example, the final edition of the Tsou genealogy, compiled in 1923, still contains a warning that all lineage members when conducting transactions over land, whether with their own relatives or outsiders, should measure the plot carefully so as to avert any subsequent complaints that the vendor was still left with part of its tax payments.[114]

In the last resort it would always be in the interests of the wealthier and more powerful landowners not to have too close a check by government agencies on the precise extent and location of their holdings. This was very probably the real reason for Yao Wen-jan's move in the 1660s to prevent the one measure that might actually have enforced it (though it is also open to doubt whether the local administration with its inadequate and venal staff ever could have carried out a really effective survey). Since the simplified form of registration that he had advocated continued in use there was little hope of real reform. As far as can be seen the most tangible result of these particular proposals by Kao P'an-kuei was an attempted improvement in the recording of population, for the figures of persons and households for 1693 do show a marked rise over the previous ones of 1672.[115]

The other major difficulty, closely connected with land registration, arose over the allocation of the *ting* charge. The county's total quota of *ting* had now risen to 9,006. Of this number 789 were still exempted, so that the tax of 0.358 taels of silver per *ting* was imposed on 8,217. As Kao pointed out, this now meant the imposition of 1 *ting* on approximately every 40 *mou* of land, which could not by any stretch of the imagination be considered a hardship since 40 *mou* was far more than one man could cultivate by himself. (It should also be remembered that he was talking in terms of the fiscal *mou*, which was larger than the standard measurement.) Despite this there were persistent attempts by 'powerful persons' to evade the charge by bribing the clerks, which inevitably meant that the burden fell more heavily on less affluent landowners.[116]

A particular variant of this abuse was the so-called 'slippery *ting*' (*hua-ting*), whereby people were retained by the clerks on the registers as being liable to *ting* payments even after all their land was sold; only heavy bribery was sufficient to remove them. Another form of it was when unscrupulous persons bribed the clerks to enter them as *ting* on the registers even though they had no land. They then went around extorting money from households in their neighbourhood ostensibly to enable them to pay the *ting* charge. If enough cash were not forthcoming they laid a legal complaint which the magistrate, having no means of ascertaining the true facts, had no option but to follow up. The only way to check this kind of practice and to deny the clerks their opportunities was to ensure that at every quinquennial registration those with 40 *mou* of land or more should be registered as one *ting*, those with 80 *mou* as two *ting*, and so on.[117]

Kao did on the other hand show some sympathy (perhaps under pressure) for the degree-holding elite when it came to the matter of exemptions. The quota of *ting* exempted was still set firmly at 789, but because T'ung-ch'eng was a county of such prosperity and academic distinction the number of persons eligible for them was far greater than this. Apart from the 'gentry' (*chin-shen*, evidently meaning holders of the two higher degrees, and those in office) there were over a thousand *kung-sheng* and *chien-sheng* (degrees frequently acquired by purchase) and seven or eight hundred *sheng-yüan*, all of whom could legally claim one *ting* exemption. Whenever a degree-holder died there was at once great competition for the *ting* exemption thus vacated, and the clerks did a thriving annual business in selling these to the highest bidder. The best that Kao could do to alleviate the problem was to order that changes in *ting* exemption should be made only on the occasion of the quinquennial registration, regardless of deaths and examination successes in the interim.[118] This does illustrate quite clearly the remarkable change in the legal privileges of degree-holders since the Ming. So far from easily obtaining *ting* exemption for their entire families, many of them were now hard put to it to acquire the small remaining exemption to which they were still legally entitled.

In his reforming zeal Kao also attempted, in 1694, to remedy similar abuses in the registration of the *chou* or sandbars along the Yangtze. The inhabitants of these paid the reed tax in silver rather than the regular land tax, and were thus in effect tenants of the government. Surveying the *chou* was extremely difficult owing to periodic landslips and changes in their boundaries, and was also frustrated by 'local bullies' who took advantage of the confusion over the liabilities of the *chou* households in order to profit themselves. Kao devised and submitted to the prefectural authorities an elaborate three-point programme for surveying and reclassifying those parts of the *chou* that lay along the river, where changes were most frequent. Yet even he was afraid to offend powerful vested interests and thereby 'cause disturbances' by ordering a government survey of the interior of the *chou*. He had to be content with offering an amnesty to those persons there who would own up to 'illegal encroachments' and volunteer to pay their proper dues.[119]

He did however select the three worst cases of tax evasion by large-scale occupiers of *chou* land as public examples. The details of their property and revisions of their tax assessment were published in the gazetteer.[120] The most striking fact about all three is actually the smallness of the amounts payable even after the revisions. The largest of these holdings totalled 446 *mou* (again possibly a large size fiscal *mou*) of arable, pasture and ponds; its total annual tax payment before the investigation was 5.253647 taels, and after it 5.75655 taels. Such figures make one doubt that taxes on the *chou*, despite the increase in the reed tax quota during the early Ch'ing, can ever have been crippling.

Something that Kao P'an-kuei evidently did not permit during his term of office was a return to the system of tax-prompting and collection by *li* heads. Any attempt to do so would probably have incurred the wrath of the elite whose goodwill was essential if his other projected reforms were to have even the slightest chance of success. Yet the method of personal delivery by taxpayers did entail considerable hardship, particularly with small items like the southern rice (*nan-mi*) which was still exacted at a different time of year from the rest of the land tax. The trouble and expense of travelling long distances in order to deliver such a small amount meant that taxpayers were even more willing in this case to allow others to contract to make the payments for them, giving further rise to the well-known abuse of *pao-lan*. In addition it provided the clerks and runners with extra opportunities for extortion and payments were often delayed. Kao's solution in this case was to request that the collection of the southern rice be finally combined with that of the land tax.[121] These kinds of malpractice were nonetheless bound to flourish as long as personal delivery of taxes continued to be enforced. Perhaps this is one reason why Kao cut the wastage fees on all items of tax, in order to relieve taxpayers of at least one charge that easily lent itself to abuse.[122]

Fears that personal delivery of taxes did penalize the average taxpayer were indeed shared by higher authorities. A few years later Liu Kuang-mei, governor of Anhwei from 1703 to 1709, was reportedly 'afraid that the yamen runners were harsh in exacting taxes and wanted to put into operation the *kun-tan* system'.[123] This method had been devised in 1700; taxpayers were to be organized in units of five to ten households, the tax-prompting agent being a member of that which owed most taxes. When its taxes were paid up the tax demand or 'rolling form' (*kun-tan*) was passed on to the next household and so on, in order of the amount of tax owed. Any household that did not pay up and pass on the demand form was punished.[124] The method did avoid the necessity of stationing runners in the rural districts but passed the responsibility of tax collection back to the households of the *li-chia* organization especially, of course, the wealthier ones, who would once again be first in line as tax-prompting agents.

This unpleasant prospect was averted by Chang Ying, who by this time was living at home again in T'ung-ch'eng in retirement. Alarmed by what he considered to be the misdirected concern of the governor he took immediate steps to have the scheme squashed. 'He recalled that in T'ung-ch'eng since the tax prompting *li* heads had been done away with the taxpayers all delivered their dues individually. The taxes were correct and the rural communities were not troubled. Superiors and inferiors were at peace with one another and there was no clash of public and private interest. He felt that while the imposition of the *kun-tan* system might be advantageous in other counties, in T'ung-ch'eng it would be better to adhere to former ways.' The luckless governor, confronted with such opposition from a former president of the Board of Rites, grand secretary and personal adviser of the monarch, had no alternative but to drop his scheme. Chang Ying's son, Chang T'ing-yü, reports that this was welcomed in T'ung-ch'eng by the inhabitants of the *li*, but one imagines that it would be the more affluent ones among them who had most cause for rejoicing.[125]

Chang Ying like Yao Wen-jan before him appears during his retirement to have taken on the role of watchdog in what he conceived to be the interests of the locality. His final act of intervention, shortly before his death in 1708, illustrates vividly the conservative and anti-commercial bias of the local elite and their concern at all costs to avert any further social unrest. In the words of Chang T'ing-yü: 'Within the boundaries of the county is much hilly land, occupied largely by graves and mourning huts. There had never been any mining there. Some years previously there suddenly appeared unscrupulous profiteers from another area who started talk of opening mines there. One or two local layabouts vied with each other in making up to them; they stirred up people's feelings and aroused uneasy fears. My late father then wrote about it to the governor, Mr Liu, speaking in the most vigorous terms of the harm that was being caused. He also pointed out that the land north and south of the Yangtze was definitely not a mining area and that never before had mines been started there. Mr Liu was fully convinced of the harm that this would cause to the people ... and the whole business was stopped.' This was followed by an imperial decree forbidding it in perpetuity, at which Chang Ying was overjoyed.[126] It was the common opinion among the upper class in Ch'ing China that miners were a feckless and impoverished lot, liable to cause disorder when assembled in large numbers.[127] Such fears in T'ung-ch'eng were no doubt magnified by the spectre of the all too recent past, so that Chang Ying's action very likely met with widespread approval.

T'ung-ch'eng in the eighteenth century, as was shown in Chapter 2, appears to have enjoyed continuing prosperity and further economic expansion. There is unfortunately much less information available on fiscal policies during this period, and on the attitudes of the local elite towards them. It is improbable however that there were any dramatic new developments. The mid Ch'ing was, as Ho Ping-ti has pointed out, a period of fairly static government demand.[128] Internal rebellion and external military threats had abated, and if revenues were adequate there was no need to risk popular antagonism by attempts to increase them. In T'ung-ch'eng once the elite had established the principle that their interests were to be respected, and tax collection procedures had settled into predictable and unchanging patterns, there was possibly less need for high-level intervention of the kind undertaken so readily by Chang Ying and Yao Wen-jan. In other words, a balance of interests appears to have been established whereby the local government, as long as it could collect the rather minimal official tax quotas, was content to let the elite conduct the affairs of the county in their own way.

It is therefore not surprising to find that very few significant changes with regard to fiscal matters were recorded in T'ung-ch'eng during the eighteenth and early nineteenth centuries. The most noticeable one was a rapid increase in registered population beginning in the 1690s, with particularly sharp rises in 1743 and 1790 (see Appendix I). These can be explained by changes in registration procedures in 1741 (when the *pao-chia* organization was made responsible for population returns) and in 1775 (when the whole system was once more tightened up).[129] Whether the figures are accurate or not is quite another matter. An increase of over tenfold in a century, to a total of nearly two-and-a-half-million in 1825, is impossible; even if the total for 1724 were far too low that for 1825 seems very improbable for a county of average size.[130] The suspicion that the figures were rather arbitrarily compiled is confirmed by the fact that the ratio of persons to households continues to be very high, fluctuating between 7 and 9 right down to 1825, despite the fact that financial incentives for household amalgamation must have diminished with the ending of most personal labour services and taxes assessed on the individual. The best that can be said is that the population was probably increasing fast, but not at that rate.

The *ting* total, as might be expected, altered very little. From 1713 it was permanently frozen, in accordance with imperial edict, at 8,231 *ting*, from which the fixed exemption of 789 had already been deducted.[131] The only increase in registered acreage occurred in 1729, when 683 *mou* were added to the existing quota, bringing the total up to 410,774 *mou*. The previous year, 1728, saw the final rationalization of the county's tax structure whereby all items of tax in silver, including *ting* (but with the one exception of the fish tax) were combined together and levied as a single surcharge on each *mou* of land. The wastage fees were at the same time standardized at a rate of 10% for each item.[132] This change was carried out on a large scale in the Yung-cheng reign as part of a general drive for administrative efficiency. It added rather little to the total tax quota and, by reducing the possibilities for illegal extortion by the clerks, probably proved a considerable even if temporary benefit to most taxpayers.

What happened to the *ting* exemption after this time is not absolutely clear. The quota of silver on the 8,231 *ting* was spread as a uniform charge of 0.0074 taels per *mou* (plus the wastage fee of 10%) but there is no mention that degree-holding landowners were excused any of this.[133] There is no strictly logical reason why they should have been, since the total of 8,231 *ting* already took into account their exemption of 789. Even if they were, the amount was obviously a minimal part of the total silver payment of 0.1029 taels per *mou* and cannot, contrary to the view of some scholars, have conferred really significant advantages on them. It therefore appears that the legal privileges of T'ung-ch'eng's degree-holders with regard to tax exemption had now reached their lowest ebb, and that there can have been little difference in this respect between them and the general population. Whether or not they resented this is unknown but seems improbable. By the eighteenth century the memory of the Ming privileges that had set the elite families so firmly apart from the rest were probably fading. If moreover the general economic situation were favourable, as it seems to have been in the eighteenth century, and official tax quotas still very low, landowning degree-holders may have come to feel it less worth their while to struggle over such a minute and comparatively unimportant item.

Even though the sources for this period present a fairly unanimous picture of prosperity and are noticeably free from laments over heavy taxes and economic distress, it should not be implied that efforts at tax evasion and concealment of landownership diminished in the slightest. Malpractice of this kind seems to have been endemic to Chinese economic life. As long as taxes continued to be delivered in person and supervised by underpaid clerks, abuses like *pao-lan* and extortion of all kinds were bound to flourish. This kind of thing undoubtedly far outweighed the regular taxes in causing trouble and inconvenience, and was very likely a major reason for the concealment of liabilities.[134]

It should be noted in this connection that the enforcement of mutual responsibility for tax payments ensured continual attempts to promote further kinship solidarity over fiscal matters. The lineage organizations which had become prominent in the county by this time were greatly concerned that their members should pay their taxes promptly and in full, mainly because failure to do so could lead to trouble and harassment for the whole group. Injunctions to this effect are commonplace in almost all the lineage rules. To take only one example, the Chaos of T'ung-pei throughout the Ch'ing dynasty ordained that if members did not meet their tax and service obligations in full and at the proper time, or substituted other items for the payments, or only paid half so that their kinsmen were responsible for making up the rest, those who suffered as a result were to report them to the lineage head for condemnation and punishment. Even stronger injunctions are found against those 'degenerate descendants', often *sheng-yüan*, who bribed the clerks to allow them to collect the taxes of others (*pao-lan*), a risky but highly lucrative practice. The Chaos provided that such persons should be denounced by the lineage head to the authorities for dismissal. If the offenders had already managed to collect some of the tax then the lineage was to arrange for a more honest and trustworthy member to take it on in their place.[135]

The lineages of T'ung-ch'eng appear from some of their rules to have played a more active role in fiscal matters than was common in other places.[136] In some instances they made provision for helping poorer members who found themselves in difficulties when it came to fulfilling their obligations promptly. The Ch'en lineage in a rule dated 1707 (which does imply the continuation of some *li-chia* duties) decreed that if their 'weaker' kinsmen were unable to render the services they owed, substitutes were to be arranged for them by the lineage.[137] At least one lineage, the Kaos of Kuan-shan, had charitable land endowed for this purpose by a member in the seventeenth century.[138] Such provisions were not made only by kinship groups, for we hear from Ma Ch'i-ch'ang that in the eighteenth century a certain Wang I-tai (who was also actively concerned in the management of his lineage's affairs) ensured that land be set aside to pay the 'miscellaneous [service] dues' of poorer families in his local *pao* registration unit.[139] It may be that during the Ch'ing, as population multiplied and it became even more difficult for the understaffed local authorities to exert any degree of direct control, collective organizations like the lineages did come to play a much greater part in maintaining local order, especially in fiscal matters. These groups were of course headed by affluent elite families and may well have proved a further vehicle for their exertion of influence in the affairs of the county. This point obviously requires more lengthy discussion and will be taken up again in the following chapter.

Evidence on fiscal administration and economic conditions in T'ung-ch'eng in the nineteenth century is still rather slight, owing to the absence of any edition of the gazetteer later than 1827, and the story will therefore have to be terminated at this point. Yet enough information is available for the period prior to 1827 to permit some provisional answers to the questions raised at the beginning of this chapter. It does appear, first of all, that the local authorities in the Ming and Ch'ing alike failed to exploit the county's rising productivity and that the best they could do throughout five centuries of expanding population and cultivated land acreage was to maintain the collection of a virtually fixed quota of taxes, albeit with the addition of the usual unspecified fees to cover handling costs, etc.[140]

They did on the other hand manage to effect one or two important innovations. These included the shifting of almost the entire fiscal burden to land and the conversion of most personal service to silver payments, a change probably welcomed by landowners in an increasingly monetized economy. They also achieved a notable success in enforcing the severe reduction in tax exemptions for degree-holders in the Ch'ing, which reduced the scope of really blatant tax evasion and helped to break down sharply antagonistic class distinctions. This change may not have been popular with the elite but was very likely accepted in the cause of averting further bloodshed.

Yet even after the upheavals of the seventeenth century, the Ch'ing local administration was in other respects apparently powerless to impose unwelcome changes on an elite determined to maintain its position and protect its vital interests. Attempts to improve the efficiency of registration and tax collection procedures were invariably blocked by members of the elite. The very fact that their active intervention in the public affairs of the county was almost always connected with taxation does in itself indicate that the protection of landed interests was paramount among their concerns. The authorities also remained powerless to check tax evasion at all levels. This persisted not so much because basic tax rates were heavy as because the inefficiency of collection methods and extortion by collection agents proved a constant incentive to avoid payment. Paradoxically, had revenues been higher in the first place it might have been possible to finance more effective and less troublesome methods of collecting them. This vicious circle is a commonplace of Chinese fiscal history but is vividly illustrated by the case of T'ung-ch'eng.

This evidence does not in itself prove that landowning was an immensely lucrative proposition but shows that its profitability is unlikely to have been very adversely affected by fiscal pressures certainly up to the early nineteenth century. It is therefore quite understandable that Chang Ying in his *Heng-ch'an so-yen* was most concerned over fundamental economic conditions such as productivity and grain prices, and dismissed taxation with merely a passing mention.

4
LINEAGE ORGANIZATION AND
SOCIAL STRUCTURE

It has by now become apparent that there existed in T'ung-ch'eng an elite group of families some of whose members were prominent in the life of the county throughout most of the Ming and Ch'ing dynasties and to whom the ownership of land was of considerable importance. It is therefore time to consider more carefully the size and composition of this group and to ascertain what were the really important elements in its long-term standing. One may suspect that the fortunes of the elite were bound up in some way with the lineage organizations that flourished in the county, and an investigation of these will occupy much of the present chapter. In particular it is necessary to discover what was their real social purpose and function, whose interests they served, and to what extent they may have helped to promote the ideals of landowning and study which Chang Ying considered the only means of maintaining a family's membership of the elite.

Owing to the abundance and complexity of the source material a very restricted approach must be adopted. The first part of the chapter will therefore be devoted to the history of Chang Ying's own family and lineage, and that of the Yaos with whom they became so closely connected, and the second to a brief description of the development and principal features of lineage organization in T'ung-ch'eng as a whole during this same period. As considerable work has been done on kinship organization by other scholars, many of the findings presented here will not be new in themselves. Most earlier studies have however concentrated on analysing the lineage and its functions at one point of time and in rather generalized terms. The present one aims to complement them by examining the historical development of a group of lineages in a limited, local context.

History of the Chang and Yao lineages
The ancestors of the Changs, like those of so many other T'ung-ch'eng families, were immigrants who came to the area from the village of Wa-hsieh-pa in Po-yang county, Kiangsi, at the very beginning of the Ming dynasty. They settled in the north-east part of the county, thirty *li* or so from the city,

and continued to live there for many generations, so that the spot in the course of time became named Chang-chia-p'ang after them.[1] They too must have occupied land and set to work to farm it; there is no evidence on the size of their early holdings but it is likely that they began in a small way and gradually built up their fortunes through the peasant virtues of thrift and hard work. These qualities, combined with a strict sense of duty that emphasized charity both to kinsmen and outsiders, were to become a strong family tradition; though later chroniclers present a rather idealized picture of their ancestors in this respect there is no reason to doubt its basis in fact.

According to Chang Ying in *Heng-ch'an so-yen* his forebears at first owned poor land but made strenuous efforts to improve it. His fourth-generation ancestor, Chang P'eng, in the late fifteenth and early sixteenth centuries, was particularly successful at this, and became 'known locally for his prosperity'; his subsequent attempts to protect his land from the incursions of powerful rivals evidently impressed his descendants.[2] It was probably he who laid the real foundations of the family fortunes, and he seems to have been regarded as a person of some consequence in the locality. He and his brother, Chang Feng, were noted for their philanthropy. The former would always give aid in any local emergency while the latter contributed large sums of money every year to help settle lawsuits and quarrels in the prefectural city and to relieve the hardships of prisoners in the county gaol.[3]

How soon their ambitions turned towards scholarly endeavour is unknown. A certain amount of literacy and learning may well have existed among them from a very early stage but the dedicated full-time effort necessary to passing the lengthy series of examinations was extremely expensive to finance. By the sixteenth century however the Changs were certainly in a position to undertake it.

It was fortunate from this point of view that the affluent Chang P'eng had only one son, Chang Mu (1520–56), who thus inherited all his property undivided. Chang Mu evidently built it up further and, by dying at the age of 36 when he had had time to father only two sons, ensured that it would be passed on for one more generation with a minimum of division.[4] This was a crucial point in the family's history, because the fact that he inherited 'extremely rich property' meant that the elder of these two sons, Chang Ch'un (1540–1612), had no need to bother about mundane matters like the family's livelihood but could devote himself instead to uninterrupted study.[5] He was rewarded in 1568 by becoming the first of the family to win a *chin-shih* degree. He subsequently had a distinguished career as a local magistrate (the Ming History lists him among its 'Upright Officials') and after serving as a prefect in Chekiang finally rose to be an administration vice-commissioner (rank 3b) in Shensi.[6]

Chang Ch'un had thus raised himself and his immediate family from being merely wealthy landowners to a social position in the top layers of the county's elite, and it was he, not Chang Ying, who was looked on as the true founder of their eminence. According to their genealogy: 'Our family first began to grow in importance from the time of Chang P'eng, but its acquisition of official rank dates from Chang Mu' (who was given honorary, posthumous rank on account of his son).[7] Chang Ch'un must have been well aware however that this individual success, though gratifying, would not necessarily be easy to repeat, and seems to have given some thought to the problem of how best to consolidate the family's social position in the long term. Here an example was provided by other T'ung-ch'eng families with claims to educational and social distinction at this time and earlier.

One of the most outstanding was that of the Yaos, whose early rise to eminence has been outlined in Chapter 2. They, being descended from a Yüan official, had had a fairly continuous tradition of education from their earliest days in T'ung-ch'eng,[8] and one of them in the second generation was said to have compiled a record of their forebears, tracing them back to T'ang times, presumably in an attempt to enhance the family's prestige. It is significant however that the first real attempt to take this up again did not occur until the time of their first *chin-shih*, Yao Hsü. His ambitious father, who had educated him strictly in the hope of an official career, strongly urged him once more to compile a genealogy for the lineage, something that he was unable to do until he finally retired from office around 1470.[9]

His ostensible motive for the compilation, stated in the preface which he wrote for the completed work, was the orthodox Neo-Confucian desire to make clear the degrees of social relationship among his increasingly numerous kinsmen, so as to ensure their good conduct and dutiful behaviour.[10] In his concern for strict accuracy he abandoned any attempt to attach the group to distinguished pre-Yüan ancestors but limited the record to those Yaos whose descent could be clearly traced to their common forebear who had first made the move to T'ung-ch'eng. His scheme of arrangement followed that prescribed by Ou-yang Hsiu in the Sung dynasty. One may suspect however that his reiterated statement that the purpose of genealogies was *not* to boast of a family's social position and exalt its descendants in fact reveals his true intentions, and that he hoped by drawing the lineage members together into a more coherent social unit to assert more effectively their new-found influence and prestige.[11] Whether these efforts were also accompanied by such measures as the provision of common land or an ancestral hall is unknown. It is interesting though that the next revision of the genealogy likewise occurred at a time of renewed academic success; it was carried out by Yao Hsi-lien's third son, Yao Tzu-yü (1541−1606), one of the *sheng-yüan* who had been so generous over protecting their kinsmen from labour services, and father of the family's second *chin-shih*, Yao Chih-lan.[12]

As will be seen, the Yaos were not the only family to undertake this kind of activity in the sixteenth century, and it is therefore not surprising that Chang Ch'un, on finally retiring from office, followed their example. His first step, around 1606–9, was likewise to compile a genealogy for the nine generations of Changs descended from their 'first ancestor' in the early Ming. This was a somewhat skeletal work, limited to tables of descent and omitting biographical details, but as the first manifestation of the Changs' corporate existence marked an important stage in their history.[13] Chang Ch'un's preface, more explicit and less modest than that of Yao Hsü, clearly reveals its purpose. He acknowledged the importance of honouring the ancestors and promoting harmonious and correct relationships among their descendants, but there is no doubt that this was with the long-term aim of inculcating the proper attitudes and ambitions among them, and in particular of fostering the tradition of agriculture and study that had already led to such success (for the Changs already numbered ten or more *sheng-yüan* among their members). 'He who plants a tree must take care to nourish its roots.' Moreover 'lineages of eminence and long standing' (which he obviously hoped the Changs would become) required worthy descendants if their glory was to be perpetuated.[14]

Chang Ch'un also at this time took the practical step of providing his lineage with some land, 26 *mou* in all, the income from which was to finance the necessary ancestral sacrifices and also to aid members.[15] The amount was not large, but some inalienable property was essential in order to prevent the lineage's corporate activities being dependent on the contributions of individual members (whose fortunes and interest in the kin group might well fluctuate with the passage of time).

Though the Changs were thus becoming one of the more distinguished local families their way of life appears not to have changed drastically, and it is clear that their landed interests were strongly maintained. Chang Ch'un's younger brother, Chang Chien (1555–1616), did not enjoy the same academic success but, being of a tranquil and unambitious nature, stayed at home looking after the property their father had left him, without adding to it much. He too was known as a good man, and during a local famine gave out grain to make gruel for the starving.[16] Of the four sons of Chang Ch'un and the five of Chang Chien at least five became *sheng-yüan* but none held office, and all seem to have devoted considerable time to their property.[17] Chang Ch'un's eldest son, Chang Shih-wei (1557–1623) managed his father's holdings in the latter's absence. He was a conscientious individual of frugal but generous disposition who may well have found compensation for his failure to pass any higher examinations in helping to build up the Changs' as yet embryonic lineage organization. He would always aid the needy among his kinsmen and relatives by marriage, especially with affairs like weddings and funerals, and assisted his father in purchasing ritual land.[18]

They must have felt that all their efforts had been justified when in 1610, just after the compilation of the genealogy, another member of the family succeeded in becoming a *chin-shih*. This was Shih-wei's own eldest son, Chang Ping-wen (1585–1639), whose achievement was said by the local people (or so the Chang genealogy claims) to be a fitting reward for the family's virtue.[19] The family's third *chin-shih* degree was won in 1631 by his cousin, Chang Ping-chen (1608–55), who served first in various Boards at the capital but by the end of the dynasty had risen to become governor of Chekiang. He had no difficulty in transferring his allegiance to the Ch'ing however, and two years before his death was made president of the Board of Punishments.[20]

Chang Ping-wen's career in provincial office, as has already been mentioned, ended less happily.[21] In the years before his heroic death at the siege of Chi-nan, however, he seems like his father and grandfather to have taken considerable interest in the lineage organization, and it was he who in 1618 secured the distinction of having a fulsome preface written for the genealogy by Ho Ju-ch'ung, the later grand secretary, with whose family they had by this time apparently made some marriage connections.[22]

The person who did most to further the family's ambitions at this period was however Chang Ping-wen's younger brother, Chang Ping-i (1593–1667), the father of Chang Ying. He had studied hard under his own father's tutelage but in over thirty years never succeeded in passing any of the higher examinations. In his case too it may well be that frustrated ambition and a self-sacrificing sense of duty found an outlet in promoting the long-term interests of both his immediate relatives and wider family. He was said to have looked after his parents, his brother's orphans and his own children with equal solicitude. As the owner of considerable property (which he appears to have recovered in full after the revolts) he could well afford to give his sons a rigorous educational training. Chang Ying has left a vivid account of the strict daily programme of essay writing and calligraphy to which they were subjected; his father's constant admonitions on the need for unrelenting effort and frugal living evidently impressed him and were later to be reflected in his own writings.[23] His mother too reinforced this training. She was a member of the Wu family, said to be renowned for its virtuous women, and on each of their successive moves during the revolts of the 1630s and 40s her first concern was always to select books to take with them.[24]

It was thus clearly advantageous to have brides from families with the correct social traditions, and Chang Ping-i spared no pains to arrange suitable marriages for his sons. His principal aim seems to have been to forge an alliance with the Yao family, without a doubt one of the most prestigious in the county. It is not easy to tell precisely when the first marriages between the two occurred but almost certainly there were none before this time. By the end of the Ming dynasty however the Changs' standing had risen so far that they too were looked upon as highly desirable in-laws. A daughter of Chang Ping-wen was obtained as a bride for Yao Wen-yen (1633–78), a younger brother of Yao Wen-jan; she was a well-educated and artistic girl, and on her early death her husband promptly married one of Chang Ping-chen's daughters, who was a talented writer of poetry.[25]

The Yaos themselves were famed for bringing up their daughters extremely strictly, which in Chang Ping-i's eyes must have made them even more suitable as wives for his sons.[26] Unfortunately his eldest son, Chang K'o-yen (1615–38), for whom he first obtained a Yao bride, died young.[27] It was therefore necessary in due course to re-cement the relationship, which he did in 1653 by marrying Chang Ying himself to the youngest daughter of Yao Sun-sen (1601–51, a son of the *chin-shih* and magistrate Yao-Chih-ch'i).[28] This was a shrewd match which was to play no small part in Chang Ying's later outstanding career, and which inaugurated a long and mutually profitable tradition of intermarriage between the two families.

Chang Ping-i was clearly concerned not merely for the welfare of his own sons but also to build up the lineage as a whole. It seems to have been threatened hitherto by somewhat haphazard management, so that part of the land donated to it by Chang Ch'un was at one stage sold off.[29] The lineage's income was moreover cut off entirely during the revolts, when its holdings went to waste. The situation was saved by the vigorous action of Chang Ping-i, who recovered the land that had been sold, purchased more and also ensured that it was rapidly brought back into cultivation in the 1640s, so that sacrifices and festivals were once more adequately financed. In addition he made provision for the welfare and education of his kinsmen, aiding 'those who were too poor to pay for weddings and funerals, those who had ambition but could not go to school, and those who were in want and could not support themselves'.[30]

It may well be that his efforts were stimulated by the effects of the revolts themselves, which for a time upset all social relationships in the county, besides decimating many important families. When the survivors returned it quite probably seemed imperative to them to find ways of reasserting their threatened position in the locality, at the same time avoiding a recurrence of the class antagonism that had led to the risings. To strengthen their lineage organizations may very likely have appeared to be one means of achieving this, for it would have the simultaneous effects of enhancing the proper hierarchical social relationships and of promoting friendly feelings among kinsmen of very different social and economic standing.

This theory is supported, as will be shown, by the evidence of the behaviour of many T'ung-ch'eng families in the aftermath of the revolts. Among them were the Yaos, who had found that after ten years of warfare and pestilence, not only were their numbers depleted but with the weakening of ties respect for the lineage had become considerably eroded.[31] When it was discovered in 1657 that around the year 1642 one unworthy and insignificant member (presumably undetected at the time owing to the prevailing chaos) had had the temerity to bury his father next to the hallowed grave of a third-generation ancestor it was decided that matters had gone far enough and that a stand should be taken.[32]

The miserable offender was accordingly denounced to the magistrate and punished by flogging and the cangue for the crime of desecrating ancestral tombs, and a set of rules was immediately devised to prevent any similar recurrence. These were termed 'prohibitions' and were of quite exceptional severity. Henceforward this particular crime was to be punishable by death, and those who cut down trees in the lineage's graveyards (an offence that had also occurred in the previous few years) were to be delivered to the authorities for punishment. Provisions were worked out for the scrupulous care and repair of all tombs, to be organized on a rota basis by the lineage head (*hu-chang*); any negligence was to be penalized by monetary fines.[33] Whether the death penalty was ever carried out by the lineage on its own authority is extremely doubtful, but that it could be invoked at all shows the seriousness with which the matter was regarded and the determination to reimpose control over members.

The principal signatory of these rules was Yao Sun-ch'u, the then lineage head. How this functionary was selected is unknown but his existence does indicate some formal basis for the management of the lineage's affairs.[34] Sun-ch'u, though presumably a capable man, does not appear to have been distinguished in any way, and it is probable that the moving spirit behind the rules of 1657, and the most important figure in the group at this time, was their other signatory, Yao Sun-fei (1598–1663). He was a son of the prefect Yao Chih-lan, a cousin of Yao Sun-sen and the father of eight sons, among whom was Yao Wen-jan. After an eventful career as a magistrate, during which he took part in the late Ming military campaigns in Chekiang, he retired home to T'ung-ch'eng where he directed his organizing capabilities to the family's affairs.[35]

In 1658, the year after the creation of the prohibitions relating to the ancestral graveyards, he initiated what he considered to be a long overdue revision of the genealogy, an arduous task that took four years. It seems to have been financed, to judge from a remark in his preface of 1661, by contributions from some lineage members in proportion to the size of their land-

holdings (an expedient resorted to by other lineages, as will be seen). His
efforts mark a step forward in the Yaos' history, for he left instructions that
in future, in order to reduce the trouble and expense of compilation and to
ensure that it would be carried out regularly and systematically every ten
years (or so he hoped), all members were to keep careful records of births,
deaths, marriages and so on, and report them to the lineage head on the
occasion of the annual sacrifices.[36]

These efforts of his distinguished relative by marriage could well have been
the immediate stimulus that in 1665 prompted Chang Ping-i to inaugurate
the first detailed compilation of the Changs' own genealogy, to replace the
earlier outlines made by Chang Ch'un.[37] The bulk of the work was however
entrusted to his favourite and most promising son, Chang Ying. The preface
which the latter wrote for it reveals clearly his desire to enhance the prestige
of the kin group (which had by now increased considerably in size), by recording in full the recent merits and achievements of all its members, humble
as well as distinguished. A sense of rivalry with the other eminent families
of the area is betrayed by his explicit mention of the Fangs, Yaos and Chaos,
and the importance of their genealogies to them. He selected as model, however, not that of the Yaos but that of the Fangs, compiled in the fifteenth
century by Fang Hsüeh-chien. Despite his desire to glorify his kinsmen, he
insisted on the need for strict accuracy and objectivity in the compilation,
and finally stated his hope that it would be carried out in future at thirty-
year intervals. (Unlike Yao Sun-fei he made no suggestions as to how this
could be systematically provided for; the management of the Changs' affairs
seems at this stage to have continued to depend heavily on the initiative of
individual members.)[38]

On the completion and printing of the work, Chang Ping-i assembled his
kinsmen en masse and harangued them at some length as to the significance
of the occasion, in an attempt to instil in them both a consciousness of their
past, with their long-cherished traditions of farming and study (the only two
permissible ways of life), and also ambitions for the future. To perpetuate
and further glorify a lineage of long standing was like living in a great mansion,
the foundations of which had to be made firm if it were not to be in danger
of collapse. This could be done only through obedience to its instructions,
aid to its members and continuous preservation of its records.[39]

When in the following year, 1667, Chang Ying himself finally succeeded
in becoming a *chin-shih*, it must once again have seemed as if their work in
building up the lineage had been directly rewarded. Yet despite his ensuing
meteoric rise in office, which was to place his family at the very pinnacle of
the county's elite, displacing even the Yaos and Fangs, it does not appear
that their austere traditions were immediately eroded by high living and con-

spicuous consumption. That they could survive the transition to court life is shown by the case of Chang Ping-chen, president of the Board of Punishments in the early Ch'ing, who was said to be extremely frugal in his habits. Even at the capital he had 'a worn-out carriage with lean horses', while at home 'he got all his supplies from his landed property'.[40]

This was even more true of those of the family, the majority, who still spent most of their lives in T'ung-ch'eng. A good example is Chang Ying's eldest surviving brother, Chang Tsai (1616–93), who was described with such approval in *Heng-ch'an so-yen*. He had studied in his youth, sufficiently to become a *sheng-yüan*, but at the age of forty finally gave up the arduous life of examinations and retired to live quietly by Pine-tree lake (hence his sobriquet, Hu-shang), where he had 'several tens of *mou* of lakeshore land and a house'. Here 'even after the Changs' rise to eminence', he continued to live the life of a scholarly recluse, supporting himself quite comfortably on the produce of his land (which he supervised in person), never going to town in thirty years. Though locally respected, sufficiently to receive courtesy calls from the county magistrate, his distrust of worldly life was such that whenever he wrote to Chang Ying at the capital he would urge him to come home and retire.[41] After their father's death he seems to have played the most active role in the management of the lineage's affairs and purchased a certain amount of ritual land on its behalf.[42] This practice was continued by his descendants, several of whom appear as managers of lineage land. His eldest son, Chang T'ing-jui, who also became a *sheng-yüan* but retired early to live a life very much like his father's, was especially active in this respect; he was able to buy more grave land with the surplus income from the ritual land, and was assiduous in providing education for any of his young relatives who lacked it.[43]

Two of Chang Ying's other brothers, Chang Chieh (1626–1704), and Chang Chia (1630–1705), despite holding minor official posts, showed similar traits. The former returned home to live in the country after spending several years as a teacher in Soochow; during the great local crop failure of 1671–2 he contributed grain from his estate to the relief programme which he helped to organize.[44] He and his descendants also took a considerable part in the management of the lineage's property, and he himself donated some land to it.[45] Chang Chia had been an assistant department magistrate but likewise retired to live on his estate in the country, 'enjoying the pleasures of ploughing and reaping'. He was frugal but generous to others, and like his father would not insist on the repayment of loans by those who were really poor.[46] They exemplify rather well the practice of living alternately in town and country advocated by Chang Ying in *Heng-ch'an so-yen*. This ability to give up city life when circumstances dictated and to live more modestly in the countryside may indeed have contributed to the family's survival in the elite.[47]

Chang Ying himself claimed not to have been particularly affluent in his early years, and even to have suffered financial difficulties. This cannot be interpreted to mean real poverty, however, for he had in 1648 been allotted 350 *mou* of land by his father, and was given another 150 *mou* in 1664. Most likely his problems can be attributed to his own admitted inexperience in managing his property (which he did from the year 1658, at the age of twenty) and to a lengthy illness which he suffered at this time.[48] The situation was said to have become so bad that his wife was reduced to pawning her jewellery. She, fortunately, was a frugal not to say puritanical woman who had been instructed by Yao Wen-jan himself in the proper principles of wifely behaviour; in 1660 she successfully took over the management of the property, so that her husband could once more devote himself entirely to his studies.[49] Even so he had to resort to selling off 150 *mou* of land in order to pay the expenses of the *chin-shih* examination in 1667.

His early years in government, as a minor official of the Han-lin Academy, were not particularly easy either, and in spite of his wife's economies it seems that they found it hard to finance the expenditures incurred in office and the affluent style of life that was almost obligatory in Peking. After Chang Ying had served as examiner at the metropolitan examination of 1673 things got so bad that the family 'went short of food for weeks at a time, and when [his wife] managed to get hold of a few *tou* of noodles the entire household had to eat noodle soup for a month'. When this came to the attention of Yao Wen-jan, who was by now back at the capital as vice-president of the Board of War, and seems to have kept an eye on his relative by marriage, 'he considered it lamentable'; he was known for his generosity and may possibly have assisted them.[50] In spite of their difficulties Chang Ying's wife, true to her upbringing, exerted all her influence to prevent him adopting the habits of venality that were so common in official life. At this same time she successfully dissuaded him from accepting a present of 1,000 taels that would have resolved their financial problems, on the grounds of the suspicion it might arouse.[51]

Their situation must have improved rapidly, however, once Chang Ying began his climb to high office and influence with his appointment in 1677 as head of the newly created *Nan-shu-fang*. Though he seems always to have been much more honest than many of his contemporaries, such as his colleague, Kao Shih-ch'i, whose peculation was the cause of much scandal, he was the frequent recipient of valuable presents from the emperor.[52] Having learned from his earlier improvidence, he took care to invest his wealth wisely. He already had a country house in T'ung-ch'eng, in the Lung-mien hills just north of the county city, and in 1682 used one of the emperor's gifts to make an extensive pleasure garden around it.[53] By the end of the century he had acquired over 1,000 *mou* of supposedly 'poor and barren land' which must have provided well for his family in his old age.[54] On his retirement early in 1702 he lived up to his own precepts by spending most of the year at another country house in the same area, and coming to live in the county city only in the winters. The 20 or so *mou* of land attached to it yielded enough produce amply to support a household of ten persons, and in addition provided him with an enjoyable hobby in overseeing farming activities.[55]

One of his major concerns during the last ten or fifteen years of his life was to continue the good work of his father and brothers by further building up the lineage, in order both to safeguard the economic welfare of its members and to prevent their traditional ideals from being endangered by increasing worldly success. He was said to have bought 'over 100 *mou* of common land which yielded over 300 *shih* of grain annually for the relief of the poor and needy in the lineage',[56] and also founded shrines at the ancestral burial places in addition to a private shrine for the use of his own immediate descendants.[57] From 1706 until his death he busied himself in making a revised edition of the genealogy, to include the achievements of the previous forty years.[58]

Chang Ying was always lavish with advice and admonitions to his relatives on practical matters, and in the late 1690s evidently decided that it would be sensible to write down his views on the management of livelihood and the proper conduct of life, so that his posterity might benefit from his rich experience. The results were, first of all, *Heng-ch'an so-yen*, and then a somewhat similar work entitled *Ts'ung-hsün chai-yü*, 'Wise maxims and instructions', written in two parts, in 1697 and 1701. These between them may have served in lieu of formal lineage instructions, which the Chang genealogy does not contain.

The first of these works has already been described and needs no further comment here. The second is a fascinating collection of essays on almost every aspect of life and conduct appropriate to a young man of good family, as well as more philosophical reflections on literary matters. It manifests strikingly Chang Ying's own fundamentally cautious and conservative cast of mind, the product alike of intensive family training and a lifetime in the dangerous world of court politics, and reveals also the attitudes and anxieties that must have been common to many of his class in this period and later.

Unfortunately there is no space here for a detailed analysis of this work. Many of its injunctions in fact repeat and elaborate on those of *Heng-ch'an so-yen*. They include such matters as the need for careful management of property, strict budgeting of expenditure and income, and control of servants, the folly of making loans, and above all, the need for frugality in every aspect of life, including food and drink, clothing, dishes and entertainments. Frequently he quotes the opinion of Yao Wen-jan, his revered teacher, who had clearly made a great impression on him.[59]

Throughout there emerges one overriding preoccupation, his anxiety for the future of his immediate descendants and of the Chang family as a whole, summed up at one point in the telling simile: 'Those who were of old termed scholar official families are like a tree which bears fruit twice a year and whose roots are eventually harmed by it.'[60] The dangers are much worse for the sons of well-established families than for 'poor scholars', for they take for granted the possession of ample resources and influential connections, while their self-confident, not to say arrogant, behaviour all too easily incurs the enmity of others.[61] He therefore warns them repeatedly of the need to behave with modesty, integrity and circumspection while in office, to choose their friends wisely and if all else fails to accept with resignation the will of fate.[62]

Nonetheless if the proper precautions are taken to maintain their educational traditions and simple way of life in their home district, the family as a whole need never sink too low. 'When you look at illustrious official families, of which the older generations have retired or are dead, you will observe that some are in decline while others are flourishing. The difference lies in the fact that in the former case none of the younger people are studying, while in the latter they still keep up their studies.'[63] The city, with its excitements and distractions, is not the proper place for study, however, and his sons and nephews are admonished to give up all frivolities and to devote themselves instead to the study of poetry and prose writing in quieter and more wholesome surroundings. This will also enable them to oversee their property in person.[64]

To preserve close contacts with their native place Chang Ying regarded as being of considerable importance to the family's stability, and it appears that his own younger sons and nephews were kept at home for as long as possible, instead of being allowed to live with him at the capital. Despite his distance from them he supervised their studies closely; they were to write nine essays per month in carefully prescribed style and to send them to him in Peking for correction. He added the severe warning that they were not to get them written by other people, 'which is the usual kind of trick that the young men of great families go in for'. Nor were they to waste too much of their time writing poetry, at the expense of serious preparation for the examinations.[65] This severe training was reinforced by the admonitions of Chang Ying's wife, whose efforts to instil in her sons a proper sense of duty in office were once publicly praised by the K'ang-hsi emperor.[66]

The dangers against which Chang Ying warned were all too real, and could, as Ho Ping-ti has shown, lead to the decline of an important individual family from national eminence to comparatively humble circumstances in the space of a few generations. In the following century or so the Changs and their relatives by marriage, the Yaos, were certainly exposed to all the temptations attendant on great worldly success, and it is instructive to see how they fared in the long term.

Chang Ying's own six sons obviously had an excellent start in life. The fourth and sixth were not able to achieve much, owing to their early deaths, but the other four all became *chin-shih* and followed in their father's footsteps by rising in their careers via the Han-lin academy, something which became traditional in their family.[67] The eldest, Chang T'ing-tsan (1655–1702), died, to his father's great grief, at the age of 47, but had even at this time risen to the post of Han-lin expositor.[68] The third, Chang T'ing-lu (1675–1745), became senior vice-president of the Board of Rites,[69] and the fifth, Chang T'ing-chuan (1681–1764), became concurrently senior vice-president of the Board of Works and a sub-chancellor of the Grand Secretariat.[70]

The most outstanding of them was of course Chang T'ing-yü (1672–1755), who in 1726 became a grand secretary and was also soon to be one of the key figures in the newly-formed office of the Grand Council, which made him in effect the most powerful Chinese minister in the entire government.[71] There seems no doubt that he used this privileged position quite systematically to advance the interests of his own family, and those of his relatives by marriage, particularly by procuring official positions for them. That this was accepted practice is suggested by the case of a great-grandson of Yao Wen-jan (Chang T'ing-yü's father-in-law), namely the noted scholar Yao Fan (1702–71), who in 1741 became a *chin-shih* and was appointed a Han-lin compiler. 'At this time Chang T'ing-yü was pre-eminent in the government and those in important central and provincial posts all looked to him for patronage. Though the Changs and Yaos had long been related by marriage, he alone, out of respect for his own learning and character, refused to become dependent on him.' Others were no doubt less scrupulous.[72]

Patronage of this kind had to be exercised discreetly, with the result that individual cases are not easy to document; however, one or two do emerge. One member of a respected T'ung-ch'eng family, Wang I-tai, despite not having passed any higher examinations, was recommended by Chang T'ing-yü for a magistracy, which however he declined.[73] Conversely it was easy for Chang to block the advancement of those whom he did not favour, and when the noted *ku-wen* scholar Liu Ta-k'uei was recommended by Fang Pao for the *po-hsüeh hung-tz'u* examination of 1736 Chang T'ing-yü rejected him, to his own later regret.[74] The value attached to his goodwill and esteem is also illustrated by the number of T'ung-ch'eng lineages which prevailed on him to write prefaces for their genealogies, something for which his father had also been in demand.[75] Towards the end of his career, however, he seems to have become careless, perhaps through over-confidence. Though there is no sign that his relatives ever formed a clique for purely political purposes, by the 1740s their presence in government posts had become so conspicuous that in 1742 the upright censor Liu T'ung-hsün memorialized in protest, and Chang T'ing-yü was warned to be more circumspect.[76]

Even at the zenith of the family's success, Chang Ying's instructions and their long-standing traditions seem to have stood the test reasonably well. His sons, despite the wealth they must have acquired (Chang T'ing-yü was once presented with a pawnshop valued at 35,000 taels), did not have a reputation for abnormally extravagant living. Chang T'ing-chuan was indeed renowned for extreme caution and abstemiousness, even at court, and 'was so parsimonious in his style of life that even his household secretly laughed at him'.[77]

A few Changs, it is true, did succumb to the temptations of sudden wealth. One was Chang Ch'eng-hsien (1683–1730), the son of Chang Ying's youngest brother. He had a lucrative post in the salt administration in Shantung and apparently attempted to emulate the extravagant way of life of the great salt merchants. His family biographer comments severely that he got delusions of grandeur, used up all his funds and exhausted his property, so that he was forced to borrow money to make it up. He had been something of a bibliomane but on his death his library of fine volumes was scattered, 'so that not one remained'.[78]

A somewhat similar case was that of Chang Ying's second cousin, Chang Ch'i (1656–1717), a provincial official who had originally owned land that brought in a rent of 3,000 *shih*. It was eventually squandered, through his generous and eccentric style of life, 'so that not a single *mou* remained'.[79] His son, Chang T'ing-ch'ing (1677–1737), despite being given local office through the special grace of the Yung-cheng emperor (conceivably through Chang T'ing-yü's intervention) was unable to rebuild the property, and their impoverishment continued.[80] Yet cases like these seem to have been somewhat exceptional, and one might suspect that even this so-called poverty was relative and did not actually entail a decline to peasant status. Ma Ch'i-ch'ang after all observed that Chang Ch'i's posterity frequently rose through recommendations, and continued to be appointed to magistracies and provincial office down to his own time.[81]

Throughout this period Chang Ying's surviving sons, led by Chang T'ing-yü, showed foresight in continuing to build up the lineage, by donating land and cash to it, and by erecting or repairing ancestral shrines.[82] Their relatives the Yaos were also keenly concerned over such matters, and it appears that the two families took an interest in, and even encouraged each other's efforts. The Yao genealogy had been revised in 1697 by Yao Shih-hung (1638–1702),

who was both a nephew of Chang Ying's wife and husband of his eldest
daughter (three of his sons and three daughters were married to Chang Ying's
grandchildren).[83] In 1727 his eldest son, the *sheng-yüan* Yao K'ung-ping
(1686–1750), with the help of another member, drew up a new set of
rules for the lineage, for, as it multiplied, the old prohibitions of 1657 had
clearly become insufficient.

The new rules reveal the increasing size and complexity of the organization.
The major responsibilities now devolved not on the *hu-chang*, of whom there
is no mention, but on branch heads (*fang-chang*). Common business could
be transacted by elders (*tsun-chang*) but the accounts were to be annually
audited by the branch heads. There is no indication as to how these were
chosen, but any neglect of duty was to be punished by dismissal at a mass
meeting of the lineage; there were further penalties for embezzlement. At-
tendance at sacrifices and meetings was compulsory for all adult male members,
on pain of fine. Though the rules regulating the conduct and professions of
members were not exceptional, they were upheld by rather severe sanctions,
including not only fines but corporal punishment, denunciation to the authorities, and expulsion from the lineage. Violation of tombs was still subject
to the death penalty, but this was to be requested of the authorities, not
directly imposed by the lineage itself.[84] All this indicates considerable corporate strength.

A decade or so later another edition was made of the Yao genealogy, at
the direct instigation of Yao K'ung-ping's mother, the eldest daughter of
Chang Ying and sister of Chang T'ing-yü. K'ung-ping himself, despite five
failures in the provincial examination, had in 1728 been recommended for
office (again, possibly by his maternal uncle) and was by this time prefect
of Soochow, so the task devolved on one of his younger brothers.[85] On its
completion in 1738 the work was provided with an effusive preface by
Chang T'ing-yü, who expatiated on its value in promoting respect for the
lineage and moral conduct among its members.[86]

Chang T'ing-yü soon began to feel that another edition of the Changs'
own genealogy was overdue. As he himself was continuously at the capital
he had to order some of his nephews living in T'ung-ch'eng to make a start
on it. It was completed in 1746–7 under the direction of his younger brother
Chang T'ing-chuan, on the latter's retirement.[87] The new edition basically
followed the old one, the only major innovation being a detailed set of rules,
fan-li, drawn up to guide future compilers as to the precise form of the
work. These however did not extend to the conduct of members (for which
Chang Ying's admonitions were presumably sufficient) nor to general principles of management.[88] The Changs, having had a later start, were a smaller
group than the Yaos, and it still seems to have been possible for the lineage's

affairs to be directed on a more or less ad hoc basis by those who took an interest in it.[89] As will be seen, however, this activity does appear to have become traditional in certain branches.

Chang T'ing-yü evidently wrote his prefaces to the genealogy in 1747 with mixed feelings and some apprehension. He was well aware that with the lineage's increased size and the worldly success of some of its members, class distinctions within it were widening and the spirit of kinship becoming 'somewhat diluted'. The remedy for this, he felt, was for those members in office to maintain a close interest in the fundamental economic basis of their success, that is, in agriculture and in their property in the countryside.[90] He knew moreover that his own position in the government was no longer so impregnable as before, and that with his passing from the scene his relatives would no longer enjoy such special favour but would be subject to the full rigours of competition.[91] He reflected at some length on the family's two hundred years of distinction and how closely the fortunes of a great lineage were bound up with government service. Even so, he felt that total decline was not inevitable. Returning to the simile his father had used, he declared that it was in the nature of some trees to bear fruit twice a year, and that harm could be averted by finding the correct way to nourish their roots. It was the same with a distinguished family, and it was for this reason that the genealogy had been compiled, as a permanent example and inspiration to the kinsmen.[92]

In the century and a half after Chang T'ing-yü's death in 1755 some of his forebodings were indeed confirmed. As Ho Ping-ti has demonstrated, the percentage of Chang Ying's own direct descendants who held official posts fell in the course of six generations from 83.3% to 19.4%.[93] They tended also to hold lower-ranking positions. The last of them to attain the third rank was Chang Tseng-i (1747—97), a *chien-sheng* and grandson of Chang T'ing-yü, who owed his rise more to the Ch'ien-lung emperor's recollection of his famous forebears than to his own intrinsic abilities.[94]

The percentage of degree-holders among them also fell, over the same period, from 100% to 30%, the higher degrees likewise occurring with less frequency. It is interesting here that the trend was not quite uniform among the sub-branches descended from Chang Ying's sons, as is shown in table 1. Paradoxically, sharp decline set in earliest among the descendants of the most successful son, Chang T'ing-yü; it was least pronounced among those of Chang T'ing-tsan. Reasons for this will be suggested later.

The extent of social decline which this represents can, however, be exaggerated. It should be pointed out that Ho's tables also show that the absolute numbers of officials and degree holders in the later generations remained reasonably constant. Considering how vastly competition increased in the

Table 1. *Degree holders among Chang Ying's descendants (adult males)**

Gener-ation	T'ing-tsan	T'ing-yü	T'ing-lu	T'ing-chuan	T'ing-kuan
2nd	1 (100%)	1 (100%)	1 (100%)	1 (100%)	1 (100%)
3rd	2 (100%)	4 (100%)	2 (100%)	2 (100%)	3 (100%)
4th	3 (100%)	15 (100%)	6 (100%)	6 (100%)	7 (87%)
5th	10 (100%)	11 (42%)	11 (84%)	10 (83%)	8 (80%)
6th	14 (50%)	10 (38%)	7 (47%)	9 (31%)	1 (10%)

*Descendants of Chang Ying's fourth son, Chang T'ing-ch'ih, have been omitted, as they were very few in number.

eighteenth and nineteenth centuries, with expanding population, this was in itself no mean achievement. It is true that the *chien-sheng* degree, which came to predominate among the Changs, could be purchased for something over 100 taels in this period, but clearly there were still quite a few of the family who could afford to do this, and the fact that some did not does not in itself prove that they were reduced to total poverty. In at least a few cases, persons without degrees were recommended for or purchased a minor post.[95] As far as can be seen, the Yaos had a similar experience, for a survey of Yao Wen-jan's descendants shows that the proportion of degree holders among them likewise fell from 100% to just under 30% in six generations, and that *sheng-yüan* and *chien-sheng* came to predominate among them. They were perhaps luckier in that they still produced one or two men of real distinction at a rather later stage, in particular Yao Nai (1732–1815), and Yao Ying (1785–1853).

It is interesting that the tradition of intermarriage between the two families, though it became somewhat attenuated, also persisted late into the nineteenth century. It remained concentrated in Chang Ying's own branch of the family. Of his six sons, three (i.e. 50%) married Yao women; in the next generation Yao marriages rose to 71%, though they fell gradually thereafter to 42.5% in the fourth generation and 30% in the fifth. Here too the trend varied somewhat among the different sub-branches, as is shown in table 2.[96]

It is noticeable that the tradition was maintained most strongly among the descendants of Chang T'ing-tsan and Chang T'ing-lu, whereas the progeny of Chang T'ing-yü after a generation or so largely renounced their Yao connections. (It must be remembered though that table 2 covers only the marriages of Chang men to Yao women; if the numerous instances of Yao men marrying Chang women were also taken into account, the pattern might well be modified.)

Table 2. *Yao marriages among Chang Ying's descendants**

Gener-ation	T'ing-tsan	T'ing-yü	T'ing-lu	T'ing-chuan	T'ing-kuan
2nd	Nil	1 (100%)	1 (100%)	Nil	Nil
3rd	2 (100%)	3 (75%)	2 (100%)	2 (100%)	Nil
4th	3 (100%)	2 (16.6%)	5 (83%)	3 (50%)	3 (37.5%)
5th	6 (60%)	2 (7.7%)	9 (76%)	3 (25%)	2 (20%)
6th	11 (42%)	Nil	2 (13%)	5 (20%)	2 (25%)

*Descendants of Chang T'ing-ch'ih have again been omitted.

It is surely remarkable that this pattern persisted as long as it did, considering the great expansion in numbers in both families over several generations, and testifies to their social cohesion and the strength of their traditions.[97]

It is quite clear, moreover, that notwithstanding their descent from their earlier heights of national eminence neither the Changs nor the Yaos ever relaxed their efforts to build up their respective lineages, something which almost certainly helped to maintain their prestige in their home community. The Yaos made a new edition of their genealogy in the 1790s, sponsored by their two most outstanding men of that time (both descended from Yao Sun-fei). One was Yao Fen, the governor of Fukien, who had earlier presented land to the county to help pay the expenses of its examination candidates, and who bought grave land and built a shrine for the lineage.[98] The other was Yao Nai, who in a lengthy preface emphasized the significance of genealogical records by attempting to show that they had been vital to the long-term survival of the great ministerial families of T'ang times and earlier.[99]

A further edition was made in 1837–9. In this a great part was played by Yao Ying (a descendant of Yao Wen-jan and Yao Fan), who was to be their most important official of the century. It was he who compiled the *Hsien-te chuan*, a collection of biographies of notable lineage members, which was henceforward published with the genealogy.[100] (He was always active in arranging help for kinsmen in difficulties and had hoped at one stage to start a charitable school for them.)[101] The arduous task of organizing the compilation was however performed by an obscurer member of the seventeenth generation, Yao Lang, who seems to have been its principal manager at that time. Investigations were carried out not only by branch heads but by sub-branch heads (*ku-t'ou*), showing that the lineage organization had become even more complex during the previous century. The common funds of the city sub-branches (from which the initiative had obviously come) were, however, too small to finance the compilation in its entirety, so contributions were solicited, and obtained, from members of all branches according to the size of their landholdings; officials on active service likewise made donations in proportion to their resources.[102]

The Changs also recompiled their genealogy, after a rather longer interval, in 1812–14. The delay had been due mainly to the lineage's expansion in numbers, which made investigation difficult. It was therefore decided that henceforth the branch heads (of whom this is the first mention) should regularly collect all the necessary information on members and send it every three years to those in charge of the ancestral hall, so as to facilitate a major revision every thirty years (a method more or less the same as that ordained for the Yaos a hundred and fifty years earlier). Managers of the lineage property were likewise to send in regular accounts of income and expenditure.[103] It is thus clear that the Chang organization too was gradually becoming more complex and more systematic.

It is obvious that they still viewed themselves, and were regarded locally, as a family of distinction (it must be remembered after all that a grandson of Chang T'ing-yü, Chang Jo-t'ing, had been president of the Board of Punishments as late as 1802). They took the opportunity to remind everyone further of this by reprinting, at the same time as their genealogy, a selection of the major writings of Chang Ying and Chang T'ing-yü (including *Heng-ch'an so-yen*) in one volume entitled *T'ung-ch'eng liang hsiang-kuo yü-lu*. Its editor, Chang Tseng-ch'ien, also compiled a substantial collection of poetry, *Chiang-yen ssu-shih shih-ch'ao*, written by ten important officials of the family over four generations.[104]

In 1837 the lineage managers organized another venture designed to promote the spirit of kinship among members and no doubt to impress outsiders, namely a tour by representatives of each branch to sacrifice at the burial places of the early ancestors, to whom they all traced their descent. This was done in grand style, for each participant was accompanied by no fewer than five chairbearers and attendants. One of their first stops was at Chang-chia-p'ang, the place where the family had first settled and where many of them still lived (though the main concentration was now further south, at Sung-shan). Here they visited with reverence the shrine in which the farming tools of these early forebears were still preserved, as a perpetual reminder and example to their descendants. The importance of their marriage connections was acknowledged by a visit to the tomb of Chang Ying's maternal grandfather, of the Wu lineage; they also passed by the main area of the Yao tombs. The account of this tour reveals clearly the sharp degree of social differentiation that by now existed in the ramified Chang lineage. Those who went on it seem to have been mainly city-dwellers of some affluence, whereas those living out in the countryside who came to join in the sacrifices with them clearly included many of humble status (the poorer ones were given gifts of grain). Some of them were stated, regretfully, to have been more interested in eating the sacrificial meal than in displaying the proper spirit of kinship.[105]

As the lineage increased in size it is likely that a smaller proportion of members came to play an active role in its management. Almost everything that is known of this has to be derived from the records of its joint land-holdings, on which the names of those managers who purchased individual items are recorded. The property in due course became quite sizeable. Up to 1747 290 *mou* of ritual land were acquired, and about as much again after that date, bringing the total in the 1820s up to 588 *mou*; the bulk of the holdings was acquired in the eighteenth century, the period of the lineage's greatest worldly success. It is interesting to find that less and less of it came from donations by individual members; up to 1747 about 66% was acquired in this way, but afterwards only about 5%. It should probably be inferred from this that owing to their descent from the higher and more lucrative government positions far fewer Changs were able to afford this kind of generosity.[106] It does not necessarily mean that interest in the lineage dwindled, for purchases of land by the managers out of the surplus built up on existing holdings continued down to 1822. They ceased after that date, a fact which possibly indicates less active management, but also, perhaps, simply that the existing property, which yielded the sizeable income of over 2,000 *shih* per annum, was by now large enough to finance all normal expenditures. Almost all the holdings were conserved down to the twentieth century and there is no obvious sign of embezzlement or malpractice by the managers. In the Tao-kuang reign (1821–50) 22 *mou* of ritual land were sold off, apparently in connection with the expenses of a lawsuit, and during the difficult years of the Taiping occupation another 56 *mou* were sold and 35 mortgaged, but they were rapidly redeemed in 1862.[107]

An examination of the names of all those known to have been responsible for managing the lineage's property over more than two centuries (even though one cannot be absolutely certain that the list is complete) shows that there was a definite concentration of management in certain branches, and that this appears to correlate rather strongly with continuing social respectability. There is an interesting and possibly significant contrast in this respect between the descendants of Chang Ying's first and second sons, Chang T'ing-tsan and Chang T'ing-yü. The former kept donating moderate amounts of land to the lineage for at least four generations and appear very prominently among its managers. As was noted earlier, the gradual falling off in numbers of degree holders was least pronounced in this sub-branch, and it was they who maintained better than any other the tradition of marriage with the Yaos. Those of them who are known to have played any part in the management of lineage land, though they often did not hold any office whereby they might have enriched themselves, all turn out to have possessed a degree of some kind (albeit often the purchased *chien-sheng*) and to have been married to Yao wives. The descendants of Chang T'ing-yü, on the other hand, began rather earlier to produce smaller numbers of degree holders, and also to make relatively very few marriages with the Yaos. Moreover, none of them, after Chang T'ing-yü himself, made any donations of land to the lineage or, apparently, played any part in its management for five generations, until a certain Chang Tsung-han (b. 1835) took it over in the 1860s (it was he who redeemed the land that had been sold off).[108]

Though the contrast should not be exaggerated, it is interesting to speculate on the possible reasons for it. One may be the very brilliance of the second sub-branch's early success. Chang T'ing-yü's sons and grandsons seem to have spent more time at the capital or in office than did those of his brothers (one sign of this is that they usually took the provincial examination not in Chiangnan but in Peking) and could possibly have been corrupted faster by worldly habits. In addition this branch became much larger than the others, very many of them being descended from Chang T'ing-yü's extremely successful fourth son, the prolific Chang Jo-t'ing, who had twelve sons (not to mention nine daughters). Rapid and repeated division of property among so many heirs could in this case have had deleterious effects (the last three of the sons emigrated to Taiwan, perhaps for this reason, and were never heard of again).[109]

It is also possible however that for some of this sub-branch the loss of close contact with their native area and the weakening of kinship ties and of interest in the fate of the lineage as a group (the very things against which Chang T'ing-yü had warned!) could in themselves after a few generations have had unfortunate results. By taking no part in the management of the lineage's joint property they had, unlike the descendants of Chang T'ing-tsan, no opportunity to share in the perquisites and social standing which this may have conferred, and it is perhaps significant that those members who in the latter half of the nineteenth century did once again take part in management did also enjoy a certain amount of affluence and worldly success. Chang Tsung-han was able to purchase a *chien-sheng* degree and to become a candidate for a minor office; he was once betrothed to a woman of the Yao family.[110] One of his brothers, Chang Shao-wen (b. 1829), was a *sheng-yüan* and eventually a magistrate, while another, Chang Shao-hua (b. 1831), managed in 1874 to become a *chin-shih* and was later a military taotai.[111] They too were active on the lineage's behalf in the late nineteenth century.

It can of course be argued that only those members who in any case already possessed education, affluence and leisure would be able to under-take the management of lineage property. Yet that the latter activity could actually help a branch to maintain these social attributes in the long term is further suggested by the history of the descendants of some of Chang Ying's brothers. None of them had outstanding or apparently lucrative careers. The eldest, Chang Tsai, as has been seen, became a complete recluse, and none of his progeny was exceptionally distinguished, yet they were involved in managing the lineage's joint property down to the end of the eighteenth century at least. The same was true of the descendants of the third and sixth brothers, Chang Chieh and Chang K'uei (1655–1703), the latter of whom became a magistrate only through recommendation.[112] The tradition of management was particularly strong here, continuing certainly down to the mid nineteenth century. It should be noted that in every single case these managers of lineage property, who were obviously men of some education, possessed at least a *chien-sheng* degree, presumably purchased. That some of them were able to do this so consistently over five or six generations, despite successive divisions of individual property and the failure to obtain official posts of any importance, does suggest that continued access to the lineage's joint property may have conferred on them social standing and financial advantages (for even if they never resorted to outright peculation the fringe benefits may have been considerable) and aided them in keeping up their educational tradition.[113]

The vital importance attached by both the Changs and the Yaos to the survival of their lineage organizations is shown by their efforts in the after-math of the eight-year Taiping occupation of T'ung-ch'eng, a period probably as disruptive and damaging as that of the revolts of two centuries earlier, and which in some respects provides a parallel to it. The Changs immediately bought back the land they had been forced to sell off, and both began very soon to make plans to produce new editions of their genealogies. This was a task of crucial importance, as many members had scattered during the troubles and contacts had been difficult to maintain. The Yaos were the first to ac-complish it, partly under the direction of Yao Ying's son, Yao Chun-ch'ang (who had become a magistrate on the recommendation of Tseng Kuo-fan). It was financed this time mainly by substantial contributions from lineage members in office (six between them gave 1,400 taels) and the surplus was used to buy more land. The whole enterprise, once started, took only two years, which shows that the lineage's methods of gathering information were still functioning well.[114]

The Changs were rather slower. Proposals for a new compilation were first made in 1869 but it was held up by lack of funds; the income from the common land had been severely reduced by the effects of the rebellion, and it was said now only to supply the expense of the various sacrifices, which indicates that it must usually have been expected to pay for far more than this. Large contributions were later made however by Chang Shao-wen, Chang Shao-hua and others, and these were gradually supplemented by the growing surplus from the common land, so that the work was completed by 1890. The major part in its organization was taken by their brother, Chang Tsung-han, though the compilers included several members of branches other than Chang Ying's.[115]

Both the Changs and the Yaos were by now clearly conscious, and regretful, of the fact that their greatest days were over and that none of them could hope to compete in distinction with their illustrious forebears.[116] They nonetheless attempted to keep up their own morale and to remind others of their glorious past by reprinting the literary works of earlier generations. In 1880 Chang Shao-wen reprinted *T'ung-ch'eng liang-hsiang-kuo yü-lu*, and in 1893 his youngest brother Chang Shao-t'ang did the same for the family poetry collection.[117] In 1897 Chang Ying's entire collected works were reprinted. These undertakings must have been expensive, for the blocks of the works had been destroyed during the rebellion. Among the Yaos, Yao Yung-p'u (the son of Yao Chun-ch'ang and grandson of Yao Ying) in 1905 compiled and printed a sizeable supplement to his grandfather's biographical collection, *Hsien-te chuan,* entitled *T'ung-ch'eng Yao-shih pei-chuan-lu.* In his preface he regretted that such heroic figures were no longer to be found in the family, but comforted himself with the thought that if any arose they would find suitable models and inspiration in this work.[118]

These projects show that both lineages, collectively and individually, could still muster considerable financial resources. Both indeed made new editions of their genealogies in the twentieth century, the Changs from 1922 to 1933, and the Yaos from 1911 to 1921. The Changs also bought more ritual land, out of common funds, in 1927.[119] The only sign that their organizations might have been weakening by this stage is that both had some difficulty in financing these final editions. The Yaos were heavily dependent on the cash contributions of one wealthy member, while the Changs, alarmed in 1927 by a report that the republican government was planning to confiscate woodlands, reluctantly decided to sell the timber in their graveyards, thereby simultaneously managing to finance the new genealogy and to retain their ancestral tomb areas.[120]

The foregoing summary account does show that both the Changs and the Yaos initially owed much of their pre-eminence in T'ung-ch'eng to their extraordinary success in academic and official life, and that after the eighteenth century they did decline considerably in these respects. Yet there seems to be no evidence that their prestige and standing in their home county dwindled sharply in proportion, nor that the descendants of their great officials were all eventually reduced to total poverty and obscurity.[121] On the contrary, it looks as if their conservative and frugal family traditions, so emphasized by Chang Ying, in general remained strong enough to prevent them from being rapidly corrupted by success, and to enable them to adjust realistically to changed circumstances. In particular their strong interest in landed property seems to have been maintained, and to have provided them with a secure financial basis.

Moreover, although their spirit of kinship may have weakened somewhat as their numbers and the degree of social differentiation among them increased, they still survived as clearly defined social groups, each with a constantly renewed nucleus of affluent and well-educated members, until well into the twentieth century. There can be no doubt that this was in part due to the deliberate efforts made by this elite nucleus to organize and perpetuate their lineages. Above all, they were anxious to give their members a consciousness of their common identity through continuous recompilation of their genealogies, despite the enormous work and expense that this entailed. That of the Yaos was revised on average every 43 years from 1661 to 1921, and that of the Changs every 53 years over much the same period, a remarkable record considering the great expansion in their numbers. The endowment of joint property provided a secure, long-term basis for lineage activities, aid for members in distress and, no doubt, indirect benefits for those involved in its management. Furthermore, the ceaseless insistence on the necessity of education in maintaining social standing, even without the formal provision of a school, must have helped to promote their scholarly traditions and to ensure a reasonably high level of literacy, especially among the better-off. Thus it may well be that, in time, merely to belong to one of these great lineages was in itself sufficient to confer a certain amount of social prestige.

Patterns of lineage organization

The question remains, how far this pattern may have been true of other important families in T'ung-ch'eng. It is clear that highly developed lineage organizations became very common in the county, for they were referred to frequently by local writers as something to be taken for granted, and exceptionally large numbers of their genealogies, representing almost seventy different kinship groups, survive in libraries.[122] Unfortunately, genealogies are not available for some of the more important lineages, such as the Fangs, and the Wus of Ma-hsi, but even so the material is so abundant as to permit fairly confident generalization.

It has already been shown that virtually all the lineages of which records survive traced their descent to comparatively humble ancestors who moved to the area around the end of the Yüan or the beginning of the Ming. This fact, and the concern for accuracy with which their subsequent history is documented, gives one faith in the general veracity of the genealogies as historical records. It is true that attempts are sometimes made to link individual lineages to remote and imposing forebears, going as far back as the Chou dynasty or even to the Yellow Emperor, but these sections are always clearly separated from the main bulk of the genealogical records, and there is never any visible sign that these have been tampered with in order to attach a group to some other local lineage of greater distinction. This was something that both Chang Ying and Chang T'ing-yü had regarded with horror.[123] In T'ung-ch'eng, competition for social prestige and interest in genealogical matters seem to have become so strong that deliberate attempts to enhance a lineage's prestige in this way would almost surely, if discovered, have had the reverse effect of bringing opprobrium on it.[124]

It is unlikely that every one of the numerous immigrants to arrive in T'ung-ch'eng in the fourteenth century can in the course of time have come to be regarded as the founding ancestor of a clearly defined lineage group. The question to be asked is, therefore, why some kinsmen descended from a common ancestor organized themselves effectively in this way and not others. It is all too often taken for granted that the Chinese lineage was a product of 'natural growth',[125] yet it has been seen in the case of the Changs and the Yaos that persistent, continuous effort was required if a lineage was to be perpetuated in the long term, and not allowed to disappear or lapse into obscurity.

Though many of T'ung-ch'eng's lineages may possibly have existed as informal groupings from a very early stage, a survey of the prefaces of the surviving genealogies and also their records of property shows that in the great majority of cases the first determined attempts at formal organization occurred in the sixteenth century, especially its latter half. This was precisely the period when the county's prowess in the examinations became really noticeable, and competition for social prestige presumably intensified. The first step was almost always the compilation of at least an outline genealogy, which was necessary to define membership and status relationships in the group, and which was accompanied (though sometimes preceded) by the provision of some common land in order to finance essential expenditures. It seems very often to have been undertaken, as with the Changs and the Yaos, by one of the first members of the family to distinguish himself, his motive being to add to his family's prestige and to help to perpetuate it.[126]

A good example among many is that of the Chaos of T'ung-pei, one of the few families whose ancestors had moved to T'ung-ch'eng towards the end of the Southern Sung. Though they had a long tradition of landowning and education, their first real successes occurred in the mid sixteenth century with two brothers, Chao Jui and Chao I (1512–69), both of whom became *chü-jen* in 1540. The former, the father-in-law incidentally of Fang Hsüeh-chien, in due course became a prefect, while the latter passed the *chin-shih* examinations in 1544 and after holding various central government posts rose to become governor of Kweichow.[127] It was apparently Chao I who made the first attempt to provide a common focus for the lineage, and a visible outward expression of its common identity, by building an ancestral shrine. He also endowed a piece of charitable land, some 19 *mou* in all, in modest emulation of the famous Fan charitable estate. The income from this both paid for the sacrifices in the shrine and aided needy kinsmen. He was assisted by his son, a *kung-sheng* and scholar of note, who carried on his efforts after his death. Their achievement was admiringly recounted by Fang Hsüeh-chien, who considered that this land was the essential prerequisite to honouring the ancestors and drawing the lineage members together, and had brought considerable prestige both to its founder and to the Chaos as a group.[128]

It must not be thought that those families who produced a *chin-shih* or an important official were the only ones to embark on this kind of enterprise, however, for those of rather less distinction soon began to imitate them. The P'ans of Mu-shan, for instance, up to the mid sixteenth century were said to have been merely 'honest gentlemen and simple farmers'. Though their lineage already existed, in the sense that it had a head, and elders, 'there was as yet no suggestion of compiling family records' (nor of undertaking any other, more elaborate, corporate activity). This was done only in 1565 at the instigation of their first *sheng-yüan*, P'an Wei-shan, a disappointed examinee who spent much of his life teaching and achieved some reputation in scholarship. He publicized his action by formally notifying the magistrate of his intention, not only to compile a genealogy, but also to build an ancestral shrine in which to carry out sacrifices. Though his avowed motive was to promote good behaviour among his kinsmen, it is probable that social ambition, and a desire to assert parity with other, more notable local families, played no small part.[129] His ambition was partly fulfilled in 1601 by his son's attaining the *chin-shih* degree (and later becoming a censor), though the lineage seems to have produced only two other *chin-shih* thereafter, and no great officials.[130]

Most lineage organizations in their early stages seem still to have been comparatively small and informal, and to have relied, like the Changs and the Yaos, rather heavily on the initiative of individuals. Almost none of the early genealogies appear to have been printed for distribution to kinsmen, but existed, like that of the Changs, only as handwritten drafts. Nor, in the majority of cases, did they apparently contain rules of any kind, to regulate either the conduct of members or the management of what property they possessed. As a result, such property was sometimes sold off and had to be refounded. The Wangs of Tung-lou were provided with a plot of charitable land by an individual member in 1578, but after his death it was sold by his relatives and not restored until 1603, by another kinsman.[131] Almost the same thing happened at around this time in one of the Chang lineages (unconnected with the famous Changs) who bought the land back rapidly because they found it impossible to finance the sacrifices every year without it.[132]

An exception in these respects was the Tso lineage (that of Tso Kuang-tou) which by 1634 had drawn up a comprehensive set of rules indicative of an attempt at fairly systematic organization. These already ordained that the genealogy be revised at thirty-year intervals, and printed, so as to prevent loss, and also required all members in office to contribute land to the group, for the aid and education of poorer kinsmen. Transgressors of the rules of conduct were to be publicly chastised by the lineage head and elders.[133] That the Tsos continued in later times to be thought of as one of the county's greatest lineages, despite the fact that they produced no really outstanding officials after the Ming, may, one surmises, be partly due to their early corporate strength and cohesion, which seems to have been maintained.[134]

It will be remembered that several of the Tso rules were aimed at checking the kind of disruptive, anti-social behaviour that had flourished among great families at the end of the Ming.[135] This must have been an even greater threat to other groups that were less well-organized and could perhaps muster little authority to control members. The ensuing revolts must have hit them still harder. What ritual land they had went out of cultivation, ancestral shrines were destroyed, and many members killed. The P'ans later claimed that entire households had been massacred or had died of disease, 'so that the lineage was barely saved from extinction'. Even thirty years later it was found that some of the scattered survivors were unable to name their ancestors and degree of kinship to each other. Many draft genealogies, including that of the P'ans, were lost.[136] The Tais only saved theirs by first hiding it and then entrusting it to one member to take into temporary exile from the county.[137]

In view of the hypothesis advanced earlier, that the deliberate renewal of kinship ties may have appeared as one means of restoring social stability in the county after the revolts, it is not surprising to discover that very many lineages in the 1650s and 1660s made determined efforts to rebuild their earlier, embryonic organizations on a firmer basis. A remarkable number, like the Changs and the Yaos, recompiled their genealogies and also printed them for the first time.[138] The P'ans began work on theirs in 1658 and completed it in 1673, mainly under the direction of P'an Chiang, a *sheng-yüan* and poet of some repute who had once been Chang Ying's teacher.[139]

Even more important than to redefine the membership of lineages was to make stricter and surer provisions for their management and finance, and also to control the behaviour of unruly or disaffected members. The P'ans, on the completion of their genealogy, at once drew up a detailed set of sixteen rules for this purpose, and similar action was taken by many other groups.[140] The Chous of Yao-shih had been greatly troubled by the lax and disrespectful conduct of their younger members, especially at the annual sacrifices, and feared that it would in time endanger and shame the whole group. In 1661 their elders finally decided that the only solution was to establish formal 'family regulations' (*chia-kuei*), and at the same time to appoint branch heads to enforce them. They were to report recalcitrant offenders to the elders in the ancestral hall for punishment, and, if that failed, to the local authorities.[141]

From this time onwards, in fact, almost all the lineages appear gradually to have organized themselves on much more elaborate and formal lines. This became more and more essential if the group was to survive as a social unit, for as numbers grew and kinsmen became more dispersed it was no longer possible to rely entirely on occasional initiatives by wealthy or public-spirited individuals. In many respects the basic methods and aims of lineage organization adopted in T'ung-ch'eng during the Ch'ing dynasty did not differ greatly from those in other parts of China, but there were some features that have special bearing on the problems under investigation here, and must therefore be briefly described.

One of the first essentials in the lineage was efficient and incorrupt leadership, to ensure that its major functions (such as the performance of the annual sacrifices, the upkeep of hall and graveyards, the periodic recompilation of the genealogy, the enforcement of rules of conduct and the disciplining of members who disobeyed them, and the settlement of disputes) were regularly and properly carried out. Almost all groups in time made formal provisions for the appointment of lineage officers, who generally comprised the usual categories of titular head (*tsung-tzu*), lineage head (*hu-chang*), branch heads (*fang-chang*) and, in the case of a very large and ramified lineage, sub-branch heads and assistants of various kinds.[142] These were persons of some authority and presumably enjoyed considerable standing in the community. The Tais actually attempted to give their lineage head official backing by having his appointment endorsed on a certificate by the county yamen.[143] There had of course to be some checks on the powers of the lineage officers, and in many cases they were subject to dismissal and replacement for abuse of their position, in particular for laxity or partiality in the discharge of their duties, or for accepting bribes.

The precise mechanism of their appointment is never made very clear (one presumes that it was decided on by the most influential members of the lineage) but what is interesting is that the rules almost invariably stress functional qualities such as ability and honesty as the main criteria for the choice, rather than emphasizing seniority and formal academic qualifications or office (i.e. 'gentry' status). This was sometimes so even in the case of the *tsung-tzu* or titular head, a title usually assumed by the most senior male member of the eldest line of descent, and carrying mainly ceremonial responsibilities. The Chaos of T'ung-pei decided that if the correct titular head in fact turned out not to be able and of good character it would be better to leave the position vacant, rather than risk his bringing the lineage into disrepute.[144] The Kaos of Kuan-shan, who expected their titular head to undertake administrative duties, specified that the choice should not be restricted to the eldest branch if it could not provide an able, conscientious and energetic man.[145] These qualities, plus a character that could command respect, were even more vital in the lineage heads and branch heads. The Wangs of Kao-lin for this reason stated emphatically that all members should be eligible to be chosen as lineage head, regardless of age or seniority; 'the important thing is virtue, not status'.[146]

It is true that persons of high academic standing might become lineage officers, and could also be extremely influential in exercising informal leadership in the group. (The P'ans for instance decreed that the 'gentry' [*shen-chin*, i.e. members holding higher degrees or official posts] should always lend their assistance in upholding decisions by the lineage and branch heads.)[147] It is nonetheless clear that they did not necessarily monopolize leadership in all lineages, simply because, even in a county of outstanding academic distinction like T'ung-ch'eng, the majority of lineages never had very many members with this kind of status. The P'ans, as has already been mentioned, had no more than three *chin-shih* in their entire history (in 1601, 1649 and 1742), and only two *chü-jen*, who did not subsequently become *chin-shih* (in 1729 and 1826). Several large and apparently well-organized lineages, such as the Tsous, the T'angs, the Kueis and the Tungs, evidently had no holders of the higher degrees whatever, for no persons of those names ever appear in the examination lists. Several lineages that did well academically in their early days later experienced a considerable falling off; the Chaos of T'ung-pei had no more than one *chin-shih* (in 1799) in the whole of the Ch'ing dynasty and the same is true of the Tais (whose last *chin-shih* was Tai Ming-shih in 1709). The Wangs of Tung-lou even admitted quite openly that, despite their long history of farming and study, they were 'not a great lineage with a tradition of official service'.[148]

That a lineage did not go on producing outstanding individuals of high status was clearly not prejudicial to its survival, which depended far more on maintaining a core of able, educated and well-to-do men, members of the local elite in the broad sense, some of whom would have time and enthusiasm to devote to its affairs. Quite often its leaders appear to have been *sheng-yüan* or failed students who found some outlet for their talents (and perhaps also a certain amount of influence and prestige) in this kind of activity, something that clearly happened in the early days of the Changs themselves. The genealogy of the Kaos of Kuan-shan in 1691 was recompiled through the efforts of a public-spirited member who apparently failed to pass any examinations at all but subsequently redirected his ambitions to increasing the prestige and fortunes of the lineage.[149] Even a lineage whose members had comparatively little worldly success could still enjoy a certain standing and respect in the locality, as long as it remained cohesive and well organized. The Kaos in fact never had any degree holder higher than a *chü-jen*, and that only in the Ming dynasty, but even so were able to have a flattering preface written for them in 1694 by Chang Ying, showing that they cannot have been considered completely insignificant on this account.[150] The Wangs of Tung-lou were likewise able to obtain a preface from the great Chang T'ing-yü himself.[151]

No lineage could preserve itself indefinitely, however, without adequate finance. This was invariably derived in the first instance from common land, whether termed ritual or charitable land (the two categories seem never to have been mutually exclusive).[152] In most cases, by the mid Ch'ing, the management of the holdings was no longer left to chance or the initiative of individuals, but was handled sometimes by the lineage head directly or, more often, by the branch heads, either jointly or in rotation. In other cases the lineage head might appoint special managers for the property; often it was specified that they be not only honest and capable, but also affluent, to reduce the likelihood of peculation.[153] Whether they were to be paid a salary is usually not stated, and in the few cases where it is mentioned the amount was very low. The Wangs of Tung-lou in 1805 allocated only 6 *shih* of un-husked grain per annum to the lineage head, who was in overall charge of financial matters, while Fang Pao in the eighteenth century considered 12 taels to be a suitable yearly recompense for managers.[154]

All lineages attempted to take precautions against malpractice by their managers, usually by insisting on strict annual accounting, as the Changs had done in 1812. The P'ans in the late seventeenth century required that all items of rent income and expenditure be entered in a printed register, to be kept by the lineage and branch heads.[155] In addition, details of all common

landholdings, including the deeds of purchase, and agreements on their management and on the use of the income, were generally printed in each successive
edition of the genealogy (though some, to save space, omitted land that belonged to the separate branches, rather than to the lineage as a whole). Sometimes, to avoid trouble and ill-feeling over rent collection, it was forbidden for
the land to be rented to lineage members. The Fangs were renowned as having
insisted on this from the very beginning, and they were imitated by the Chous
of Yao-shih when the latter established their first ritual land in 1598; they
repeated the prohibition in 1822.[156] The Lis of Yen-p'ing forbade their
managers to exact illicit fees from tenants.[157] If all this failed, the managers
were usually to be disciplined by the lineage and branch heads, often at a
mass meeting, though it was not always explicitly stated that they should be
dismissed and others appointed in their place.

It is difficult to tell how effective all these provisions were. It does seem
extremely probable, as has already been explained, that managers might
often enjoy considerable unofficial perquisites from the property under
their care. It must on the other hand be stressed that in T'ung-ch'eng, after
the Ming, there appears to be virtually no evidence to suggest the kind of
flagrant mismanagement and illicit sale of common property that characterized
the history of the Fan charitable estate at Soochow.[158] Cases of managerial
incompetence do occur but seem to have been fairly effectively dealt with.
To take one instance, the second branch of the Wang lineage of Tung-lou
usually had a comfortable annual surplus on its ritual land, but the managers
appointed in 1813 proved so inept (or possibly corrupt) that this rapidly
changed to a deficit. Concern at once become so acute that in 1819 the lineage
head had them replaced by two former managers, who not only made good the
deficits but created enough surplus to enable them to buy more land.[159]
This suggests that in T'ung-ch'eng (whatever the case may have been elsewhere), not only was loyalty to the lineage and its ideals fairly strong, but
also the long-term benefits of maintaining the organization with its inalienable
property intact were so substantial as to discourage managers from endangering
its survival by really selfish and short-sighted profiteering, especially if in so
doing they were likely to incur immediate censure and protest from other
elite members of the group.

Though almost all lineage holdings were inaugurated through the donation
or bequest of one or two wealthy, public-spirited members, and gifts of this
kind did continue, most lineages came to feel that it was unrealistic to rely
on the spontaneous but sporadic generosity of individuals, and therefore in
time devised more systematic ways of adding to their property. One was
actively to solicit contributions. The Tsos in 1634 had required all members in
official posts to give part of their salary for the purpose of buying land, while

one of the Hu lineages at a later stage promised that members who did this would be eligible for the position of greatest honour in the ancestral hall after their death, giving them priority over virtuous persons, good scholars, meritorious lineage heads, filial sons and, lastly, illustrious officials. The Hus also insisted that all private property belonging to members who died without heirs was to revert to common ownership (the original owner to be rewarded with either a special shrine or a place in the ancestral hall, depending on the size of the property); even if an heir was adopted the lineage was still to get 20% of the property.[160] The surest way of raising funds to buy more land was, however (as will be explained), to loan the surplus income from existing holdings at interest. The P'ans had a detailed rule to this effect as early as 1673, and it seems to have become universal practice in the course of the Ch'ing dynasty.[161]

It is difficult to estimate the average size of a lineage's total holdings, but none seems to have been enormous and most were very likely smaller than the Changs' 588 *mou*.[162] Whether the property was termed ritual or charitable land, the income which it yielded was always used in the first instance to finance the annual sacrifices, the symbolic expression of the group's corporate identity. Next came the upkeep of the ancestral hall and the care of communal graveyards. Any surplus that was not reinvested in more land was generally used to aid members, particularly, as will be explained below, with the expenses of education, though the usual kinds of relief were also given to orphans, widows and the poor. No attempts were ever made to give per capita grants to all members, for which resources would have been insufficient.[163]

There were however some very desirable or necessary projects that required very large sums of money to be raised all at once and could not therefore be financed entirely from the income on land. These included, at some stage, the building of an ancestral hall, but also, even more vital, the periodic re-compilation of the genealogy. The expense of the latter does seem to have been kept down to some extent by the expedient, already noted in the case of the Changs and the Yaos, of keeping up-to-date records of all births, deaths, marriages and important events of any kind. The Suns in 1732 had even specified corporal punishment, of ten blows, for those who were remiss about noting down such details and communicating them to their branch heads for delivery to the ancestral hall.[164]

Genealogies were nonetheless huge works (in up to thirty separate volumes) that required the full-time labour of many compilers and were extremely costly to print. On these occasions therefore recourse was often made to the somewhat unusual expedient of, in effect, imposing a tax on every member of the lineage.[165] Numerous examples are to be found from the early Ch'ing onwards. The P'ans had done it in a small way in 1673 to finance the building of their ancestral hall; on the birth of a son or grandson, or an important birthday of an elderly person, 0.1 tael was to be paid to the lineage head, and made to yield interest for this purpose.[166] The Tais in around 1700 held a discussion with lineage members (taking advantage of an occasion on which many scholars were gathered together for the local examinations) on the financing of the first printed edition of their genealogy, and decided that the fairest and safest method was to exact a standard contribution of 0.1 tael from each male member (though the really poor were permitted to give only what they could) and in addition a levy of 5 *fen* of silver on every *mou* of land they owned. Larger contributions were of course welcomed.[167]

Some lineages seem to have done this on the occasion of every new edition. The Chous of Yao-shih in 1730 imposed a levy of 0.1 tael on each male adult, to be collected by the branch heads in three instalments; women were to pay one *sheng* of rice and one *fen* of silver. This was felt at the time to be a much surer method than that of relying on voluntary contributions from wealthy and distinguished households.[168] It was applied again, in an even more systematic way, in 1893, when each branch was ordered to draw up a register of members and the acreage they owned, so that contributions could be correctly assessed. The rates were 70 cents per adult male and 70 cents also on rice land (though it is interesting that the basic unit of measurement on which this was to be paid was not the fiscal *mou* but the seedage, that is, the amount of land that could be sown with one *shih* of seed, probably a much more reliable gauge of its true productivity). Half-rates were levied on mort-gaged property and non-paddy land. The money was collected in two instal-ments by branch heads and managers.[169] The P'ans had likewise resorted to this method in 1846, levying 200 cash per *mou* and double that on any who tried to evade payment. A per capita levy of 200 cash was also imposed on each male adult, though it was permitted for poor ones to have it made up for them by their branch hall. The organization of the collection was extremely careful and complex, and every precaution was taken to ensure fairness.[170]

Though this was essentially a system of progressive taxation, that bore most heavily on wealthy, landowning members, the rates were low and there seems to have been no great resistance to paying them. That it was a successful means of raising funds is of course proved by the fact that the genealogies were in due course compiled and printed, often in a fairly short space of time. Such an achievement suggests once again a rather exceptional degree of cor-porate strength in those lineages that managed it, and shows that they were very far from depending solely on one or two wealthy individuals to finance their activities.[171]

The other major function of the lineage and its leaders, apart from ensuring the continuation of all the activities necessary to the survival of the group as such, was to regulate the behaviour of members, so as to perpetuate desirable traditions and values and to prevent clashes with the authorities. For this purpose almost all the lineages devised rules, in most cases, as far as can be ascertained, by the eighteenth century (many are dated and it is fairly safe to assume that even those that are not were in existence before the final edition of the genealogy, in the late nineteenth or early twentieth century). It should be stressed that in virtually every case the rules include not only *chia-hsün*, 'family instructions' (fairly general injunctions on correct moral behaviour), but also much stricter and more explicit *chia-kuei*, 'family regulations'. It was these latter that covered the really substantial matters, like management of property, and also attempted to deal with all types of anti-social behaviour by members that might harm the standing and survival of the group as a whole (non-payment of taxes always comes in this category). The widespread existence of regulations of this type can be considered as a yet further indication of these lineages' organizational strength.[172]

It is clear also that serious efforts were made to enforce them. The Tais, as a preventive measure, had extra copies made of their rules and given to the branch heads, who were to ensure that they were read aloud and clearly explained to all the kinsmen at the annual Ch'ing-ming sacrifices.[173] Transgression almost invariably incurred punishment of some kind, usually to be administered by the lineage and branch heads. Quite often the penalties were specific and even severe. Fines were fairly frequent, and sometimes the actual rates were stated, as by the Chaos of T'ung-pei, who required monetary payments from all those who failed to attend the annual sacrifices, graded according to their circumstances.[174] For worse offences corporal punishment was sometimes imposed. The Suns in 1732 laid down a scale of between ten and forty blows, depending on the seriousness of the matter; those who persisted in really outrageous behaviour (such as the violation of ancestral tombs) were to suffer the severe penalty of being expelled from the lineage, or denounced to the authorities, in one case (that of gross filial impiety) with a request for the death penalty.[175]

Mention of the death penalty is in fact found more than once in the T'ung-ch'eng rules (it has already been noted in the case of the Yaos).[176] The Chaos of T'ung-pei ordered that dishonest members who persisted in robbing outsiders (thus bringing trouble on the lineage) should be forced to commit suicide; those guilty of offences that carried the death penalty in the civil code were indeed to be executed, though whether the lineage intended to carry this out on its own account is not absolutely clear.[177] In one case however there is no doubt. One of the Hu lineages, in a rule dating from the years after the Taiping occupation, ordained that members who became bandits were to be tracked down and captured by the heads of their own branch and their assistants, and then strangled to death at the ancestral tombs, 'regardless of whether the authorities have already discovered the matter'.[178] This may have been an exceptional reaction after a period of dangerous social upheaval (it will be remembered that the Yaos first specified the death penalty in the years immediately following the late Ming revolts), but that such severe rules could even be formulated is indicative of the strength of lineage corporate authority.

There is no space here to discuss in detail the contents of the various instructions and regulations, except to say that they cover abundantly all the categories so ably analysed by Hui-chen Wang Liu. It is worth noting in passing, though, that injunctions on making suitable marriages with families of the appropriate moral standards and traditions (rather than allowing wealth to be the only criterion) are frequent, and appear, from the evidence of marriage patterns noted so far, to have been taken seriously. That a tradition of this kind could be maintained indefinitely can be seen from the remarkable fact that the Fang lineage, after a feud towards the end of the fifteenth century, avoided all marriage relations with the Nis from then on, a prohibition that was said by Ma Ch'i-ch'ang to have lasted to his own times.[179]

From the point of view of this investigation the most interesting feature of all these rules is their concern over the occupations and way of life of members. There was absolutely universal agreement that the most desirable goal for intelligent kinsmen was study, for this was 'the only way for a lineage to become great'.[180] Yet many seem to have been realistic enough, in times of constantly intensifying competition, not to set their sights mainly on the attainment of higher degrees and official posts. The Hus in 1878 stated that they considered obtaining the first degree, the *sheng-yüan*, to be the first priority, while the P'ans, as early as 1673, had felt that even this was not absolutely essential; the main thing was simply to keep up a constant scholarly tradition in the family, for by these means their descendants, in the words of the *Yen-shih chia-hsün*, 'would never in a thousand years be reduced to commoners (*hsiao-jen*)'.[181] Only if their basic educational standards were kept up could there be any possibility of members ever attaining real eminence.[182]

The ways of achieving this varied. Most of the lineage rules insisted that private initiative was vital, and that all members should try to provide schooling for any of their younger kinsmen who showed promise.[183] Many went further, however, and provided aid and incentives for study. In a remarkably large number of cases the first priority for the use of surplus income from ritual land was not relief for the needy nor help with weddings and funerals, but 'paper and brushes' for poor but ambitious scholars.[184] Many also provided help with the expenses of the examinations, including travelling expenses, and also large cash prizes for the successful. One of the Chang lineages in 1779 offered 100 taels to members who managed to become *sheng-yüan*, 180 to *chü-jen* and 300 to *chin-shih* (though it is of course unlikely that these amounts had to be paid out very often).[185]

One or two lineages even went so far as to set up a special school and to endow a separate holding of land for its upkeep and the payment of teachers. The Tais aimed to do this, apparently in the eighteenth century, at the same time as building their hall, in order that the talents of bright boys from farming families might be saved from going to waste.[186] The Chaos of T'ung-pei did it in the nineteenth century out of concern that their educational standards were falling; all able kinsmen were to be eligible for instruction and tests were to be carried out monthly.[187] The Hus in 1878 re-endowed a piece of school land that was traditionally allowed to be managed by the students themselves, as an added incentive to study.[188]

If one seeks an explanation for the county's truly remarkable academic record from the sixteenth century onwards, and for the scholarly habits of life there which are described with such approval in the gazetteer, it seems unnecessary to look further than this constant striving by lineages for educational attainment. This must undoubtedly have been stimulated by intense competition amongst themselves (for academic distinction and official careers were the surest way to win high social prestige in the short term), and the competition was probably even further sharpened by the really amazing success of one or two families like the Changs and the Yaos. This collective desire to compete for esteem in academic matters is shown also by the action of several lineage halls in ostentatiously sponsoring the creation of a county academy in 1826.[189]

The lineages were not concerned merely to ensure that some of their members become scholars, but also that the rest should not disgrace the group and themselves by improper modes of life. The professions of merchant and artisan, though not regarded with enthusiasm, were generally considered acceptable, as were geomancy and medicine.[190] There was a universal ban however on the occupations of yamen clerk and runner, which were regarded with particular loathing perhaps precisely because of the county's outstanding tradition of government service; for a member to sink to the position of corrupt yamen menial may well have constituted extreme social disgrace in the eyes of the lineage's elite and reduced its standing in the community. The Ch'ens indeed claimed that for several hundred years not a single member had become a clerk.[191] Also banned were the professions of actor, musician, servant and Buddhist or Taoist monk. The penalty for any of these offences was almost always expulsion from the lineage.

It was clearly expected however that the great majority of kinsmen would follow the basic and highly commendable profession of farming, or at least possess some land. It is no doubt for this reason that rules relating to land-ownership are extremely frequent, particularly those noted earlier enjoining prompt payment of taxes and forbidding abuses such as *pao-lan*, lest they bring trouble on the group as a whole.[192] Many lineages seem to have taken an interest in the disposal of members' private property. The Chaos of T'ung-pei had extremely detailed rules and penalties on this subject, ordaining not only that kinsmen should have rights of pre-emption on all sales of land or houses, and that family property should be divided early among heirs to enable them to get on in the world, but that the lineage should protect the rights of young orphans who were left with property. If their uncles tried to appropriate it, they were to be reported to the ancestral hall for public 'fine and castigation'.[193] The Ch'is also attempted to safeguard the rights of orphans and widows in this way and they seem not to have been the only ones to do so.[194]

It is interesting also to find that several lineages laid down provision for the treatment of tenants and servants, two matters over which Chang Ying had manifested great concern in his *Heng-ch'an so-yen*. The Tais insisted that tenants not be treated too harshly, especially over rent arrears, for fear of arousing resentment.[195] Very many others stipulated that servants be properly managed; they should be made to know their place and not allowed to assert themselves. In particular, they should not harry people over debts, nor appropriate land and property, offences which might bring their masters into disrepute.[196] Such anxieties seem often, as in Chang Ying's case, to be a clear legacy of the social unrest of the late Ming. Chang Ying's other principal injunctions, on the need for frugality, careful management of property and budgeting of resources, are also echoed in every set of lineage rules.

In the absence of massive biographical documentation one cannot of course be sure that these instructions, especially those on the fundamental importance of the professions of farming and study, were always obeyed. Yet it is worth citing one interesting individual case to show that these ideals were not just conventional formulas, but could be held with profound conviction by indi-vidual lineage members. This is an autobiographical account by one of the Wangs of Tung-lou in the eighteenth century, a man of no great personal importance who seems to have been regarded as a good example by his kins-men. The eldest of three brothers, he came of a landowning but not particularly well-off family; he studied hard in his youth but was forced to give up examin-ations at the age of twenty owing to difficulties caused by his mother's death. He then became a geomancer of some skill but also helped to make ends meet by farming a small amount of land allocated to him by his father, and by various business ventures, which were not always successful. He was thus able to undertake several acts of charity to kinsmen, such as providing burial sites for his parents and grandparents, paying off one brother's debts and redeeming the land which the other had unwisely sold to their uncles. Yet throughout his varied and difficult life he still clung firmly to the security of his original landholding, and ended his account by reaffirming his faith in the long-term value of landowning and study as a means for his descendants to get on in the world.[197] In this case at least it appears that an insignificant member of a T'ung-ch'eng lineage had the greatest reluctance to abandon completely what were considered the twin bases of economic and social life, even when under great pressure from unfavourable outside circumstances.

Virtually all of these lineages appear to have survived the holocaust of the Taiping rebellion in the 1850s and afterwards to have resumed all their normal activities very rapidly. Ruined halls were rebuilt, genealogies recompiled and more land bought. All this was still going on even in republican times (by which stage a large lineage might apparently number several thousand male members) and it is hard to detect obvious signs of weakening.[198] It was occasionally acknowledged that social circumstances had changed somewhat (the Suns in 1922 admitted that their former rules of conduct of 1732, with their detailed corporal punishments, were now hard to apply and that the latter could now be considered inoperative),[199] but this was not sufficient to bring activities to a halt nor to prevent the compilation and printing of some massive new editions of genealogies as late as the 1930s. Clearly, lineage organizations were by now so entrenched in the county's social life that they had acquired a kind of momentum of their own, that could only be finally halted by a major revolution, as one can presume must have happened in 1949.

To sum up, it is clear that the T'ung-ch'eng lineages were in general remarkable both for their long survival and for the strength and complexity of organization which they attained. Many lasted for three or four hundred years from the time of their conscious inauguration, and the vast majority were able to produce three or four, or even five or six editions of their genealogy in that time. By their later days they had become more or less self sustaining and were very far from being entirely dependent on the efforts of the occasional outstanding individual. Though it is impossible to tell, owing to the incompleteness of the sources, just how all-pervasive they were, there can be no doubt that they played a major role in the social life and scholarly activities of the county and may, one surmises, have helped to promote more effective social control, especially after periods of upheaval and antagonism such as the mid-seventeenth-century revolts and the Taiping rebellion.[200]

It is evident moreover that one of the major purposes of founding and building up these lineage organizations was to maintain the prestige of individual kinship groups and their position in the local elite. This is not to claim that most of them produced a continuous stream of higher degree holders and officials, *shen-chin* or 'gentry' in the narrow sense. On the contrary, though this was a very desirable feat, and one that conferred great glory on those few groups, such as the Changs and the Yaos, that managed it for a time, it was clearly very exceptional indeed, and by no means essential to a lineage's actual survival and standing in the local community. For this, collective wealth and strong organization were probably even more essential, but they could not be achieved without the constant production and renewal of a nucleus of educated, affluent and leisured men, who would enjoy membership of the local elite in the broad sense and provide the manpower necessary to keep the lineage organization going. Even though certain branches in a lineage might prosper as others declined, there is no doubt of the essential continuity of the elite core.[201]

The key to the dual process of prolonging the lineage organization and maintaining its prestige was indeed Chang Ying's favourite prescription of land and study. Some inalienable property, no matter how small, was essential to the group, or else it would have been impossible to keep up its corporate activities and its aid to members. Private landholding seems likewise to have been considered of vital importance to individual members, hence all the attempts to encourage its acquisition and to regulate its disposal. Educational traditions had to be perpetuated, both privately by individuals and publicly by lineage sponsorship, for without it there was a risk that the vital elite nucleus might become attenuated or even disappear.[202] One might conclude that the lineage functioned in fact rather like a long-term collective insurance scheme. Even if the benefits from its joint assets and organization might go mainly to those members who already enjoyed some degree of wealth and social privilege, and even if they were not sufficient in themselves to bring about great affluence and academic success for individuals, they may still have helped to rescue some from falling too far down the social ladder and to ensure that the lineage's elite membership never declined.[203] It is not going too far to claim, therefore, that lineage organization and joint property did indeed exert a 'decisive influence on the shaping of Chinese traditional society' in this one area, and probably did assist in the growth of a semi-permanent 'gentry'.[204]

5

CONCLUSION: LAND AND LINEAGE
IN CHINESE SOCIAL HISTORY

While it must always be remembered that the findings presented in this study are from one limited area and have no claims to universal validity, they nonetheless constitute extremely valuable evidence bearing on the current controversies concerning the nature of the Chinese ruling class and its hold on wealth and power, and also, more immediately, on Chang Ying's arguments in *Heng-ch'an so-yen* as to the vital role played by land in the fortunes of the elite.

It is evident, first of all, that when one attempts to describe and define this elite in a strictly local context, rather than from the standpoint of the central government, it is extremely difficult to make clear-cut distinctions between persons with formal academic qualifications and office and those without. This is so regardless of where the line is drawn; whether, like Ho Ping-ti, one considers the elite to include only officials and higher degree holders ('potential officials'), or whether, like Chang Chung-li, Ch'ü T'ung-tsu and others, one takes them to include all degree holders. Even in a county of outstanding academic distinction like T'ung-ch'eng, individuals with this kind of formal status were surprisingly few in number (approximately 1,800 at the end of the seventeenth century, out of a population of probably over 200,000) and the vast majority had relatives, friends and in-laws who, despite their lack of such qualifications, still lived in the same economic and social milieu as themselves. The wealthy, educated and influential in T'ung-ch'eng were in fact a larger group than this narrowly defined, academic-official elite, and can for the most part be identified as members of important families and lineage organizations.

These latter had a long history, dating back to the middle of the Ming dynasty or earlier. They began to be founded at precisely the period when the county was first experiencing real academic success, and it is clear that one of their main purposes was in fact to try to consolidate and perpetuate the position of successful or aspiring families. To this end they adopted a dual strategy, on the one hand gradually building up the joint resources and organization of the group, so as to enhance its control over members and its position and prestige in the community, and on the other, strengthening its educational traditions, so as to ensure that some kinsmen always remained members of the local elite.

One of the principal aims of education was of course the attainment of degrees and office, but these seem to have been valued more for their usefulness in promoting a family's power and prestige in the county than as ends in themselves, leading to a political career. Chang T'ing-yü did not advance his relatives and in-laws in office with the intention of creating political support for himself, but rather, almost certainly, in order to provide lucrative opportunities for them and to use power and patronage as a means of enhancing the Changs' prestige and influence over those of other local families. Yet while it is true that the degree of influence that an individual or a family might wield in T'ung-ch'eng did correlate with the eminence they attained in office (men like Yao Wen-jan and Chang Ying were able to intervene with provincial authorities at the highest level) it cannot be claimed, as Chang Chung-li tends to, that officials and degree holders monopolized the conduct of all public affairs and projects in the county, for there are many cases where charitable or educational undertakings were founded and run by persons of low formal status or none at all, and this is even more true of lineage management.[1]

Thus there gradually emerged in T'ung-ch'eng a hierarchy of lineages, one or two with very high prestige and influence derived from large numbers of office holders, but most of them much less distinguished, though still able to consider themselves as 'notable lineages' simply by virtue of their effective organization and corporate wealth. This hierarchy was further defined and reinforced by systematic patterns of intermarriage which deserve much fuller study. It is clear in particular that prolonged intermarriage took place between some branches of the greatest lineages of the county, notably the Changs, Yaos, Fangs, Tsos and Wus, and it appears moreover that these traditions were often strong enough to survive temporary or even long-term fluctuations in their academic and official standing, provided that their lineages' collective resources and organization remained impressive.

The history of lineage organizations in T'ung-ch'eng thus confirms Fei Hsiao-t'ung's view that they were deliberately used by the elite to perpetuate themselves and their privileges. It also confirms the suspicion voiced earlier, that the reason why interest in kinship organization began to revive so strongly in the Sung dynasty, following the final demise of the old aristocracy with its automatic claims to political power on both local and national levels, was precisely because the new bureaucracy had to try to find ways to shore up its social position and power in the long term, and insure against the hazards of the competitive examination system. This hypothesis derives further support from the fact that in T'ung-ch'eng the really decisive stimulus to more intensive efforts at lineage organization came in the mid seventeenth century, when the elite found themselves faced with unprecedented threats, not only from violent revolts, but also from tax changes that drastically reduced their accustomed financial privileges. Henceforward it was even more difficult for a family or wider kinship group to rely on the protection of a few degree-holding members; they had in addition to protect their interests by building up the corporate wealth and authority of the lineage. This activity continued strongly to the end of the Ch'ing dynasty and beyond, and perhaps partially accounts for the basic cohesion and stability of local society, and its resilience in the aftermath of major disasters.

All this of course has considerable implications for the much-debated question of the degree of mobility in Chinese society. It is obvious, as Ho Ping-ti has demonstrated, that upward and downward mobility among the very tiny proportion of the population that ever held important national office was very high indeed, but at the local level the picture was very different. The history of T'ung-ch'eng was dominated by the same families and lineages — the Fangs, Yaos, Changs, Tsos, Mas and many others — for hundreds of years. Though in time they became larger and more diffuse, and some branches declined or even disappeared, there is no doubting the essential social continuity in these kinship groups, or their long-term membership in the local elite. This must surely have been true of other places, besides T'ung-ch'eng, where lineage organization was strong; there are clear indications of it in Hui-chou prefecture, in southern Anhwei (where powerful kinship ties and academic prowess also went hand in hand), and also in Chia-hsing prefecture, Chekiang, whose great families were studied by P'an Kuang-tan.

Whether there can have been high mobility into this broad elite group in T'ung-ch'eng is rather doubtful. It took shape substantially in the mid to late Ming, and there appear to have been very few lineages founded after the seventeenth century. Moreover the overwhelming majority of surnames found on the county's examination lists, especially after the Ming, are those of known lineages, a fact which suggests that few outsiders now rose in this way. Even if such persons did occasionally manage to pass a higher examination, it was possibly harder in later times, when population and pressure on resources intensified, for them to build up from scratch the lineage organization that was a major means of perpetuating this success for any length of time. It is, however, plausible that there was some upward mobility within lineage groups, in view of their educational facilities and interest in promoting the careers of gifted kinsmen. Downward mobility obviously must have occurred, even within a lineage, but it was by no means inevitable that a family would be reduced to poverty or actual peasant status even after many generations (protestations of dire poverty by once-great families should usually be seen in relative terms), as the history of Chang Ying's and Yao Wen-jan's descendants shows. Chang T'ing-yü was essentially right; if the roots were made firm the tree need not perish.

It thus appears that, after the early Ming, class structure in T'ung-ch'eng was much more stable and less mobile in the long term than one would imagine from the studies of Ho Ping-ti and Chang Chung-li. It was so stable in fact that the society seems hardly to have been affected by the passing of the examination system and of the Ch'ing dynasty itself. As long as some lineage members still enjoyed wealth and education they would still have access to power, and the supposedly shattering change is signified by no more than a casual mention in some genealogies (including that of the Changs themselves) to the effect that the system of recording official ranks and positions in the biographical entries had now in consequence had to be altered.[2]

There can be no doubt moreover that one major element in the survival of the enduring elite of T'ung-ch'eng (as Ho Ping-ti indeed noted at one point) was its continuous effort to secure its wealth in the form of land.[3] All the great families of the county were built up in their early days on land, and its attractions seem to have been increased, not diminished, by the growing commercialization and monetization of the local economy, especially the increased opportunities to sell rent grain on the market and to multiply the proceeds by usury. In any case, commercial development and manufacturing here obviously never reached the level of sophistication that they did in the lower Yangtze region, and probably never offered really attractive and safe investment substitutes.

The value of land undoubtedly did fluctuate in response to changes in grain prices, and population increase, but it can hardly have been reduced by tax pressures, for these were low, and the elite were in any case able to mount effective resistance to unwelcome fiscal changes. Nor does it seem to have been reduced in the long term by freer tenantry and the disappearance of serfdom in the Ch'ing dynasty. There is no evidence to suggest that land-owners as a whole ever had severe difficulties over collecting rents, for even Chang Ying considered that farm tenants were basically reliable if chosen carefully, and the nineteenth-century edition of the county gazetteer still described the population as being 'meticulous over rent payments'. Nor is there any sign here, contrary to Chang Chung-li's assertions, that formal academic standing always made a decisive difference to a landowner's ability to collect rent and to resist extortion by tax collectors; in this latter respect, wealth and family connections were probably more significant. The long-term advantages of investing in land were not as severely diminished by alienation and by repeated division of property through inheritance as has often been thought. There were persistent attempts by lineages to ensure that property circulated mainly within the kinship group, and it was certainly possible, as has been shown, for enterprising individuals to build up holdings even on the basis of a small inheritance. Very many well-to-do landowners in T'ung-ch'eng, if Chang Ying's family are any guide, did take a personal interest in their property even if they lived in the city, and were anxious to get the maximum return from it.

This is not to assert that landowning, especially in later times, was in itself the way to acquire a huge fortune and maintain a highly affluent style of life, even though its proceeds could be enormously increased by usury. There were other ways of doing this, as Chang Chung-li has shown, the most lucrative of which was a spell in office. Yet the importance of these to the average member of the local elite (whose life-style was not necessarily luxurious) can be exaggerated. Comparatively few of them actually got a chance to enrich themselves through office, and in T'ung-ch'eng it appears that teaching and the management of local projects were not always very profitable. Most individuals who had to make a living by teaching seem not to have been rich, and the few affluent teachers, like Fang Hsüeh-chien, usually turn out also to have been landowners. Projects like charitable granaries seem in fact to have entailed considerable expense for those who founded them and there is no evidence that they provided managers with large salaries. The most reliable income of this type was probably the perquisites derived from the management of lineage property, and these went by no means only to degree holders. If wealth were amassed by any of these methods it seems to have been rare for at least some of it not to be invested in land, as the only security that might enable a family to keep up its educational standards and membership in the elite throughout long periods without any access to office. That land was an essential security, even down to the twentieth century, is further shown by the fact that no lineage could do without a moderate holding if it was to continue to finance its corporate activities. It is therefore impossible to claim that in T'ung-ch'eng academic degrees and office were the sole precondition of wealth; rather, they were the occasional results of it.

One may thus conclude that Chang Ying, for all his old-fashioned Confucian moralizing, was indeed a hard-headed realist in financial matters, and that the strategy of land investment and education which he advocated actually worked, both for some of his individual descendants and for the lineage as a body. Though in terms of social organization T'ung-ch'eng may prove to be an extreme case, its economic development is more likely to have been typical of central China than is that of the much more advanced Yangtze delta. In general the evidence from this one area does corroborate to a striking extent the views of Fei Hsiao-t'ung on Chinese class structure and its economic foundations, as presented in his article 'Peasantry and Gentry'. Whether these will be confirmed or modified by other local studies remains to be seen, but one thing is certain, namely that it is unwise when studying these questions to confine one's attention to the tip of the iceberg, the tiny, academically qualified elite, rather than to attempt to investigate the submerged mass, the solidly entrenched local elite on which it rested.

TABLES OF REGISTERED POPULATION, ACREAGE AND TAX QUOTAS

Table 3. *Registered population of T'ung-ch'eng county, 1383–1825*

Date	Persons	Households	Ratio of persons to households
1383	58,560	10,427	5.6
1481	109,650	9,601	11.4
1631	58,560	10,417	5.6
1645	25,530	5,010	5.0
1657	33,250	6,123	5.4
1662	40,345	7,310	5.5
1672	45,255	9,112	4.9
1693	109,165	12,407	8.8
1705	124,808	14,783	8.5
1717	159,780	17,085	9.3
1724	204,411	19,787	10.3
1734	261,792	22,348	11.7
1743	432,796	49,252	8.8
1753	622,655	78,965	7.9
1765	850,168	114,758	7.4
1790	1,330,876	179,959	7.4
1797	1,482,180	182,486	8.1
1809	1,818,984	218,698	8.3
1819	2,119,994	263,802	8.0
1821	2,236,156	269,481	8.3
1825	2,443,750	274,599	8.9

Sources: *TCHC* (1490), 1.21a; *TCHC* (1696), 2, *hu-k'ou*, 2a–3a; *TCHC* (1827), 2.39b–42b.

Table 4. *Registered acreage*

Date	Total acreage, to nearest fiscal *mou* (including ponds)
Yüan	201,383
1391	392,702
1481	410,388
1581 (before survey)	410,063
1588 (before reconversion)	419,705
1588 (after reconversion)	410,061
1666	410,061
1729	410,744
1827	410,744

Sources: *TCHC* (1490), 1.21a; *TCHC* (1696), 2, *tien-fu*, 41a–42b; TCHC (1827), 2.21a–22b.

Table 5. *Tax quotas*

The following simplified table shows the total grain tax and service charges which the local authorities in T'ung-ch'eng were officially required to collect throughout the Ming and Ch'ing. Minor, miscellaneous items are omitted, but would not add a great deal to the total.

Date	Land tax (husked rice, *shih*)	Summer tax (wheat, *shih*)	Service charges including *ting* (silver, taels)
1391	21,835	3,535	miscellaneous
1481	22,245	3,634	levies and services (amount unknown)
1566*	20,500		36,000 (plus wastage fees)
1672	21,592		36,592
1728	21,628		37,109+
			3,711 (wastage fees)
			40,820
1827	21,628		40,820

Sources: *TCHC* (1490), 1.21a–22a; *TCHC* (1827), 2.1a–3b, 21a–22b.

*The quotas for the period of the Single Whip reform have been calculated approximately by deducting from the 1672 quota the small surcharges added in that year. The pre-1672 Ch'ing quota was almost certainly based directly on that of the late sixteenth century.

APPENDIX II
NOTES ON CONDITIONS OF
LANDOWNERSHIP IN T'UNG-CH'ENG

It would be extremely desirable to have solid statistical information from which to document the real productivity and profitability of land in T'ung-ch'eng over the centuries, and to be able to estimate accurately the size of holdings, the conditions of tenancy and so on. Unfortunately this kind of evidence is either all too often lacking or else extremely difficult to interpret. The best that can be done at present is to set out briefly the few facts which seem certain and to see how they fit into the general picture presented so far and with the statements made by Chang Ying. The following discussion is necessarily rather technical but it seems preferable to give it here, rather than scattered in the notes to *Heng-ch'an so-yen.*

It is clear first of all that by the seventeenth and eighteenth centuries the holdings of individual landowners, even the more affluent ones among them, were not enormous. To take a few examples, Chang Ying in *Heng-ch'an so-yen* states that he himself had bought a total of 1,000 *mou*, besides the few hundred *mou* that he inherited. His father, Chang Ping-i, probably had more; from Chang Ying's account it is possible to work out that he distributed among his sons a total of over 2,300 *mou*.[1] This is actually the largest individual holding found so far. Yao Wen-jan when dividing land among his five sons gave them 120 *mou* each, so that the total distributed to them must have been 600 *mou*; it seems unlikely that this constituted his total property, however.[2] Yao stated on one occasion, already mentioned, that *li-chia* heads generally possessed around 500–700 *mou*.[3] The joint property of lineage organizations was likewise not immense. Chang Ying's own lineage by the early nineteenth century was in possession of 588 *mou* of arable, as well as a considerable amount of hill land used for graves.[4] These figures are consistent with the findings of Ray Huang that holdings of over 2,000 *mou* were relatively rare from the late Ming onwards.[5]

To get an idea of the productivity of and returns on such holdings is very difficult. Many deeds of land purchase, dating from the sixteenth century to the twentieth, are preserved in the genealogies of the county's lineage groups. They include details of rents, prices and so on but are almost impossible to interpret, owing to uncertainties over the fertility of the soil, the size of the measurements used and the fact that a plot of land usually included many variable extras such as ponds, irrigation wheels, threshing floors, cesspits, sheds and even houses, the value of which in relation to that of the land itself cannot be estimated.

The most interesting fact about almost all T'ung-ch'eng holdings, of whatever date, is that the rents seem on the face of it to be extremely high. Again to cite only a few typical examples, the rents on the ritual land owned by the Chang lineage, mentioned above, work out to between 2.5 *shih* per *mou* (though such a low figure is very rare) and over 5 *shih* per *mou*, the average appearing to be around 3 or 4. The rents on the school land owned by the county in the seventeenth century also range between 3 and 5 *shih* per *mou*.[6] Yao Wen-jan when dividing land among his sons stated that the rent income to be expected was 3.6 *shih* per *mou*.[7] Assuming the rent to be roughly half the main crop this would mean rice yields (in unhusked rice) of anything from 5 *shih* (at the very lowest) to 7 or 8 and even well over 10 *shih* per *mou*, figures which are impossibly high. Both Ku Yen-wu in the seventeenth century and Fang Pao in the eighteenth century considered a yield of 3 *shih* per *mou* to be normal in the Soochow and Nanking areas respectively, and modern ·scholars have found much the same.[8] D. H. Perkins gives figures for yields in Kiangsu and Kiangsi (he does not include Anhwei) in the Ming and Ch'ing that vary between 2 and 4 *shih* of unhusked rice per *mou*,[9] while Ray Huang has found yields of between 3 and 5 *shih* per *mou* on top-quality land in Hang-chou *fu*, Chekiang.[10]

One should not deduce from this that land in T'ung-ch'eng was abnormally productive. A much more probable explanation, as was already mentioned in Chapter 3, is that the *mou* given in these deeds, and in fact the *mou* generally referred to by T'ung-ch'eng writers, is the large-sized fiscal *mou*. This is confirmed by more than one contract in which the acreage is actually stated to be 'converted *mou*'.[11] As the precise conversion rate is always unknown the real acreage of the piece of land in question cannot be discovered, nor can its actual yield.

In T'ung-ch'eng land deeds the stated acreage, in other words, simply represents the fiscal liability of the land. The fact that yields per fiscal *mou* were so high confirms the supposition made in Chapter 3 that tax rates here were in effect remarkably low, even by the standards of the times. The basic rate per *mou* in the sixteenth and seventeenth centuries after the Single Whip reform was 0.051 *shih* of husked rice and 0.083 tael of silver (not counting wastage fees, in theory around 10%); the latter was slightly increased to 0.1 tael (including wastage fees) after the rationalization in 1728.[12] This compares favourably with the rates elsewhere in Chiangnan, where the average assessment in grain was 0.078 *shih*, and with Kiangsi, where it was 0.065 *shih*; rates in silver were also comparable.[13] In most places, however, these rates were imposed on an average *mou* of rather nearer the standard size. Huang has calculated that on the most conservative possible estimate taxes at this level took between 3.3% and 10.8% of farm income on a standard *mou* (the latter figure assuming very low grain prices).[14] This would mean between 6.6% and 21.6% of the landlord's rent income. In T'ung-ch'eng it is probable therefore that the effective rate of basic taxation was markedly lower even than this.

It thus seems reasonable to assume that throughout most of the Ming and Ch'ing (before the nineteenth century), in conditions of general economic expansion, the returns to be had from fertile agricultural land in T'ung-ch'eng were at least as good as could be obtained in most parts of China, and better than in many. Chang Ying in *Heng-ch'an so-yen*, calculating annual income in silver against the price of the land, considers a return of approximately 5% per annum on capital to be average in the 1690s. This is somewhat lower than some later estimates for other places, but it should be remembered that Chang Ying was writing during a period of abnormally low grain prices.[15] Rice at that time in T'ung-ch'eng cost only 0.04 taels per *shih*[16] which was low even for the K'ang-hsi reign (a period of falling prices, when the average was around 0.07 taels).[17] It is probable therefore that returns on land were now at absolutely rock bottom level, which may well explain the timing of Chang Ying's essay. Once the eighteenth-century inflation set in and grain prices rose (to an average of 1.0 tael per *shih* in the Yung-cheng reign and 1.7 or 1.8 in Ch'ien-lung) profits for landlords must have improved considerably, even taking into account a rise in the price of land. Examples of eagerness to buy land are numerous in the eighteenth century in many parts of China, and seem to be largely explicable by rising grain prices.[18]

It must be stressed, however, that in T'ung-ch'eng, as in most other places, landowners were by no means entirely dependent on the vagaries of the grain market for their income. In rural China the most readily available source of credit was usually the landlord, and usury was a highly profitable way of multiplying rent income.[19] In the Ming a rate of at least 3% per month (36% per annum) could be expected on private loans, and in the Ch'ing 2% per month.[20] Chang Ying in *Heng-ch'an so-yen* rather disapproved of this practice owing to the risks involved (especially if the profits were not immediately reinvested in land) and the ill-feeling it aroused; his attitude may well have been conditioned by memories of the savage reprisals suffered by wealthy landowners during the late Ming revolts.

There can be no doubt however that moneylending by landowners was a fairly common practice in this area. Chang Ying's own father and at least one of his brothers are known to have made loans,[21] and the managers of lineage joint landholdings, especially from the late seventeenth century onwards, appear to have done it systematically as a means of amassing capital in order to buy more land. Most of the lineage rules on the management of ritual land prescribe that this be done with the surplus income, and some go into great detail on the matter.[22] The P'ans of Mu-shan even specified precisely the amount of security in the form of rent income that members were to put up if they wished to borrow from the common fund.[23] The most striking example of this kind of thing is to be found in the instructions given by Fang Pao for the management of ritual land which he bought in the early eighteenth century. He reckoned that the annual surplus income after the ritual expenditures had been made would be 20–30 taels. It was to be saved up until it amounted to 100 taels and then handed to a trustworthy pawnshop. When it had been multiplied to 600–700 taels it was to be used to buy more land. He stated that it would be possible in this way to double the size of the holding every ten years.[24]

If the lineage organizations did this as a matter of course it is impossible to believe that private landlords would not have done it also. An astute property owner could presumably build up his holdings considerably in this way, which is one reason why one should not assume that the division of property by inheritance necessarily meant the rapid impoverishment of successive generations of the family. One lineage, the Chaos of T'ung-pei, even advocated the early division of some family property, long before the death of the parents, on the grounds that ambitious young men would be penalized by being forced to live in common with their brothers, and would profit from the opportunity to manage their own resources.[25]

It should also be noted that in T'ung-ch'eng, as in other places, property was not freely alienable by individual owners; the rapid dispersal of holdings was checked by the rights of relatives to intervene in sales and to demand compensation.[26] Niida Noboru has discussed many deeds of sale from T'ung-ch'eng, of Ming and Ch'ing date, in which the transaction was carried out jointly by father and sons or other male relatives, and most of his examples also contain provision for dealing with objections to the sale by other family members.[27] I have discovered other deeds in which female relatives, usually the mother, also participated.[28] Quite sizeable sums in compensation had sometimes to be paid to the interested parties after the sale had taken place; in one example from the Ma lineage, dated 1762, this amounted to 30 taels in addition to the basic price of the land of 100 taels.[29] The Chaos of T'ung-pei had a definite rule that when members sold land or houses they were to offer them first to their own kinsmen, on pain of punishment.[30] If this kind of thing was general practice, and it seems very possible, it would also help to explain why Chang Ying stated that one of the advantages of land as an investment was that it was hard to sell in a hurry, even by reckless young men.

It should finally be noted, though it constitutes only negative evidence, that in T'ung-ch'eng one can indeed find no sign of any other investment that was regarded as remotely comparable in reliability. When lineages made cash income through usury it was invariably reinvested in more land, unless used for some specific short-term purpose like the building of an ancestral hall; this holds true right down to the twentieth century. Though other sources of income were undoubtedly available to members of elite families the combination of landowning and usury seems likely always to have provided the most secure basis for livelihood. This would help to explain the continuing tradition of landownership by the elite already described in Chapter 2, and also to provide further confirmation of Chang Ying's theories.

APPENDIX III

TRANSLATION OF *HENG-CH'AN SO-YEN* (REMARKS ON REAL ESTATE) BY CHANG YING

In the three dynasties and earlier, land was bestowed on the basis of the well-field system. People received it at the age of twenty and returned it at the age of sixty. Every foot and inch of land was the property of the state and the people could not own it privately. From the Ch'in onwards the well-field system was abolished and paths between fields were created. The people for the first time could buy and sell land privately. Thus in the three dynasties and earlier even the highest nobles and the very rich had not been allowed to acquire several hundred *mou* of land and bequeath it to their descendants. When later generations obtained the right to buy it, they took advantage of nature's soil and state maps, and allowed people to draw and delimit boundaries; they fixed written contracts, estimated values and traded it. Even though the emperor might change, the landowners remained as before. Tung Chung-shu of Chiang-tu was distressed, on the people's behalf, that the poor had not enough ground on which to stand an awl while the fields of the rich stretched from one path to the next. Though he wished to pass a law limiting people's occupation of land and to establish restrictions on it, it was never accomplished. With a minimum of effort, their forefathers finally came into full possession of the land and enabled their successors to enjoy its products. If they preserved it carefully and did not lightly give it up, then, throughout a hundred generations of their descendants, provided it was not involved in upheavals or revolts, the land assuredly could not pass into the hands of others. Having reflected on it thus far, one should consider the means of preserving it.[1]

Young men from an early age are accustomed to read Mencius. Each is familiar with the work but does not examine it carefully. Now Mencius, owing to his talent as an adviser to kings, counselled Hsüan of Ch'i and Hui of Liang; his discussions were comprehensive and his ideals lofty and far-reaching. He observes however that while there are many causes of sickness there is only one medicine to be used. He says: 'He who has permanent property will have a constant heart',[2] and speaks of 'homesteads of five *mou*' and 'fields of one hundred *mou*'.[3] He also says: 'In good years the young people are for the most part to be relied on.'[4] It repeatedly appears that if you take Mencius as a whole, the substantial points consist of no more than these few sections. And finally he says: 'The treasures of the princes are three; land, the people and government.'[5]

I have moreover read the collected works of Su Shih, whose natural genius is startling and unrestrained; there is no one in his class in ancient or modern times.[6] It almost seems as if he is unconcerned about the subject of making a livelihood, for in his poem 'Travelling to Chin-shan' he says: 'I have land but, like the waters of the Yangtze, cannot go back',[7] and in the poem 'Travelling to Chiao-shan' he says: 'I have no land and nowhere to retreat to; it is surely better not to be covetous.'[8] But in the poem 'On Wang Chin-ch'ing's picture of the misty river and towering cliffs' he also says: 'I did not know that there were places like this anywhere in the world of men. I long to go straightway and buy two *ch'ing* of land there.'[9] One may be sure that this had long been on his mind, for he frequently formed this kind of project. All his life he wanted to buy land in Yang-hsien but even in old age his desires were not realized.[10] Nowadays people are keen to talk of talented men, famous scholars and outstanding personages but they do not pay attention to their family's livelihood, so that when finally they have to do something about making a living they are quite without recourse. Thus they defy Mencius' warnings without second thoughts. How can one fail to be deeply pained at this?

As regards the things of this world, those that are new invariably become old. Houses after a long time collapse in ruins, clothing eventually wears out. Serfs, cattle and horses after lengthy service grow old and die. Something which in the beginning was bought for a heavy price may not be old after ten years, but after another ten years its value has depreciated to nothing. Only land is a commodity which even after a hundred or a thousand years is always as good as new. Even if agricultural labour is not intensive, if the land is poor and the produce meagre, as soon as it is manured and irrigated it will be renewed. Even if the land is gone to waste and the homestead is covered with weeds, once it is reclaimed it will be renewed. If you construct many ponds, poor land can be enriched, and if you vigorously uproot the weeds then barren soil can be made fertile. From ancient times to the present day there has never been any fear that it will decay or fall into ruin, nor anxiety lest it abscond or suffer attrition. This is really something to be treasured!

I have a friend, Mr Lu, with the personal name Yü-lin and the courtesy name Hsün-jo. He is a Chekiang man and at present he is second-class sub-prefect of Kuei-te.[11] He is very experienced in the affairs of the world and self-confident in financial matters. In the days when he was at the capital I used to meet him frequently, and one day the conversation naturally turned to the subject of securing one's livelihood, in particular, how one may actually succeed in this. Mr Lu thought it over for a long time and then said: 'In my long experience of the world I have found that pawnbroking, trade and usury inevitably mean sharp practice. Though they initially provide large profits, these always in the end turn to an "empty nothing".[12] Only land and houses can be preserved for a long period of time. If you compare the two, you will find that buildings are not as good as landed property. Why do I say this? With houses, when you demand the rent from people, every time the end of the year comes round you have to have a manager put on full dress, cap and

boots, and go and bawl and shout at them to get it. If they do not pay up
you lay a complaint before the authorities. Every time it results in a quarrel
and a lawsuit and, what is worse, there are occasions when you have to
compel them by force, which produces yet other calamities. But you will
not get it by showing any weakness over the matter either. This is not the
case with land rents however. Even if your descendants have become commoners and are extremely poor and weak, and their servant goes to the tenants'
door wearing merely black shoes and cloth socks and carrying an umbrella,
they will not dare treat him with disrespect. When the autumn grain is ready
they must pay the landlord's rent in full before they pay their private debts.[13]
If you take what they actually have, and do not demand what they do not
possess, neither the giver nor the receiver need be troubled. Furthermore
agricultural workers are all honest people, not like the crafty merchants of
the market places. If you consider it in this light you will realize that property consisting of buildings is not nearly as good as land.' Up to this day I
have found substance in Mr Lu's words.

In reading the Ya and Sung sections of the Odes I have sighed admiringly
over the fact that the men of old valued the lands of their forebears in this
way.[14] In the 'Ch'u tz'u'[15] and 'Ta t'ien'[16] odes the nobles and ministers all
have estates. The Chou had hereditary ministers and the estates of their
grandfathers and their fathers were passed on to later generations, which is
why it refers to 'the descendant'.[17] When one actually looks at the words,
they say: 'We draw boundaries, we divide them into sections'[18] and 'Our
fields are good.' They talk about 'our glutinous and our panicled millet' and
'our granaries and our stacks'.[19] The farmers loved the descendant, for it
says: 'The descendant is not annoyed.'[20] The descendant loved the farmers,
for it also says: 'That is the happiness of the husbandmen'[21] and 'They take
the provisions of those who come bringing food to the field workers and taste
them to see if they are good.'[22] They cut up the gourds 'by the boundaries
and divisions' and 'present them to the august ancestors'.[23] How honest and
simple the customs of these people were, that superior and inferior should be
as close to each other as this. Not only were there wealthy homes and satisfied
people, who did without improper schemes for livelihood; there is moreover
in the wind-borne, lingering cadences of the Odes a pleasure which is most
beneficial.[24] When posterity have property handed down to them by their
forefathers they should tour the dikes and inspect the sowing, and go on their
donkeys to keep a watch on the ploughing. If they have the splendour of the
Ya and Sung Odes right in front of their eyes, yet regard them as low and
rustic, and never pay any attention to them, then what can be the outcome?

In the present age the young men in a family have elegant clothing and
spirited horses and are always dancing and carousing. The cost of one fur
garment may go up to several tens of taels and that of one feast may be as
much as several taels.[25] They do not reflect that in my home area for the
past ten years or more, grain has been cheap,[26] and that more than a full ten

shih are insufficient to provide one feast and a full hundred *shih* or more are not enough to pay for one garment. How can they know the farmers' sufferings? Labouring all year round with soaked bodies and muddy feet, how can it be easy for them to get those hundred *shih*? How much less so when there is unseasonable rain or drought and one year's harvest cannot be made to last until the following year? I have heard that in Shensi, whenever there is a famine, the price of one *shih* of grain goes up to six or seven taels. At present it is considered a commodity like jade or pearls, yet they sell it at a lower price in order to get the cost of a fur garment or a feast. How can one fail to be deeply alarmed at this?[27] The men of old had a saying: 'You should use the products of the earth sparingly and then their hearts will be good.'[28] Therefore the young men certainly should not fail to direct their attention to the hardships of farming households. When they open the granaries and sell the grain they should issue the people with tallies and, on the assumption that an able-bodied man cannot lift more than one *shih*, the amount that can be lifted by four or five men should be priced at only one tael. But if they [the young men] squander their resources, then the granaries will have been emptied with nothing to show for it.[29] If the young men have a modicum of good sense they will not tolerate things being thrown away extravagantly. How can they live sheltered lives knowing what it is like to have full stomachs and warm clothing, but paying no attention whatever to the conservation of resources and indeed casting them away in the mire?

When possessions are accumulated in this world there are constant worries about floods, fire and thieves, and the most precious, rare things easily attract the swiftest misfortunes. Country people who have savings of even ten taels cannot sleep at ease, whereas those whose possessions consist merely of their land worry neither about flood and fire, nor about thieves. Even a strong and violent man cannot after all snatch away a single foot or inch of land, and even one with the strength to lift ten thousand *chün* likewise cannot run away with the land on his back. Property consisting of thousands of *ch'ing* of land which may be worth ten thousand taels is no trouble for one man to protect.[30] Even if people should have to leave their homes because of the ravages of war and rebellion they will return when things have quietened down. There may be nothing left of their houses and stores worth asking about, yet the plot of land which belonged to the Chang family will still belong to the Changs and that which belonged to the Li family will still belong to the Lis; when the wilderness has been cut down and the land reopened to cultivation they will still be prosperous families as before.[31] When it comes to the material commodities of this world it is not enough merely to compare their strength and solidity; one should think of the means by which they can be preserved.

When I have casual conversations with people from different places I make a point of inquiring what are the products of their native soil and thus come to the topic of their landholdings. In most cases the land yields a very small return,

less than three or four parts of what you would get from commerce.[32] In
the whole empire only the people of Hsin-an and Shansi are good at trading
because they are by nature extremely frugal and can hold on to their profits
securely.[33] People of other regions cannot do this at all and there are frequent
cases of their coming to grief. In the case of returns from land, even if they are
insufficient reckoned over a month, there may be a surplus when reckoned
by the year, and even if they are inadequate over a year there may still be a
surplus when reckoned over a generation. I have seen the young men of a
family get tired of the slow rate at which land yields its slight returns and
covet the speed and abundance of returns from trading. But when it comes to
selling property in order to carry on business there has definitely never been
a case when this did not lead to utter ruin. I personally have verified that this
is the case and have seen people who were like this; I have not made one
mistake in a thousand or a hundred. It is not only the stupid and feeble who
are unable to do it; even the clever and competent likewise invariably fail
to manage it. Young men should never harbour any misapprehensions on this
score.

People are intent on gaining wealth from others but it is better to take
riches from Heaven and Earth. I have seen cases of people lending out money
at interest so as to mortgage someone's land.[34] If after three or five years the
creditor has got a return as great as the sum lent, the other party may then
get disputatious about it [feeling that he has rewarded the lender sufficiently].
Or else it may gradually happen that the borrower, being resentful at heart
though grateful on the surface, refuses to pay back even the principal.[35]
Occasionally when a very poor scholar has saved up several tens of taels of
silver he may invest it in this way for a short period, but when he becomes a
bit richer he can no longer do it.[36]

The merit of land is that it alone is not like this. If you sow thinly you
will reap a meagre harvest but if you nourish the land generously then you
will get a generous return. In some cases you may get three harvests in the
four seasons or you may plant twice in one year. The central fields can be
sown with rice or wheat and the side plots and banks can be planted with
things like hemp, pulse and cotton for clothing. There will be some trifling
income from every foot and inch of earth. This is why it is said, 'The earth
does not grudge its riches', a very apposite remark.[37] A man with land first
supports his grandfather and father and then looks after his sons and grandsons. He has neither an air of self-satisfaction nor an appearance of weariness,
nor any objection to enjoying pleasures and exerting loyalty to the full. When
good things are renewed and increased every day and every month he can
accept them without shame and enjoy them without anxiety. Though he
gains them by many means he does not have the stigma of raking in profits.[38]
He can address Heaven and Earth above and face the gods and spirits in the
world below. He does not trouble himself over clever schemes nor is he
envied or hated by others. And there is even more to it than this, for he can
by these means use surpluses to make up deficiencies.[39]

I have already spoken of land as something that should not be sold, yet there have been frequent cases in all ages of landed property being sold. Even intelligent people often do it. The basic reason for this must lie in the burden of debt. The fact that debt arises is due to expenditure not being regulated. If a man does not know how to make expenditures on the basis of income, when it comes to the point where the total interest owed is already great and there is nothing in the accounts to pay it, then there is no alternative but to sell land which has been in the family for many generations. Therefore not regulating expenditure is the cause of debt, debt is the cause of selling land, and selling land is in turn the cause of hunger and cold. If therefore you wish to avoid the basic cause of selling land then you must definitely begin by regulating your own expenditure.

If you require a way of managing a household and keeping wants simple over a long period, there exists the method of Lu So-shan for making expenditure on the basis of income.[40] His method is to reckon up the total income for one year, deduct contributions to the lineage and the government, and divide the rest by three. You reserve one-third for extra expenses incurred during years of bad harvests and divide the other two-thirds into twelve, one for each month's expenses. If there are abundant harvests every year then this corresponds to the practice of the ancients in tilling three parts and reserving one. If it happens that the harvest is deficient one year then it will be made up by what is left over from another year, and if there is a deficit for several years in succession it will be made up from the remainder accumulated over several years. In this way debts will never be incurred. If one year's income merely supplies one year's expenditures, as soon as you encounter flood or drought it will not be possible to preserve the property. This is an extremely obvious principle, but people do not pay attention to it. Lu So-shan's method is very explicit. Even property worth one hundred taels may be run on these lines; it is a great mistake to think you have to be wealthy before you can operate it. Actually by his method you further divide the twelve parts each into thirty small parts but I fear this is very troublesome, so I merely make twelve parts. If you want to know the significance of the ancients it lies entirely in making economies in small matters. If there are deficits in large-scale management they arise from lack of care in small things, and if there are deficits in monthly accounts they are due to daily expenditure being excessive. If you can follow So-shan in dividing each month into thirty parts then your finances will be even more secure.[41] Every month there are the expenses of eating and drinking, and obligations to entertain people to feasts. You should economize that little which can be economized, and if, with what is left over from this one month, you set up a separate fund to assist poor relatives in small emergencies, you will feel even greater peace of mind and satisfaction.[42]

Thus failure to regulate expenditure is undoubtedly the major reason for incurring debts and selling property. Apart from this, however, gambling, depravity and wastefulness also lead unquestionably to ruin. Again, there are those who sell their property because of marriage expenses, which is absolutely ridiculous. As long as there are men and women there will always be marriages, but you should measure your resources and regulate the style of the affair on the basis of a good year's savings. Why should you sell something which has been the mainstay of the family for generations in order to make a fine show on one particular occasion? How, after the wedding is over, can you have a full stomach without eating or be warm without clothing? This too is the height of folly.[43] I have already said that land should definitely not be sold. Nonetheless, what recourse is there for families who do sell land? If in normal times expenditures are not regulated this will bring about debts and the sale of land, as I have already explained clearly. When in normal life a man practises the method of adjusting expenditure to income he will of course avoid ruin, but in difficult times he may regard his property as an encumbrance and will even bear resentment against his forefathers for preserving such a troublesome thing and passing it on to their descendants. I have seen quite a few of these cases also. But what is the solution? If you do not want to sell property then you should think about safeguarding it, and if you want to safeguard it then you must make the most of the land's productivity.[44] There are two ways of doing this. One lies in selecting tenants and the other in promoting irrigation.

There is a proverb which says, 'It is better to have good tenants than good land', and this is a very accurate statement. Even if the landowner is energetic and intelligent, if the tenant is lazy and inferior then the land will daily get worse. One may compare it to the case of a father and mother; though they may love their infant, if they give it over to the hands of a cruel maidservant how will they be able to know of its sufferings?[45] There are three advantages in having good tenants, namely that they are on time with ploughing and sowing, they are energetic in fertilizing, and they are resourceful in conserving every drop of water.

The men of old used to say: 'The most important thing in agriculture is doing everything at the proper season.' If you plough a month early you will have the advantages of an extra month; therefore winter is best for it and spring next. And if you plant a day early you will have the advantages of an extra day, so the late crops will be sown at least a day before the beginning of autumn.[46] As for fertilizing, it is what was referred to by the ancients as 'manure for a hundred *mou*'. They also used to say: 'It is not enough to manure the land only in bad years.' The Odes say: 'The smartweed decays while the millet flourishes.'[47] With diligence like this, one *mou* may yield the produce of two. Without the land being extended or the acreage increased, the tenant will have a surplus and the landlord too will profit by it.[48] In the conservation and use of water everything depends on speed and timing. Damming up the waters, waiting, and then releasing them, all have to be done at the proper time. Only good and experienced farmers know about this.

There are three disadvantages with inferior farmers, namely that they are not on time with ploughing and sowing, they are not energetic in fertilizing and they are not resourceful in conserving water. If there happens to be a good year and rain falls at the proper time, the lazy and inferior farmers will also reap a harvest, despite their negligence, and will conceal the harm they have done so that it is not noticed. But when a drought occurs then their incompetence will immediately be revealed. In a bad year the landlord will get one *shih* of rent when it ought to have been two *shih*.[49] How great must be his regret at the injury he has suffered on account of his inferior tenant!

People's servants, who manage the affairs of the farm, are always pleased with inferior tenants and dislike good ones. Good tenants have prosperous families and good standing and are unwilling to curry favour with others. They are moreover sturdy and simple by nature and frugal with their food and drink; they do not heed the illicit orders of the servants. Inferior tenants are invariably lazy and poor; they flatter the servants and obey their commands, and thus indulge their greed. The two differ in all kinds of ways, and this is the reason why servants by nature like bad tenants and dislike good ones. But the fate of their master's fields is something which they disregard entirely. They are actually delighted at floods and droughts which mean that it will be impossible to make up the full amount of rent and that they can take advantage of its fluctuations. How can anyone be unaware of these accumulated evils and corrupt practices?[50] But good tenants' houses are neat and tidy, their plots and orchards flourishing and their trees luxuriant. These are all things which the landlord's servants cannot attain even by striving for them, whereas the good tenant brings them about naturally. Bad tenants are the opposite of this in every respect. This shows that selecting tenants is a matter of the first importance.

When the grain is in the fields its fate depends on water. There is a proverb; 'Rich fields are impoverished by lack of water.' Even extremely fertile soil, if it has insufficient water, will still be classified as barren land. In Chiangnan there are many ponds and dikes.[51] Of old when a man opened up one *mou* of land there, he had to have a *mou* of water to irrigate it. Because people have subsequently become accustomed to years of plentiful rainfall, the ponds and dikes have not been properly maintained; the dikes burst and do not retain the water, while the ponds are shallow and leak so that they do not hold the water either. Every year in early spring there are several heavy rainfalls but they allow the water to flow away unrestrictedly. When summer comes, with its hot, dry weather, they are completely helpless and can only look up to Heaven and heave deep sighs. People's servants manage the affairs of the farms and the few stones to be used for banking up ponds and repairing houses are merely the pretext for making a new entry in the accounts and pretending that 'the top of the pagoda is completed'.[52] How could a spadeful of earth ever reach the ponds and dikes?

Ponds ought to be deep and strong. Once when I passed through the south district of Chiang-ning, where the land is reputed to be very well-watered and fertile, I observed that their ponds were extremely small, not as much as half a *mou* in extent.[53] When I inquired of some of the local people I found out that the ponds were deep and steep-sided, some as deep as twenty feet, so that they could irrigate dozens of *mou* of land and not run dry. In my locality there are many ponds; some of the bigger ones are several *mou* or over ten *mou* in extent, but they are shallow and leak.[54] Even after a heavy rainfall they are not full, and the bottom shows whenever there is a slight dry spell. The fate of the fields depends on them, but what use are they? In future, when it comes to constructing ponds and building dikes, you must supervise the matter in person; if in a rainy year the ponds are still not full, the leaks should be discovered and the dikes at once built up further. In general, bad farmers are lazy by nature, and their knowledge is superficial; they regard it as good luck if there is a very rainy year, but they make no preparations for it. Since the servants have already falsely entered this as an item in the accounts, it is not expedient to mention it again to the landlord. As soon as there is a hot, dry spell the grain withers right away, and as the days and months wear on the fields are barren and the farms ruined. The rent income decreases daily and the situation leads inevitably to the sale of the property. This shows that promoting irrigation is the other matter of vital importance. If you are unaware how necessary it is to pay attention to this but speak merely of conserving inherited property, then how can you have any control of the situation?

I have bought over one thousand *mou* of land, all of which is poor and barren. It is not that I like poor land but that I cannot afford a great price, and so would rather have poor land.[55] Someone with great energy would make it rich and fertile but I cannot do it. The price of fertile land is, when you consider, several times that of poor land. In time of flood and drought, income from even fertile land is always reduced and if there is a year of good harvests the poor land will likewise give a yield, and the rent return [in terms of capital investment] is double that on fertile land. The only real advantage of fertile land is that when you sell you can get a good price for it. In normal times you will get a *shih* of grain from both and there will be no great difference between them.[56] Moreover, if fertile land is not well managed, in only a few years it will have changed into land of medium quality, and in another few years it will have become inferior land. If poor land is well managed, then inferior land may be transformed into medium-quality land and medium-quality land into good land. Even if you can't make a great change you can still raise it one grade. Thus later men's ability or inability to preserve it obviously does not depend on the quality of the land.[57]

Furthermore, a well-known, prosperous estate may easily become coveted by a powerful family. When the young men sell the land they will have to sell the good parts first. My family's forebears occupied very poor land but at that time they improved it and made it so good throughout that it was termed rich soil. When my fourth generation ancestor Tung-ch'uan died he instructed his descendants that he should be buried to the left of the house, saying, 'I am afraid that otherwise the land may be appropriated by some powerful family.'[58] One can see from this that in those days there was never a time when it was not good land, and it is only in the present day that it has become poor soil. You can tell just by looking if people are good managers or not. I have on occasion seen waste, barren land which was taken over by one or two experienced local peasant families. The land was put under cultivation, the ponds were repaired, the crops were abundant, the homesteads in good order, and bamboos and trees growing all around. Yet at the same time as they, contrary to expectations, had got their property into good shape, the fields of official families were going to waste and were not fit to be seen. People like you should examine this phenomenon carefully.

The young men of the family should in the spring and autumn of every year go in person to the farms and inspect them thoroughly. In the slack season also they should get on their nags and take a trip there. But it is no use going just for the sake of it. The first important thing is that they should know the boundaries of the fields, but these are not easy to recognize. They should get some old peasant to point them out; they may not memorize them all at once but after two or three times or, most likely, five or six, they will be familiar with them. If there are doubtful points they should ask about them. They must not hesitate to repeat questions they have already asked, just because they are afraid that people will laugh at them. In that case they will never find out these things all their lives.

The second thing that they should do is see whether the farmers are industrious or lazy in their work, if the ploughing and sowing are early or late, if the stores are abundant or meagre, if men and beasts are many or few, if expenditure is extravagant or moderate and if the land is being well managed so as to improve its quality. The third thing to do is to examine carefully to see whether ponds are shallow or deep and whether dikes are strong or unsound, so that they can be built up. The fourth thing is to inspect the trees on the hillsides to see if they have gone to waste or are flourishing. The fifth thing is to inquire whether the price of grain at the time is high or low. I hope that they will gain accurate knowledge of all this.

If, however, a man heeds the talk of the servants and enters deep under the thatched eaves, once he has sat down, had a meal and spent the night there he will not see the fields with his own eyes nor walk along the paths on his own two feet. The servants will gather the tenants round him shouting and making an uproar, some wanting to borrow seed grain, others to borrow food against their rent, some claiming that the ponds are leaking and others that their houses are falling down. They shout their complaints to the landlord, who finds it very distressing and cannot get away fast enough. If he asks about boundaries then he will not find out and, similarly, if he asks who is industrious and who lazy, or about trees and prices, he will not find out these either. When he goes back into the town and meets his friends, one salutes him with

the words, 'I see you have returned from inspecting your property', while another says with a smile, 'You must be just back from a tour round your estate', whereas he himself says, 'I have just come from the village — what a wearisome business it was.' Alas, how can there be any benefit in this?[59]
This is what I myself experienced when young and I am ashamed of it to this day. In general the young men of a family definitely should not consider the management of property a vulgar, common thing, and avoid it for fear of incurring such a reputation, but neither should they consider it simply a matter of precedent and thus actually incur this kind of reputation. If you think carefully about such matters as these and compare them to the alternative, of going around with an alms bowl, whining, to solicit alms from people, who will win and who will lose, who will be honoured and who despised?[60]

For a family the two words 'wealth' and 'honour' signify merely transient glory. To raise their sons and grandsons they rely ultimately on agriculture and study.[61] Only if the young men have two or three thousand taels worth of land will they be able to live in the city. Why is that? Two or three thousand taels worth of land in a good year will produce an income of over one hundred taels. Their own fuel, vegetables, meat, fish and pickles, and also such things as help for relatives and the repayment of hospitality by giving feasts, all have to be obtained and paid for out of this money. In a good year grain is cheap and even in a bad year it may not rise all that much, so on this income they may not be able to do more than just get by, or avoid being ruined. If the property is worth less than a thousand taels then they should definitely not live in the city.[62] The reason is that if they live in the country they can inspect the ploughing and keep a count of the acreage, so that their rent income will be doubled and they will be able to feed eight mouths. Chickens and pigs will be reared in pens, and beans and vegetables grown in the kitchen garden; fish and shrimps will be raised in the ponds, and firewood and charcoal obtained from the mountains. They will be able to manage for weeks and months on very little money. Moreover if they live in the country there are few relatives to be entertained and little hospitality to be repaid, and if guests should come they need only be provided with chicken and millet. If the women and children work hard they can manage the spinning; they will wear garments of cloth and ride lame donkeys. There is no need of refinements. These are all things which people living in the city cannot have.

You can pursue farming and your studies at the same time; it is likewise very simple to engage a teacher to instruct the children. If you have little surplus wealth, how can it attract thieves? Old Mr Hu-shang in my family obtained great pleasure in this way.[63] He did not leave any great amount of property but the life he led was much richer than that of people with several thousand taels' worth of property who lived in the city. Among the mountains and rivers you can stroll about at ease and repeatedly enjoy satisfying pleasures, without being oppressed by anxieties or probing deeply into the sorrows of mankind. When finally you succeed in your studies and are given an official appointment you may live in the city. Thus you move back to the city, but after one or two generations it is proper once more to live in the country, so you again move to the country to live. In this way agriculture and study, country and city life succeed each other in cycles and may be great and long-lasting. What a fine and auspicious thing this is! Further, as regards the ancestral property, living in the city you will get merely the nominal rent[64] out of it and let slip much profit from the mountains, forests, lakes and pools, for this is something which you cannot appropriate simply by being powerful. But if you are poor and live in the country you may still obtain these lost profits and not merely the rent from the land. You should be aware of this point also.

I am an official and am supposed to be acquainted only with official matters, so how can I know anything about farming? But I associate with eminent men from all parts of the country and moreover have had long experience of the world. In the past fifty years I have seen quite a number of people's offspring succeeding and failing, selling land but becoming poor, or conserving it and growing wealthy. A thousand men, and all follow the same course. This is why I repeatedly issue these salutary warnings on behalf of people like yourselves.

My late father in the *wu-tzu* year [1648] divided the property, and I got over 350 *mou*. Later, in the *chia-ch'en* year [1664], it was again divided, and I got over 150 *mou*.[65] It was in the *wu-hsü* year [1658] that I first set up a separate household and began to manage the affairs of the farm.[66] Just at this time the land in my locality was at its cheapest.[67] When someone asked me, 'Was there any money when your father divided the property?' I replied, 'No, there was merely the land', and that was the end of his questions. I also said at one time, 'It is not that land is no good; I am merely sorry that it is difficult to sell quickly.' After the *ting-wei* year [1667] because of the *chin-shih* exam I raised a loan, and then sold the 150 *mou* of land that had been allotted to me in the division of the *chia-ch'en* year.[68]

Before I was forty I had no idea that land should be valued, which was why I made light of giving it up in this way. Later, because I was in office, it was not expedient to buy it back from people. Now I have at last realized that the really intelligent way to divide property is to have no money with it.[69] If you are well off in the early years you become accustomed to it, but when after one or two years your allotted share is exhausted you are bewildered to have lost what you relied on. The real advantage of land lies in its being difficult to sell in a hurry.[70] If it were easy to sell then it would be a very simple matter to let it slip out of your hands. This is something which I have come to see in my later years but it was not at all the same when I was young. I say all this as a result of great and bitter experience. You should think it over and not disregard it.

NOTES

A list of the abbreviations used throughout this work will be found with the bibliography.

Ch. 1 THE CHINESE ELITE AND THE FOUNDATIONS OF ITS POWER

1　Among the most important individual studies on the Chinese elite are: Chang Chung-li, *The Chinese Gentry* (Seattle, 1955) and *The Income of the Chinese Gentry* (Seattle, 1962); Ho Ping-ti, *The Ladder of Success in Imperial China* (New York, 1962); Robert M. Marsh, *The Mandarins: The Circulation of Elites in China, 1600–1900* (Glencoe, Ill., 1961). For useful discussion of the subject see: Ch'ü T'ung-tsu, *Local Government in China under the Ch'ing* (Cambridge, Mass., 1962), pp. 168–92; Jonathan D. Spence, *Ts'ao Yin and the K'ang-hsi Emperor* (New Haven, 1966), pp. 77–81; Philip A. Kuhn, *Rebellion and its Enemies in Late Imperial China* (Cambridge, Mass., 1970), pp. 3–5. I deliberately avoid a definition of the much abused term 'gentry' at this point. Throughout this chapter the term 'ruling elite' and 'ruling class' are used simply to denote the upper stratum of society that had enough wealth to enable it to enjoy leisure and education and thus, potentially, power on the local or national level.

2　Details of all these works will be found in the bibliography.

3　A short biography of Chang Ying is given in A. W. Hummel, ed., *Eminent Chinese of the Ch'ing Period* (Washington D.C., 1943–4), pp. 64–5. There are numerous accounts of him in Chinese, reference to which can be found in: *Index to Thirty-three Collections of Ch'ing Dynasty Biographies*, 2nd ed. (Tokyo, 1960), p. 259. See also Spence, *Ts'ao Yin*, pp. 141–4. Considerable attention is devoted to Chang Ying and his descendants by Ho Ping-ti, *Ladder*, pp. 137ff. and *passim.*

4　More information on the Chang family will be found in Chapter 4, below, and in the notes to the translation of *Heng-ch'an so-yen*, Appendix III. Chang Ying gave his views on the proper training and education of young men in upper-class families, and also further enlarged on matters discussed in *Heng-ch'an so-yen*, in a companion work, *Ts'ung-hsün chai-yü* (Wise maxims and instructions) written at about the same time for the same audience. It will also be discussed in Chapter 4.

5　An article by Nakamaya Mio, which in general supports the points made here concerning *Heng-ch'an so-yen*, unfortunately appeared too late to be consulted during the writing of the present work. See Nakayama Mio, '*Heng-ch'an so-yen* ni tsuite', *Tōyō Gakuhō*, 57:1, 2 (1976), 171–200.

6　This point will be discussed in Chapter 3.

7　As the following sections are based very largely on well-known secondary sources listed in the bibliography, annotation will be kept to a minimum. Detailed references on some matters alluded to briefly here are given in the notes to *Heng-ch'an so-yen* (Appendix III).

8   I follow here the views of Ikeda On, expounded in his draft chapter for the *Cambridge History of China* (forthcoming), 'The Decline of the T'ang Aristocracy'.

9   For a summary of these changes in the T'ang dynasty see D. C. Twitchett, 'Merchant, Trade and Government in Late T'ang', *AM* 14:1 (1968), 63–95. The most comprehensive account of commercial development in Sung times is that by Shiba Yoshinobu, now partially translated by Mark Elvin as *Commerce and Society in Sung China* (Ann Arbor, 1970).

10   The two main views are those of the Kyoto school, led by Miyazaki Ichisada, and the Tokyo school, whose main protagonist is Sudo Yoshiyuki. Many of their quarrels appear to have arisen because they used evidence from quite different areas. They are summarized by Kusano Yasushi in an article 'Daitochi shoyū to tenko sei no tenkai' in the recent series published by Iwanami Kóza, *Sekai rekishi* (Tokyo, 1970), IX, 345–82. It should always be remembered however that tenancy was by no means predominant even in the Yangtze valley at this stage; one estimate is that 60% of the farm population was still free peasantry. See D. C. Twitchett, *Land Tenure and the Social Order in T'ang and Sung China* (London, 1962), p. 29.

11   For a succinct discussion of the limitations on alienability of property in the Sung and later, see H. F. Schurmann, 'Traditional Property Concepts in China', *FEQ*, 15: 4 (1956), 507–16.

12   The standard work on the Fan clan is that of D. C. Twitchett: 'The Fan Clan's Charitable Estate, 1050–1760' in Nivison and Wright, eds., *Confucianism in Action* (Stanford, 1959), pp. 97–133, and 'Documents on Clan Administration: I. The Rules of Administration of the Charitable Estate of the Fan Clan', *AM*, 8 (1960–1), 1–35. Though work has been done on lineage rules by Hui-chen Wang Liu and Hu Hsien-chin, on joint property by Shimizu Morimitsu, and on genealogies and other aspects of lineage organization by Taga Akigoro and Makino Tatsumi (for all of which see bibliography), Twitchett's are almost the only studies to date (apart from the present one) on the long-term history of individual lineage organizations.

13   Cf. E. A. Kracke, Jr, 'Family vs. Merit in the Examination System', *HJAS*, 10 (1947), 103–23. His findings cannot be considered conclusive, however, owing to absence of information on collateral and maternal relatives of *chin-shih* winners, a criticism that can also be applied to Ho Ping-ti's study of social mobility in the Ming and Ch'ing. See the end of Chapter 1.

14   For a discussion of Chinese communist views on China's economic history see A. Feuerwerker, ed., *History in Communist China* (Cambridge, Mass., 1969), pp. 216–46.

15   It has been estimated that, between 1573 and 1644 alone, silver worth over 100,000,000 (Chinese) dollars entered the country. Quoted by Ch'üan Han-sheng in 'Mei-chou pai-yin yü shih-pa shih-chi Chung-kuo wu-chia ko ming ti kuan-hsi', *CYYY*, 28 (1957), 540.

16   This account of commercialization in the Ming draws heavily on the two classic works of Fu I-ling, *Ming-Ch'ing shih-tai shang-jen chi shang-yeh tzu-pen* (Peking, 1956) and *Ming-tai Chiang-nan shih-min ching-chi shih-t'an* (Shanghai, 1957). On trade see also in particular Fujii Hiroshi, 'Shin-an shónin no kenkyū', *Tóyó Gakuhó*, 36: 1–3 (1953), 1–44, 32–60, 65–118, and on the development of the highly complex, interlocking system of local market towns the pioneer article by G. William Skinner, 'Marketing and Social Structure in Rural China', *JAS*, 24:1 (1964), 3–43.

17   Ho Ping-ti, *Ladder*, p. 81. For the business interests of officials in the early Ch'ing see Li Wen-chih, 'Lun Ch'ing-tai ch'ien-ch'i ti t'u-ti chan-yu kuan-hsi', *LSYC*, 5 (1963), 96, and, more especially, Hatano Yoshihiro, *Chūgoku kindai kógyóshi no kenkyū* (Kyoto, 1961), Ch. I. The readiness of the Chinese elite to make the most

of commercial opportunities open to them is striking, but to argue from this that some of them were becoming 'bourgeoisified' at this time, as Fu I-ling sometimes tends to (*Shih-min ching-chi*, Ch. 5) is reminiscent of attempts to prove that England from the sixteenth century onwards witnessed the rise to power of the middle class. For a stimulating challenge to this view, showing that strong commercial interests and attitudes could perfectly well be shared by the landed aristocracy and gentry without altering their social dominance as a landed class, see J. H. Hexter, 'The Myth of the Middle Class in Tudor England' in *Reappraisals in History* (London, 1961), pp. 71–116.

18   A useful work that discusses the profitability of commercial farming from the peasant's or tenant's point of view is E. S. Rawski, *Agricultural Change and the Peasant Economy of South China* (Cambridge, Mass., 1972). On the growing trend towards commercialization of agriculture in the early Ch'ing, see Li Chih-ch'in, 'Lun Ya-p'ien chan-cheng i-ch'ien Ch'ing-tai shang-yeh-hsing nung-yeh ti fa-chan' in *Ming-Ch'ing she-hui ching-chi hsing-tai ti yen-chiu* (Shanghai, 1957), pp. 263–357.

19   Ch'en Heng-li, *Pu-nung-shu yen-chiu* (Peking, 1958), p. 13.

20   A brief account of the controversies surrounding these measures of the Hung-wu emperor is given by Frederic Wakeman Jr, in note 71 to his paper 'Localism and Loyalism during the Ch'ing Conquest of Kiangnan: The Tragedy of Chiang-yin' in F. Wakeman, Jr and C. Grant, eds., *Conflict and Control in Late Imperial China* (Berkeley and Los Angeles, 1975), pp. 43–85.

21   Ku Yen-wu, *Jih-chih-lu chi-shih*, 10.17a. By the sixteenth century, owing to the pressures of private landownership, the distinction between government (*kuan-t'ien*) and private land (*min-t'ien*) was being obscured; it was the write-off of the latter and the reallocation of the dues paid on it to private landholdings that largely accounts for the very high tax rates in the Yangtze delta (where as much as 70% of the total land area had been government owned). Discussed by R. Huang, *Taxation and Governmental Finance in Sixteenth Century Ming China* (Cambridge, 1974), Ch. 3.

22   Huang, *Taxation*, Ch. 3. Huang's work has thrown a vast amount of new light on the Ming financial administration and certainly constitutes the most important secondary source on the subject.

23   The rates of exemption are given in *Ta-Ming Hui-tien* (1587), 20.19b.

24   Quoted by Fu I-ling in *Ming-Ch'ing nung-ts'un she-hui ching-chi* (Peking, 1961), p. 75.

25   This is an extreme oversimplification of the nature and purpose of the reform, which is undoubtedly one of the most complex and least understood problems in Chinese fiscal history. In general Huang's work on this supersedes earlier studies, including that of Liang Fang-chung, *The Single Whip Method of Taxation in China* (Cambridge, Mass., 1956).

26   Fu I-ling, *Shih-min ching-chi*, p. 34.

27   Huang, *Taxation*, Ch. 4.

28   This certainly seems to be borne out by the findings of twentieth-century surveys, such as that of J. L. Buck, *Land Utilization in China* (Nanking, 1937) which show that the really large landlord had by then become a comparative rarity. It must of course always be remembered that, even in the Ming and Ch'ing, estates were very small by European standards.

29   The major work on serfdom in pre-modern China has been done by Niida Noboru, especially in his *Chūgoku hōseishi kenkyū: dorei nōdo-hō, kazoku sonraku-hō* (Tokyo, 1962). Fu I-ling (*Nung-ts'un she-hui*) has investigated the system in detail as it worked in Hui-chou *fu* and in Fukien, and reproduces many original contracts.

30   Landlords frequently resorted to using unfair, i.e. extra large, measures in collecting rent. One of many examples is cited by Fu I-ling, *Nung-ts'un she-hui*, p. 89.

31   Pressures were of course even more intensified by the absence of primogeniture, which kept younger sons on the land.

32   Fu I-ling, *Nung-ts'un she-hui*, Ch. 5.

33   The origins of the *i-t'ien liang-chu* system are discussed in detail by Niida Noboru, *Chūgoku hōseishi kenkyū; tochi-hō, torihiki-hō* (Tokyo, 1960), pp. 164–215. He considers that it was often originally a right given to the tenant as a recompense for his efforts in reclaiming land. Fu I-ling in *Nung-ts'un she-hui*, Ch. 3, investigates the system as it operated in one part of Fukien.

34   Fu I-ling, *Nung-ts'un she-hui*, p. 19.

35   Chang Ying in his *Heng-ch'an so-yen* evidently felt that it was advisable to treat tenants with humanity. Another seventeenth-century landowner who shared his views was Chang Li-hsiang of T'ung-hsiang *hsien* in north Chekiang, author of a well-known treatise on agriculture that forms the subject of Ch'en Heng-li's *Pu-nung-shu yen-chiu*. On one occasion he wrote to a friend who was having trouble with his tenants over rent payments advising him that to punish them was unwise and would only cause further resentments and difficulties. See Ch'en Heng-li, *Pu-nung-shu*, pp. 73–4.

36   For a convincing reconstruction of Ch'ing grain prices see P'eng Hsin-wei, *Chung-kuo huo-pi shih* (Shanghai, 1954), pp. 560–1. Another reason for their general stabilization in the later seventeenth century was the temporary check in the supply of silver entering the country, foreign trade being banned until 1683 on account of the Ch'ing campaigns against resistance in Taiwan. That changes in the price of grain could sharply affect the demand for land is shown by the well-known case of Sung-chiang prefecture, where in the 1640s and 50s people had frantically bought up real estate because of the high price of grain after the revolts. Many of them were bankrupted in the 1660s and 70s by increased labour services (imposed as a consequence of the revolt of the Three Feudatories) and sold this land very cheaply to 'powerful families'. In the 1680s the situation was eased somewhat by a reduction in labour services and, as grain prices gradually rose, that of land also increased. With a subsequent fall in the price of rice, however, the demand for land also slackened somewhat. See Yeh Meng-chu, *Yüeh-shih-pien*, 1.18a–19a.

37   For detail on the Chiangnan tax clearance case and its effects see Hsiao I-shan, *Ch'ing-tai t'ung-shih* (Shanghai, 1927), I, 425–8.

38   Both Hatano, *Kōgyōshi*, p. 5, and Li Wen-chih, 'T'u-ti chan-yu', p. 81, are agreed that this meant the end of all exemptions, a point which Hsiao Kung-ch'üan in *Rural China: Imperial Control in the Nineteenth Century* (Seattle, 1960), pp. 125–6, appears not to accept.

39   For more detail on this, especially as it affected T'ung-ch'eng, see Chapter 3, below.

40   Hsiao Kung-ch'üan, *Rural China*, pp. 124–139.

41   Land-tax rates remained stationary and taxable acreage increased very little after the mid eighteenth century. The case is convincingly argued by Wang Yeh-chien in his article 'The Fiscal Importance of the Land Tax During the Ch'ing Period', *JAS* 30:4 (1971), 829–42. See also Ho Ping-ti, *Studies on the Population of China, 1368–1953* (Cambridge, Mass., 1959), pp. 210–11.

42   A good selection is given by Li Wen-chih, 'T'u-ti chan-yu'.

43   Ho Ping-ti, *Studies*, p. 220.

44   M. Elvin, 'The Last Thousand Years of Chinese History: Changing Patterns in Land Tenure', *Modern Asian Studies*, 4:2 (1970), 100.

45   Hatano, *Kogyoshi*, pp. 17–19. He makes much of the fact that the notorious imperial favourite Ho-shen (1750–99), the richest man of the eighteenth century, had only 2% of his vast wealth in land, but even this 2% apparently comprised some 126,000 *mou*, a colossal holding by the standards of the time.

46   Muramatsu Yüji, 'A Documentary Study of Chinese Landlordism in Late Ch'ing
      and Early Republican Kiangnan', *BSOAS*, 29 (1966), 566–99. Jack M. Potter in
      Capitalism and the Chinese Peasant (Berkeley and Los Angeles, 1968), pp. 23, 40,
      also cites cases of landlords in the New Territories of Hong Kong living comfort-
      ably off their rents in the late nineteenth and early twentieth centuries.

47   Rent resistance in the Ch'ing has been studied by Imabori Seiji, 'Shindai no kôso
      ni tsuite', *Shigaku Zasshi*, 76: 9 (1967), 37–61, but he does not come to the
      conclusion that only landlords with formal *shen-shih* status were able to overcome
      this problem.

48   Chang Chung-li, *Income*, p. 125.

49   D. C. Twitchett, 'A Critique of Some Recent Studies of Modern Chinese Social-
      economic History', *Transactions of the International Conference of Orientalists
      in Japan*, 10 (1965), 28–41.

50   Max Weber, *The Religion of China*, translated by Hans H. Gerth (New York,
      1964), p. 129.

51   It is true that *shen-shih* status could be purchased, especially in the nineteenth
      century, but this does not mean that every person able to do so would necessarily
      take advantage of the opportunity. Equally it could mean that at certain periods
      wealth became a major determining fact in the acquisition of social status. Ho
      Ping-ti, *Ladder*, p. 47.

52   Fei Hsiao-t'ung's views are set out most clearly in his article 'Peasantry and Gentry:
      An Interpretation of Chinese Social Structure and its Changes', *American Journal
      of Sociology*, 52 (1946), 1–17.

53   Olga Lang, *Chinese Family and Society* (New Haven, 1946), p. 180; Morton H.
      Fried, *Fabric of Chinese Society* (New York, 1953), p. 181.

Ch. 2   T'UNG-CH'ENG COUNTY

1   *TCHC* (1490), preface.

2   For a description of the present-day climate and characteristics of the region see
      Buck, *Land Utilization*, pp. 65–72.

3   *TCHC* (1490), 1.1a–b.

4   *Ibid.*; *TMITC*, 14, 24b–25a.

5   Shiba Yoshinobu, 'Urbanization and the Development of Markets in the Lower
      Yangtze Valley', paper prepared for Sung II Conference (Aug.–Sept. 1971),
      pp. 9–11.

6   It is impossible to obtain satisfactory maps of the county, especially ones showing
      place names, which appear to have changed continuously over the centuries. The
      1696 and 1827 editions of *TCHC* both have traditional-style sketch maps; there is
      a rather better one in *Chiang-nan An-hui ch'üan-t'u* (1896). The best modern map
      available seems to be in the series L500 published by the U.S. Army Map Service
      (Washington D.C., 1954), sheets NH 50–2, 50–3, 50–6, 50–7, scale 1:250,000.

7   *TCHC* (1696), 1, *shui-li*, 17b. The county appears to have shifted closer to Peking
      throughout the last few centuries. *TCHC* (1490), 1.3a, estimates the distance at
      4035 *li* (1,378 miles); *TCHC* (1696), 1, *ch'iang-yü*, 14b, gives 3,000 *li* (1,000
      miles), while *TCHC* (1827), 1.1a, puts it at 2,397 *li* (799 miles)! Perhaps this
      symbolizes the growing importance of the capital to T'ung-ch'eng's inhabitants,
      as they were drawn more into the sphere of national life.

8   *TCHC* (1696), 2, *feng-su*, 3a–5a; *TCHC* (1827), 1.28a–b.

9   *TCHC* (1696), 2, *feng-su*, 1a–b. The information is said to be derived from the
      Sui-shu.

10   *TCHC* (1490), preface, p. 1a.

11   All information on the county's examination results cited in this chapter is taken
      from the most complete list available, that in *TCHC* (1827), Ch. 7. T'ung-ch'eng's

one official in the Sung was Chang Han-ch'ing, on whom see *TMITC*, 14. 37b, and
TCHC (1490), 2.17b–18a.

12   Shiba, 'Urbanization', pp. 25–6.
13   *TCHC* (1827), 3.1b.
14   *Ibid.*; *TCHC* (1490), 1.1a–b.
15   On the revolts in general see Wu Han, *Chu Yüan-chang chuan* (reprinted Hong
     Kong, n.d.); the campaigns in the Po-yang area are described in Ch. 3.
16   Fang Hsüeh-chien, *T'ung-i hsü*, 1.17a; *TCHC* (1490), 2.14b.
17   *Po-yang HC*, 14.10a, 15b; 27.9a–b.
18   *Wu-yüan HC*, 17. 4a–5a.
19   There must have been an equally large movement of people to nearby Su-sung
     county, to judge from the following: 'From the beginning of the Ming many
     people came here from the Jao-chou area which is why the simple, honest
     customs of Kiangsi are still preserved here.' See *Su-sung HC*, 2.35b. Ho Ping-ti,
     Studies, p. 138, considers that voluntary movement of population in this period
     was probably of greater importance than government-sponsored migration, but
     finds it hard to document.
20   *Tai STP* (T. 1136), 22.1a–3a. The first ancestor of the Ts'ai family, a Yüan
     official, was also from this same village. Once the fighting started 'there was
     hardly any safe place there, so the local gentlemen aided each other and scattered
     to avoid the revolts'. *Ts'ai STP* (T. 1046), 1.1a–3a.
21   *Mao STP* (T. 19), second preface, p. 2a.
22   These are rough estimates made on the basis of those genealogies (the majority)
     which record the place of origin of the lineage's first ancestor.
23   *Chang STP* (T. 656), 26.1b.
24   *Wu-yüan HC*, 15.2a–b.
25   Among them however were two of the most important, the Fangs and the Yaos,
     whose ancestors moved to T'ung-ch'eng in the Sung and mid-Yüan respectively.
     Ma Ch'i-ch'ang, *T'ung-ch'eng ch'i-chiu chuan* (1911), 1.14a; *Yao STP* (T. 428),
     1.1a.
26   *Lien-hsi Chou STP* (C. 290), 24.7b.
27   *TCHC* (1490), 1.21a. Ho Ping-ti, *Studies*, p. 4, considers that this registration was
     more accurate than most. Surviving registration certificates of the year 1370
     preserved in various of the genealogies show that some effort was made to register
     all household members, including old, young and women.
28   *Tai STP* (T. 1136), 4.1a–b; 22.1a–3a, 15a–18b. In later times it seems to have
     been accepted that 10–15 *mou* of rice land was about the maximum that one
     farmer and his family could easily cultivate unaided. See Ho Ping-ti, *Studies*, p. 225.
29   *Mu-shan P'an STP* (C. 818), 1, *lieh-chuan*, 2a.
30   *Ch'eng STP* (T. 878), 1.1b.
31   *TCHC* (1827), 9.3b; *TMITC*, 14.29a.
32   *TCHC* (1490), 1.17b–19b. Figures for registered acreage are given in *TCHC* (1696),
     2, *t'ien-fu*, 41a–42b.
33   *TCHC* (1490), 1.19b–20b; *TCHC* (1827), 22.37b. On taxes see Chapter 3, below.
34   *TCHC* (1490), 1.2b.
35   *Ibid.*, 1.6a, 31b.
36   Tai Ming-shih, *Tai Nan-shan wen-ch'ao*, 6.1a; 4.39b. More information on Tai Ming-
     shih and his family will be found later in this chapter.
37   *Tso STP* (T. 126), 2, *hu-t'ieh*, 1a–b.
38   *Yao STP* (T. 428), *Hsien-te chuan*, 1.1b–2a.
39   *TCCCC*, 1.6b–9a.
40   *Ibid.*, 4.4b; *Tso STP* (T. 126), 2.32a–33b. This case will be discussed in rather
     more detail in Chapter 3.

41 *Chang STP* (T.656), 26.2b, 3b–4a.
42 *TCHC* (1827), 9.4a.
43 It should be noted that some of the county's natives listed in *TCHC* (1490),
    2.18a–b, as becoming officials did not have *chü-jen* or *chin-shih* degrees, con-
    firming that at this period criteria for office-holders were not as strict as they
    later became. Of the 22 T'ung-ch'eng magistrates up to 1490, 15 possessed
    neither of these degrees. *Ibid.*, 2.14b–15b.
44 Ho Ping-ti, *Ladder*, p. 264.
45 I have been unable to find any copy of the Fang genealogy, which is particularly
    unfortunate because they are in many ways the most remarkable of all the kinship
    groups in the area, indeed of the entire Ming-Ch'ing period. I have had to identify
    their most important members and reconstruct their relationships by working
    through all the Fang biographies given in Ma Ch'i-ch'ang's work, supplementing
    this with information from their own writings and from one or two other sources.
46 *TCCCC*, 1.4a–b; Fang Hsüeh-chien, *T'ung-i*, 1.9a–10a, 2.6a.
47 *TCCCC*, 1.6b–9a.
48 *Ibid.*, 1.16a.
49 *Ibid.*, 9.14a–b.
50 *Ibid.*, 1.7b, 12b–14a.
51 *TCHC* (1827), 3.2b; *TCHC* (1490), 1.29b. On these local schools see T. Grimm,
    Erziehung und Politik im Konfuzianischen China der Ming-Zeit (1368–1644)
    (Hamburg, 1960), pp. 139–144. Those in T'ung-ch'eng had all lapsed by the
    seventeenth century.
52 *TCHC* (1490), 1.5a; preface, p. 3a.
53 That commercialization in the lower Yangtze region at this time resulted in
    greater agrarian prosperity is shown by the work of Fu I-ling. It is also demon-
    strated by Rawski, *Agricultural Change*, much of whose research follows that of Fu.
54 *TCHC* (1490), 1.21a. See Appendix I.
55 Ho Ping-ti, *Studies*, p. 264, estimates a rise in population from approximately
    60m. to 100m. between the late fourteenth century and the year 1600.
56 *TCHC* (1827), 9.6a–b. It should be noted that, despite continuing reclamation,
    the figures for officially registered acreage increased very little between 1391
    and the late Ming; indeed, between then and the late Ch'ing. The implications of
    this will be discussed in Chapter 3, below.
57 *TCHC* (1696), 1, *shui-li*, 17b. This method of reclamation, by enclosing large
    areas with dikes and draining out the water, is described most succinctly by
    Tamai Zehaku, *Shina shakai-keizai shi kenkyū* (Tokyo, 1942), pp. 355–414.
58 *TCHC* (1696), 7.67a. See Chapter 3, below, for more on this.
59 *TCHC* (1696), 2, *fang-wu*, 2a ff. This description of local crops and products
    dates from the early Ch'ing but must apply also to an earlier period; it is incon-
    ceivable that such development should have occurred entirely within thirty years
    or so.
60 *Ibid.*, 14a–b.
61 *TCHC* (1696), 1, *ch'iang-yü*, 15a–b.
62 *TCHC* (1696), 2, *feng-su*, 3a; 1, *ch'eng-chih*, 4a.
63 *TCHC* (1827), 9.6a–b.
64 Fujii Hiroshi, 'Shinan shōnin no kenkyū', *Tōyō Gakuhō*, 36:1 (1953), pp. 22–3.
65 Confirmed in *An-ch'ing fu-chih*, 4.226a.
66 In Wu-wei *chou* for instance, somewhat further east along the Yangtze, conditions
    seem to have been remarkably similar to those in T'ung-ch'eng. Here even at a
    much later date it was stated that local handicrafts were not in general specialized,
    and that few of the inhabitants became professional merchants or artisans. See
    Wu-wei chou-chih, 2.17b–18a; 8.23a.

67   Fang Hsüeh-chien, *T'ung-i hsü*, 1.6a—b.
68   Fang Hsüeh-chien, *T'ung-i*, 3.1a.
69   *TCHC* (1696), 2, *feng-su*, 3a ff.
70   *Wu-wei chou-chih*, 2.18a.
71   *Lü-chiang HC*, 2.46b—47a.
72   There is some evidence to suggest that holdings of land could be further built up on the proceeds of agricultural surpluses. In the late Ming one of the Yin family is said to have worked hard at farming and to have accumulated land worth 1,000 taels solely by these means. See *TCCCC*, 4.10b.
73   *Tso STP* (T. 126), 2.69a.
74   *TCCCC*, 4.3b—4a; *Yao STP* (T.428), *Hsien-te chuan*, 1.3a—4a.
75   *Chang STP* (T. 656), 26.4b, 9a.
76   *TCCCC*, 2.14a—b.
77   Fang Pao, *Wang-hsi hsien-sheng ch'üan-chi, wen-chi*, 17.4a.
78   *TCCCC*, 4.14b.
79   *Chang STP* (T. 656), 26.23b.
80   *TCHC* (1696), 1.14a—b.
81   *TCHC* (1827), 3.5b. The amounts were not large, 44 *mou* and 21.9 *mou* respectively. By the late seventeenth century much more had been acquired.
82   *TCHC* (1696), 2.11b—12a.
83   *Ibid.*, 2, *feng-su*, 3a.
84   Ho Ping-ti, *Ladder*, pp. 244ff., gives records of outstanding *chin shih* success for prefectures rather than counties, which makes comparison difficult. T'ung-ch'eng's record is certainly respectable when compared with that of one or two counties in Fukien that prospered greatly from foreign trade in the Ming, for example Hai-ch'eng, with its 11 *chin-shih* in the late sixteenth century. See Rawski, *Agricultural Change*, p. 90. Populations of counties of course varied, so any comparisons are bound to be impressionistic.
85   Ho Ping-ti, *Ladder*, p. 227, table 27.
86   *TCHC* (1827), 3.3b.
87   J. B. Parsons, 'The Ming Dynasty Bureaucracy: Aspects of Background Forces', in C. O. Hucker, ed., *Chinese Government in Ming Times* (New York, 1969), pp. 175—231. On T'ung-ch'eng see p. 190.
88   *TCCCC*, 4.1a—2a. For a fuller account see Yeh Ts'an, *Fang Ming-shan Hsing-chuang*, 1a—4a, in Fang Ch'ang-han's *T'ung-ch'eng Fang-shih ch'i-tai i-shu*. (I am indebted to Willard Peterson for this reference.) It was Fang Hsüeh-chien's biographical compilations on virtuous individuals of the county, *T'ung-i* and *T'ung-i hsü*, that later served as model and inspiration for Ma Ch'i-ch'ang (see *TCCCC*, 11.37a—b). He wrote another highly moralistic work, *Erh-hsün*, in twenty *chüan*, in which individual case histories are used to illustrate certain categories of good conduct, such as frugality, hidden acts of charity, the proper instruction of families and so on. This emphasis on moral teaching rather than abstract speculation was to remain characteristic of many of T'ung-ch'eng's thinkers, particularly the eighteenth-century 'T'ung-ch'eng school', who will be mentioned later in this chapter. On Chang Hsü's influence on the county's scholars in the late sixteenth century see *TCHC* (1827), 9.11a—b. He was in turn a disciple of Keng Ting-hsiang (1524—96), then director of education in Nanking.
89   Yao Ying, *Shih-hsiao-lu*, 5.25a—26a (in his collected works, *Chung-fu-t'ang ch'üan-chi*).
90   This preponderance of certain surnames has been noticed by J. B. Parsons, 'Ming Dynasty Bureaucracy', pp. 212—13. He points out that, of T'ung-ch'eng's officials in the Ming, seven were named Fang and six Chang, though he is wrong to assume automatically that they were all from the same families (one of the Changs at least was unrelated to the others). Only five other counties in Anhwei show this

concentration of names among their officials and three of them were in Hui-chou prefecture, where it is significant that lineage organization had been strong from Sung times.

91 This early connection is remarked on by Yao Nai in a preface which he wrote for a Fang genealogy, reprinted in his *Hsi-pao hsüan ch'üan-chi, wen-hou-chi*, 1.197–8.

92 *TCCCC*, 4.2b.

93 Fang K'ung-chao wrote an essay in praise of these three ladies, reprinted in *TCHC* (1696), 7.19a–20b.

94 Chang Ying, *Tu-su-t'ang wen-chi*, 4.31a–32a.

95 Tai Ming-shih, *Tai Nan-shan wen-ch'ao*, 4.40a–41a.

96 Tso Kuang-tou's career is described at length by Charles O. Hucker, in *The Censorial System of Ming China* (Stanford, 1966), especially pp. 281–5.

97 *Ibid.*, p. 199; *TCCCC*, 4.14b–16a.

98 *TCCCC*, 4.18a–19a. On the campaigns in general see Hucker, *Censorial System*, pp. 224–30.

99 *TCCCC*, 4.14a–b; 5.18a; *MS* 260.2953. Another from T'ung-ch'eng to be implicated was Yeh Ts'an, president of the Board of Rites at this time; see *TCCCC*, 5.16a.

100 Most of the members of the Fu-she who came from T'ung-ch'eng are listed in *Fu-she hsing-shih chuan-lüeh*, 4.14a–17a (a reference kindly supplied by Jerry Dennerline). Ma Ch'i-ch'ang in *TCCCC*, Ch. 6., gives biographies of the more important. For further detail on their activities, especially after the rebellions, see my paper 'The Alternative to Resistance: The Case of T'ung-ch'eng. Anhwei', in J. D. Spence and J. E. Wills, Jr, eds., *From Ming to Ch'ing: Conquest, Region and Continuity in Seventeenth Century China*, New Haven (forthcoming).

101 *Yao STP* (T. 428), first preface.

102 *TCCCC*, 4.1a–2a.

103 Fang Pao, *Wang-hsi hsien-sheng ch'üan-chi, chi-wai-wen*, 8.9a; *TCCCC*, 4.13a–14a.

104 *Ibid.*, 2.15a.

105 Yao Nai in 1809 wrote an account of the various mansions that the family had owned in T'ung-ch'eng city since the early seventeenth century; many of them were still in its possession. See Yao Nai, *Hsi-pao hsüan ch'üan-chi, wen-hou-chi*, 10.312.

106 Tai Ming-shih, *Tai Nan-shan wen-ch'ao*, 6.1a.

107 *TCHC* (1827), 9.6b–7a; *TCHC* (1696), 1, *ch'eng-chih*, 2a–b.

108 *TCHC* (1827), 23.11a.

109 *TCHC* (1696), 2, *feng-su*, 3a–b.

110 The account of the revolts given in *TCHC* (1827), 23.11a ff., is identical with Tai Ming-shih's *Chieh-i lu* (Record of a survivor), in his *Nan-shan chi*, Ch. 14, except that some material at the beginning and end has been trimmed. Except where otherwise stated, the following discussion is based on this source.

111 This version of events comes from a work entitled *T'ung-pien jih-lu* (A diary of the revolts in T'ung-ch'eng), by the notable local scholar and Fu-she member Chiang Ch'en, one of whose works was proscribed in the Ch'ing (see note 89, above). It appears, regrettably, not to exist in any Western or Japanese library, but is quoted by Fu I-ling, *Nung-ts'un she-hui*, p. 98. Tai Ming-shih is much less explicit on the origin of the revolts.

112 *Tai STP* (T. 1136), 22.33b; *TCCCC*, 5.21a.

113 *TCHC* (1827), 23.11b.

114 *Ibid.*, 9.9a.

115 *TCCCC*, 3.17a; 8.26a.

116 *Chang STP* (T. 656), 26.26a, 14b–15a.

117 This was the famous occasion on which the president of the Board of War, Chang

Feng-i, scornfully retorted that Chiangnan was in no danger because the rebels, being from the north-west, could not survive on a diet of southern rice, nor could their horses eat the local fodder. See *TCHC* (1827), 23.12a.

118   *Yao STP* (T. 428), *Hsien-te chuan*, 2.19a. Chang Ying's father's cousin, Chang Ping-chen, also helped to organize the city's defences; see *Chang STP* (T. 656), 26.28a–b, and Chapter 3, below.

119   Wakeman, 'Localism and Loyalism', pp. 48–53, in discussing the resistance to the Manchus at Chiang-yin in 1645 notes that here too local defence efforts were kept firmly in the hands of the *tien-shih*, precisely because he did not have local ties. When in 1644 a memorial was sent to the emperor urging him to allow the formation of gentry militia, T'ung-ch'eng was cited as one of the places where this was being done (by the *sheng-yüan* Chou Ch'i) but it is hard to find confirmation of it. At least one local man, Wu Chin-chao, did form a band to fight the rebels, but was soon defeated and killed. See *TCCCC*, 6.11a.

120   According to J. B. Parsons, *Peasant Rebellions of the Late Ming Dynasty* (Tucson, Arizona, 1970), p. 210, it was from T'ung-ch'eng that Chang Hsien-chung obtained his most important gentry adherent, Wang Chao-ling, who later pushed Chang into using even more terroristic methods. Wang must have been from a well-connected family (his elder brother was apparently a *chin-shih*) but no further information on his background has come to light.

121   Fang I-chih and one or two others did attach themselves to various of the southern Ming courts, but in general there seems to have been very little loyalist feeling among the T'ung-ch'eng elite after the conquest. For more detail on this, and on the course of the revolts in T'ung-ch'eng, see Beattie, 'Alternative'.

122   *TCHC* (1827), 23.6a, 21a.
123   *TCHC* (1696), 2.2a–3a.
124   *TCHC* (1827), 2.1a ff. See also Chapter 3, below.
125   This certainly seems to have happened in neighbouring Lü-chiang *hsien*, where there was likewise a tradition of landowning by rich households. After the revolts, when 'nine out of every ten' houses were left empty, it was said that much of the land reverted to their possession. 'The rich grew steadily richer and the poor poorer.' See *Lü-chiang HC*, 2.46b–47a.
126   *TCCCC*, 3.17a.
127   *TCHC* (1827), 23.21a–b.
128   *TCHC* (1696), 1, *shui-li*, 17b.
129   *Ibid.*, 1, *hsiang-i*, 11a–13a.
130   *TCCCC*, 6.19a.
131   *TCHC* (1827), 2.39b–41b; Ho Ping-ti, *Studies*, p. 47, and also p. 59 for population figures of some other counties around this time. See also Appendix I, below.
132   *TCHC* (1827), 1.27b–28a.
133   Crops and products are listed in *ibid.*, 22.1a ff.
134   D. H. Perkins, *Agricultural Development in China, 1368–1968* (Chicago, 1969), p. 44, asserts that double-cropping of rice was unknown in Anhwei before the 1930s. The gazetteer of Ch'ien-shan, another of the counties of An-ch'ing, does state that two crops of rice were grown there before 1920, when the gazetteer was compiled; see *Ch'ien-shan HC*, 1.6a–b. More research is obviously needed.
135   *TCHC* (1827), 1.28a–29a. The cotton cloth of the area was still known as 'local' or 'home-weave' cloth even in the nineteenth century, and was said to be coarse and hard-wearing.
136   The accounts of crops, products and local customs given in the gazetteers of all the counties surrounding T'ung-ch'eng (see bibliography) present a very similar picture of a basically agrarian economy in which non-farm occupations were of marginal importance, even in the nineteenth century.

137 *TCHC* (1827), 3.14b.
138 This statement is based on the rules of the various T'ung-ch'eng lineages, which in many cases date from the eighteenth and nineteenth centuries. The general attitude is summed up by the injunction found in *Tai STP* (T. 1136), preliminary chapter, pp. 35a–36b: 'The professions of merchant and artisan easily lead to loss of integrity and the gentleman of high purpose does not follow them ... ' For further discussion see Chapter 4, below.
139 Ch'üan Han-sheng has shown that most commodity prices (notably grain and land prices) were rising from about the middle of the K'ang-hsi reign (1662–1722) onwards and that the rise became particularly acute in the second half of the eighteenth century. This he attributes not merely to population increase but also to the growing influx of American silver in this period. See in particular 'Mei-chou pai-yin', pp. 517–50. This is also confirmed by the work of P'eng Hsin-wei, *Huo-pi shih*, especially pp. 560–1.
140 *TCHC* (1827), 3,14b–15a.
141 The list in *TCHC* (1827) is of course incomplete and has had to be supplemented with information from Fang Chao-ying and Tu Lien-che, *Tseng-chiao Ch'ing-ch'ao chin-shih t'i-ming pei-lu*, Harvard-Yenching Index Series, Supplement 19 (1941), and also from *An-hui TC* (1877), 164.4a ff., which gives *chü-jen* results up to the year 1876.
142 Ho Ping-ti, *Ladder*, p. 228, table 28. Some of the outstanding counties listed on p. 254, such as Yang-chou (Kiangsu) and Chia-hsing (Chekiang) did very little better than T'ung-ch'eng in terms of *chin-shih* production; most of them moreover had the advantage of being large urban centres.
143 Shang Yen-liu, *Ch'ing-tai k'o-chü k'ao-shih shu-lu* (Peking, 1958), pp. 77, 79–80; Ho Ping-ti, *Ladder*, p. 186.
144 Ho Ping-ti, *Ladder*, pp. 137ff. and *passim*, devotes considerable attention to the Changs though his main concern is to use them as an example of long-range downward social mobility. That they declined in terms of holding high government office is undeniable but whether this drastically affected their social position as one of T'ung-ch'eng's more eminent families is much less certain, and will be discussed in Chapter 4.
145 Most of these men have entries or mentions in Hummel, *Eminent Chinese*. It should be noted that all the Fangs eminent enough to qualify for a separate biography in this work are from T'ung-ch'eng (remarkable, considering that Fang is a common surname). It is true that the sixth branch of the Fangs seem to have lived mainly in Nanking but they do appear to have maintained close contact with their original home, as is suggested by the fact that Fang Kuan-ch'eng of the sixth branch was adopted into the first, which still lived in T'ung-ch'eng; see *TCCCC*, 9.8b–14b. Fang Pao himself restored some of the ancestral property in T'ung-ch'eng (that belonging to Fang Ta-mei) as ritual land; see *Wang-hsi hsien-sheng ch'üan-chi, wen-chi*, 17.4a.
146 See in Hummel, *Eminent Chinese*, under Fang Pao and Tai Ming-shih; also L. Carrington Goodrich, *The Literary Inquisition of Ch'ien-lung* (Baltimore, 1935). The standard account of the affair is *Chi T'ung-ch'eng Fang Tai liang-chia shu-an*, reprinted in *Ku-hsüeh hui-k'an* (1912–13).
147 Mary C. Wright, *The Last Stand of Chinese Conservatism* (Stanford, 1962), pp. 59–60.
148 Entered as a postscript to *Chieh-i-lu* in Tai Ming-shih, *Nan-shan-chi*, ch. 14. See especially p. 4a.
149 *TCCCC*, 9.16b–18a.
150 Ho Ping-ti, *Ladder*, p. 138.

151   *TCHC* (1827), 3.12a ff.
152   *Ibid.*, 10b–11a.
153   *Chung-kuo ti-fang-chih tsung-lu* (2nd ed., 1958), does list a later gazetteer for
      T'ung-ch'eng, compiled in 1871, but no copy of this appears to exist in any
      library outside mainland China.
154   *TCHC* (1827), 2.42b.
155   *Ibid.*, 22.1a ff.
156   A survey of two individual sub-branches in the Chang and Yao lineages from the
      seventeenth century onwards (see Chapter 4, note 97) suggests that there may
      have been a fairly steady rise in mortality and decline in fertility among both.
      Whether this can be interpreted as evidence of generally falling living-standards
      in the nineteenth century is uncertain, as it is doubtful whether these families
      can be regarded as typical of the general population.
157   *TCCCC*, 10.34b–35a.
158   *Ibid.*, 11.17ff. On Lü Hsien-chi see Hummel, *Eminent Chinese*, p. 949. What is
      known of *t'uan-lien* formation in T'ung-ch'eng agrees with the picture presented
      by Philip A. Kuhn in *Rebellion and its Enemies*.
159   *TCCCC*, 10.34a.
160   Hummel, *Eminent Chinese*, pp. 870–2. See also the biographies of Fang Tsung-
      ch'eng and Fang Tung-shu, pp. 237–40. A younger relative of Wu Ju-lun was the
      anarchist Wu Yüeh who in 1905 was accidentally killed by his own bomb in
      attempting to assassinate the five ministers commissioned to investigate consti-
      tutions in Europe. Ironically, he had been aided earlier in his career by his dis-
      tinguished kinsman; see *Chung-hua min-kuo k'ai-kuo wu-shih nien wen-hsien*,
      1st collection, XIII, 581. I am indebted to Martin Bernal for this reference.
161   Hummel, *Eminent Chinese*, pp. 871, 239.
162   *TCCCC*, 11.37a–b.
163   *Ma STP* (T. 495), 4.52b–55a.
164   Chang Ying, *Tu-su-t'ang wen-chi*, 4.12a–b.

Ch. 3 LAND AND TAXATION

1   The best-known exposition of this popular but somewhat dubious view is by
    Wang Yü-ch'üan, 'The Rise of Land Tax and the Fall of Dynasties', *Pacific Affairs*,
    9: 2 (1936), 201–220. At present scholarly opinion seems to be veering against
    it. See Ray Huang. 'Fiscal Administration during the Ming Dynasty', in C. O.
    Hucker, ed., *Chinese Government in Ming Times* (New York, 1969), pp. 73–128,
    especially pp. 125–8; and also Wang Yeh-chien, 'Land Tax'.
2   *TCHC* (1490), 1.21a–22b. For a comprehensive discussion of the early Ming tax
    structure see Huang, *Taxation*, Chs. 3 and 6.
3   The standard account of labour services in the Ming is that of Heinz Friese, *Das
    Dienstleistungs-System der Ming-Zeit (1368–1644)* (Hamburg, 1959). In the
    very beginning of the dynasty, services were fairly light but increased sharply in
    the fifteenth century. See Huang, *Taxation*, Ch. 3.
4   On the development and decline of the Ming registration system, see Wei Ch'ing-
    yüan, *Ming-tai huang-ts'e chih-tu* (Peking, 1961).
5   There has been considerable debate over the reliability of Ming acreage figures.
    These were compiled for fiscal purposes and most authorities consider them in
    general (with the exception of the national total for 1398 given in *Ta-Ming hui-
    tien* which may have included much uncultivated land) to have been under-
    reported. See in particular the discussion by Ho Ping-ti in Ch. 6 of *Studies*; also
    Huang, *Taxation*, Ch. 2. Dwight H. Perkins, *Agricultural Development*, pp. 222 ff.,
    contests this view in an attempt to prove that 'population grew much faster than

cultivated acreage, and hence this population could only have been fed by an increase in per acre yields'. As will be seen, the evidence from T'ung-ch'eng does not on the whole support this thesis.

6   *TCHC* (1490), 1.21a. On *kuan-t'ien* see Chapter 1, note 21, above. All figures for acreage, tax quotas and population are collected in Appendix I.

7   Methods of converting actual to fiscal acreage are described by Ho Ping-ti, *Studies*, pp. 103 ff. Unfortunately no modern estimate is available of the county's present cultivated acreage for purposes of comparison, but all the evidence to be discussed later in this chapter indicates that the early-Ming figure was only a small proportion of the later total.

8   *TCHC* (1490), 1.21a; see also beginning of Chapter 2, above.

9   *T'ung-pei Chao STP* (T. 977), 21.2b–3a.

10   Rawski, *Agricultural Change*, p. 170.

11   See note 8, above.

12   *TMITC*, 14.34b. See also note 3, above.

13   Friese, *Dienstleistungs-System*, p. 97; Huang, *Taxation*, Ch. 3.

14   *T'ung-pei Chao STP* (T. 977), 21.1b.

15   Ho Ping-ti, *Studies*, pp. 14–15; table 3, p. 10. Rawski has also found household amalgamation to be prevalent in Fukien; see *Agricultural Change*, pp. 170–2. Shimizu Taiji in *Mindai tochi seido shi kenkyū* (Tokyo, 1968), p. 448, describes both methods of evasion as being practised in Ch'ang-chou *fu*, Kiangsu, in the late sixteenth century. There the wealthy families and great lineages with much land found that if they split up their services were heavy, but that if they amalgamated they were counted as one for the performance of service. 'Medium' families with only a hundred *mou* or so found on the other hand that if they did not divide up then their services were heavy; if they did, they had a chance of escaping them altogether.

16   *Huang STP* (T. 838), first preface, pp. 2a–b.

17   *TMITC*, 14.35a.

18   *Tso STP* (T. 126), 2.32a–33b; *TCCCC*, 4.4b–5a. Cf. Chapter 2, p. 30, above.

19   *TCHC* (1490), 1.23a.

20   See note 18, above. Tso's action was invoked by the family as a partial explanation of the heroic career of his descendant, the censor Tso Kuang-tou, during the Tung-lin episode in the 1620s.

21   His name does not appear in the lists of degree-winners and officials given in *TCHC* (1490), Ch. 2.

22   Huang, 'Fiscal Administration', p. 86.

23   Friese, *Dienstleistungs-System*, pp. 33–7, shows that *sheng-yüan* in practice had this rate of exemption from at least the 1440s, though it was officially defined only in 1545 when all exemption rates were finalized; see *TMHT* (1587), 20.19b. They ranged from 30 *ting* and 30 *shih* for grade one central government officials down to 2 *ting* and 2 *shih* for the lowest degree holders, and 1 *ting* and 1 *shih* for very minor functionaries. The grain exemption was apparently not from the land tax itself but from the amount of service levy that the local government imposed on that number of *shih* of the basic tax payment; see Huang, *Taxation*, Ch. 3. The annual *sheng-yüan* quota in T'ung-ch'eng was at first 20 but this was doubled in 1428 and a further, indefinite number was allowed to be added from 1447; see *TCHC* (1827), 3.4a. This scale of increase was nationwide. Ho Ping-ti, *Ladder*, p. 175, considers that *sheng-yüan* numbers multiplied greatly after 1500. By the seventeenth century their exploitation of their exemption privilege had become so flagrant that Ku Yen-wu wrote of them as a menace to the social order and demanded their abolition. Quoted by Friese, *Dienstleistungs-System*, pp. 37–8.

24   *Yao STP* (T. 428). 1.8a–9a; *ibid.*, *Hsien-te-chuan*, 1.3a–b.

25 *Ibid., Hsien-te chüan*, 4.1b—2a.
26 *Ibid., Hsien-te chuan*, 2.6a—b.
27 *Ibid.*
28 *TCHC* (1827), 9.6a—b.
29 On the varying terms used for the Single Whip reform see Liang Fang-chung, *Single Whip*, pp. 25—6. Some of the ways in which it was put into operation, and its limitations, are discussed by Huang, *Taxation*, Ch. 3.
30 This supposition is confirmed by surviving land deeds of the period after the 1560s. One found in the genealogy of the Chous of Lien-hsi, and dated 1609, states explicitly that service and land tax were to be paid according to the acreage of the land; *Lien-hsi Chou STP* (C. 290), 24.7a—b.
31 Ho Ping-ti, *Studies*, pp. 119—20, considers that the 1581 survey was a straightforward attempt to increase revenues, but this view is not substantiated by the findings of Shimizu Taiji, *Tochi seido*, pp. 563ff., nor by those of Huang, *Taxation*, Ch. 7.
32 Huang, *ibid.*
33 *TCHC* (1696), 2, *t'ien-fu*, 36a. It should be noted that there is no mention in these surveys of the category of *kuan-t'ien* or government-owned land. Most probably it had by this time become indistinguishable from the rest, as happened elsewhere. See Chapter 1, note 21, above.
34 *TCHC* (1696), 2, *t'ien-fu*, 39b.
35 *Ibid.*, 39a—40b. The survey was carried out by the rural district heads, *hsiang-chang*, and their assistants.
36 *Ibid.*, 40a—41b. Ho Ping-ti, *Studies*, p. 120, states that in general during the Wan-li period the officials and local people were successful in defending their existing land-tax quotas, though he cites no specific examples. The case of T'ung-ch'eng is an extreme one; it is clear however that anxieties here were mainly over the weight of the service assessment rather than that of the land tax.
37 *TCHC* (1696), 2, *t'ien-fu*, 37a—39a, gives all the details of the conversion scheme.
38 According to Ho the usual practice was to measure top-grade land in standard *mou* and adopt proportionately more generous conversion rates for the lower grades. See *Studies*, pp. 105 ff.
39 *Ibid.*, pp. 111—12.
40 On the decennial compilation, *ta-tsao*, of the yellow registers, and the abuses connected with it, see Wei Ch'ing-yüan, *Huang-ts'e*, pp. 186—7.
41 *TCHC* (1696), 2, *t'ien-fu*, 40b.
42 The type of malpractice common in T'ung-ch'eng was *kuei-chi* and its variants, i.e. false registration of land under other people's names and often without their knowledge. This is described in some detail by Wei Ch'ing-yüan, *Huang-ts'e*, pp. 186—7, by Liang Fang-chung, *Single Whip*, p. 13, and by Shimizu Taiji, *Tochi seido*, pp. 451—3, who notes that the Board of Revenue had as early as 1492 laid down regulations dealing with it similar to those proposed by the T'ung-ch'eng magistrate in 1588.
43 *TCHC* (1696), 2, *t'ien-fu*, 41a.
44 For examples see the deed dated 1632 in *Tung STP* (T. 929), 5, *ch'i-shu*, 1a—2a; and that of 1609 in *Lien-hsi Chou STP* (C. 290), 24, *ch'i-ch'üan*, 7a—b.
45 *Yao-shih Chou STP* (C. 291), 2, deeds of the ritual estate, 1598. That land deeds give fiscal rather than real acreage must be kept in mind when assessing the returns on the land. See Appendix II, below.
46 *TCCCC*, 4.26a—27a. The precise date of Hu Tsan's retirement is unfortunately unknown. A brief account of his career is given in *MS* 223.2578—9.
47 This method of assessing *ting* completely on land acreage was still fairly exceptional at this time, according to Ho Ping-ti, *Studies*, p. 29.
48 Hu's use of the term *i-kuan* rather than *shen-chin* is interesting in that it implies

the wealthy and leisured as a class, rather than simply the narrow group of degree holders.

49 *TCHC* (1696), 2, *t'ien-fu*, 20b.

50 *TCCCC*, 4.25b.

51 In the early Ch'ing, an exemption of 1,597 *ting* from the total quota was permitted, which must have been a continuation of Ming practice. See *TCHC* (1696), 2, *t'ien-fu*, 20b–21b.

52 Hu Tsan was certainly from a landowning family. It was one of his nephews who was mentioned in Chapter 2 as having found his holdings virtually undamaged when he returned to T'ung-ch'eng after the revolts; see *TCCCC*, 3.17a.

53 *Tso STP* (T. 126), 2, *chia-hsün*, 12a–13a.

54 Huang, 'Fiscal Administration', p. 118. The surcharges are not mentioned in the T'ung-ch'eng gazetteer but were certainly universally imposed.

55 See Chapter 2, note 79, above.

56 *Chang STP* (T. 656), 26.28a–b.

57 *TCHC* (1827), 23.17a, 21a–b.

58 *Chang STP* (T. 656), 26.33a–b.

59 *TCHC* (1696), 2, *t'ien-fu*, 36a ff., simply reprints the account of the conversion system followed in 1588 as being that currently in use. It mentions only one case in which land was upgraded after the 1640s, apparently because of a great increase in its population; see *ibid.*, 36a.

60 *Ibid.*, 5a–8b. See Appendix II, below. The Ch'ing almost always put local tax rates back to what they had been before the late Ming surcharges; see Ho Ping-ti, *Studies*, p. 120.

61 *TCHC* (1696), 2, *t'ien-fu*, 20b–21b. The continuing assessment of *ting* on acreage is probably the reason why the Ch'ing population figures did not exceed the Ming total for most of the seventeenth century. See Appendix I, below.

62 Huang, *Taxation*, Ch. 6.

63 *TCHC* (1696), 2, *t'ien-fu*, 23a–25a.

64 *Ibid.*, 25a. The name Kuo was common to the generation of Tso Kuang-tou's sons.

65 This confirms the generally favourable picture of conditions in the first half of the Ch'ing dynasty given by Ho Ping-ti, *Studies*, pp. 208–13.

66 *Chang STP* (T. 656), 26.33a–b.

67 The changes are summarized by Li Wen-chih, 'T'u-ti chan-yu', p. 81. Hsiao Kung-ch'üan, *Rural China*, p. 125, simply notes the reduction of the exemption privilege in 1657, but does not really consider its implications. The change in the *sheng-yüan* exemption is explicitly noted in *TCHC* (1696), 1, *hsüeh-hsiao*, 8b.

68 See Chapter 1, above.

69 Chang Ying relates this episode in his obituary notice of Huang Chen-lin, *Pei-chuan-chi*, 93.9b–11b.

70 *Yao STP* (T. 428), *Hsien-te chuan*, 1.5b–6b. From a search of the Chang genealogy it appears that there was no other member of the family alive at this time who had the word *liu* ('six') in any of his names.

71 Yao Wen-jan has entries in several of the standard Ch'ing biographical collections, including *CS*, 264.3896–7, but the fullest available biography is that in *Yao STP* (T. 428), *Hsien-te chuan*, 2.12a–18b.

72 *Ibid.*, p. 16a.

73 His proposals are to be found in *TCHC* (1696), 7.40a–42a.

74 An edict of 1657 authorized rewards for magistrates who managed to raise local *ting* quotas by 2,000 or more. See Hsiao Kung-ch'üan, *Rural China*, p. 89.

75 See the list of successive *ting* increments in *TCHC* (1696), 2, *t'ien-fu*, 20b–21b. From Yao Wen-jan's account it appears that the same method of assessing *ting* on land acreage was used throughout the rest of the prefecture.

76 The magistrate Kao P'an-kuei in the 1690s stated quite explicitly that the *ting* charge could not possibly be considered a hardship. For his attempts to prevent evasion of it see later in Chapter 3. Total tax quotas for 1672 are given in *TCHC* (1827), 2.2b–3a.

77 *Ibid.*, 13a.

78 Hsiao Kung-ch'üan, *Rural China*, pp. 88–9.

79 *Sheng-tsu shih-lu*, 8.4a–b.

80 *TCHC* (1827), 9.12a.

81 *Ch'ing-ch'ao hsü-wen-hsien t'ung-k'ao*, 1.7501.

82 *Yao STP* (T. 428), *Hsien-te-chuan*, 2.16a.

83 *TCHC* (1827), 2.22a.

84 T. C. Smith notes likewise that in eighteenth-century Japan, owing to the infrequency of land surveys, 'improved land was taxed at a lesser rate in relation to productivity than unimproved land'. See *The Agrarian Origins of Modern Japan* (Stanford, 1959), p. 100.

85 Huang, 'Fiscal Administration', p. 122.

86 *Sheng-tsu shih-lu*, 15.6b–7a.

87 On the operation of the *li-chia* tax collection system in the Ch'ing see Hsiao Kung-ch'üan, *Rural China*, pp. 95 ff., and Ch'ü T'ung-tsu, *Local Government*, pp. 135–9. It is not clear how soon the attempt to abolish it took place; Hsiao describes the change on p. 98 but mentions no precise date. One suspects, though it will be hard to prove, that it may have been regarded as a means of conciliating the elite for the reduction of their exemption privileges in 1657.

88 *Yao STP* (T. 428), *Hsien-te chuan*, 2.11a–12a (biography of Yao Wen-lieh).

89 *TCHC* (1827), 9.12a. The fact that action over the matter was taken not by him but by his successor suggests that the protest occurred at the very end of his term of office.

90 See note 88, above.

91 *TCHC* (1827), 9.12a.

92 The complete text is given in *TCHC* (1696), 7.51a–53b.

93 Magistrate Kao P'an-kuei in the 1690s requested that the southern rice be combined with regular grain tribute; his account makes it clear that this item was now delivered only to An-ch'ing. See *TCHC* (1696), 7.63a.

94 *Ibid.*, 65a–66a.

95 *TCHC* (1827), 9.12a.

96 *TCHC* (1696), 2, *t'ien-fu*, 34a. In 1671 it was ordered that the small extra levy imposed on the land tax in that year should be subject to the method of official collection and delivery, *as with the regular items of tax*; see *ibid.*, 12a.

97 *CSLC*, 9.27a.

98 Chang Ying describes the friendship in the adulatory memorial account which he wrote for Hsü Kuo-hsiang. See *Pei-chuan-chi*, 66.4b–6a. On his exemplary career see also *Ta-Ch'ing chi-fu hsien-che chuan*, 3.28a–b. Hsü had earlier been provincial treasurer of Anhwei and so had had considerable time in which to build up contacts in the province.

99 Chang T'ing-yü, *CHYWT*, 15.24a.

100 *TCHC* (1696), 2, *t'ien-fu*, 34a–b. The notice is prefaced by a statement, p. 32a, that the prohibition was 'requested' of the governor but it does not say by whom.

101 *Ibid.*, 30a–31b.

102 Almost all surviving local land deeds of Ch'ing date do contain a provision to this effect, and further attempts were made to enforce it in the 1690s. See later in this chapter.

103 Ch'ü T'ung-tsu, *Local Government*, p. 291. Hsü Kuo-hsiang in 1684 was transferred to be governor-general of Hukwang, where he also abolished the *li-chang*

system. It is perhaps significant that on his way to his new post he met Chang Ying in T'ung-ch'eng and had lengthy discussions with him on administrative matters. See *Pei-chuan-chi*, 66.5b.

104   *TCHC* (1696), 2, *t'ien-fu*, 21b–23a. The total annual amount was under 1,300 taels, less than half the *ting* quota.

105   In most places by the late sixteenth century it appears that the fish tax was covered with the proceeds of the land tax. See Huang, *Taxation*, Ch. 6.

106   Chang T'ing-yü, *CHYWT*, 15.23b.

107   *TCHC* (1827), 2.37a. It may be that one of Chang Ying's reasons for objecting to the measure was that the addition of any extra item would provide further opportunities for extortion by the clerks, but Chang T'ing-yü does not actually say so and there is no means of proving it.

108   *TCHC* (1827), 9.12b–13a.

109   For a general account of registration procedures in the Ch'ing see Hsiao Kung-ch'üan, *Rural China*, pp. 88–91.

110   *TCHC* (1696), 7.43a–44b.

111   *Pien-shen t'iao-i, TCHC* (1696), 7.45a–50b.

112   *Ibid.*, 47b–48a. The 'actual collection registers' are the only documents that would enable one to gauge the real level of taxation in a locality, but no trace is ever found of them in official records. Presumably they were monopolized by the yamen staff. See Huang, *Taxation*, Ch. 4, and Ch'ü T'ung-tsu, *Local Government*, pp. 133–4.

113   *TCHC* (1696), 7.48a–b.

114   *Tsou STP* (T. 953), 2, *chia-kuei*, 13b.

115   See appendix I, below. The rise in 1693 was to roughly the level registered in 1481, so is still unlikely to have been accurate.

116   *TCHC* (1696), 7.46a–b.

117   *Ibid.*, 46b–47a. It is not absolutely clear whether those with less than 40 *mou* of land were to be charged fractions of the *ting* payment. The account of this type of malpractice confirms that local mutual responsibility for tax payments was enforced (on which see also the end of this chapter).

118   *TCHC* (1696), 48b–49b. There is one indication that exemptions may have been allocated to lineages on some kind of quota basis. In the Ch'en rules, dated 1707, it is stated that a poorer member who became eligible for *ting* exemption might use one of his own branch's exemptions; if these were all used up he might try another branch. See *Ch'en STP* (T. 760), 1, *chia-cheng*, 2b–3a.

119   For his proposals and the reply of the prefectural authorities see *TCHC* (1696), 7.67a–72b.

120   *Ibid.*, 73a–78b.

121   *TCHC* (1696), 7.63a–64a. On the abuse of *pao-lan*, frequently practised by lower degree holders or members of powerful families, see Hsiao Kung-ch'üan, *Rural China*, pp. 132–2; Ch'ü T'ung-tsu, *Local Government*, p. 187; and also the end of this chapter.

122   *TCHC* (1827), 9.12b.

123   Chang T'ing-yü, *CHYWT*, 15.24a.

124   On the *kun-tan* method see Hsiao Kung-ch'üan, *Rural China*, p. 96; Ch'ü T'ung-tsu, *Local Government*, pp. 137–8.

125   See note 123, above.

126   *Ibid.*, 15.24b. This particular decree does not appear to be in the *Shih-lu* but it is interesting that in 1713, five years after Chang Ying's death, the grand secretaries recommended to the emperor that the opening of new mines should be prohibited, and that existing ones should be operated by local people, not outsiders. See *Sheng-tsu shih-lu*, 255.3b–4a.

127 These attitudes are well described by E-tu Zen Sun, 'Mining Labor in the Ch'ing Period', in Feuerwerker, Murphey and Wright, eds., *Approaches to Modern Chinese History* (Berkeley and Los Angeles, 1967), pp. 45–67; see especially pp. 46–8.

128 Ho Ping-ti, *Studies*, p. 211.

129 *Ibid.*, pp. 39–41 and 47ff.

130 Ho Ping-ti, *Studies*, pp. 53–5, considers that exaggeration of population totals in this period is rare, but T'ung-ch'eng must certainly be such a case. For some comparative figures for the populations of other counties around this time, see *ibid.*, p. 59.

131 *TCHC* (1827), 2.20a–21a. The *ting* quota for the entire country was frozen in 1712. See Ho Ping-ti, *Studies*, p. 211.

132 *TCHC* (1827), 2.21a–22a.

133 *Ibid.*, 21a. The evidence from T'ung-ch'eng thus appears to support the view of Li Wen-chih, 'T'u-ti chan-yu', p. 81, that degree holders from this time on had no way to avoid paying the *ting* charge. Hsiao Kung-ch'üan, *Rural China*, pp. 125–6 asserts the contrary, and considers that this still conferred considerable financial advantages on 'gentry who had extensive landholdings'. It seems doubtful in the case of T'ung-ch'eng.

134 It is well known that many extras and fees were always collected besides the regular taxes, and that the latter could often be arbitrarily increased by the clerks, so that there is no way to discover the actual amounts collected from the population. Ch'ü T'ung-tsu, *Local Government*, pp. 141–4, cites some horrifying examples of these practices but they are all from the nineteenth century. It must be stressed that in T'ung-ch'eng there is not a shred of evidence to suggest that extortion reached these levels before 1827. It undoubtedly caused considerable annoyance and may well have resulted in hardship in individual cases, but there is no sign that it reduced the peasantry to desperation, let alone the more affluent landowners.

135 *T'ung-pei Chao STP* (T. 977), *chia-yüeh*, quoted in Taga Akigorō, *Sōfu no kenkyū* (Tokyo, 1960), p. 739.

136 The rules on tax matters quoted by Hui-chen Wang Liu, *The Traditional Chinese Clan Rules* (New York, 1959), pp. 152–4, are mainly limited to injunctions on the prompt payment of taxes.

137 *Ch'en STP* (T. 760), 1, *chia-cheng*, 2b.

138 *Kuan-shan Kao STP* (C. 404), 1, *K'o-ch'i i-t'ien-shuo.*

139 *TCCCC*, 8.34b. By the mid eighteenth century, the *pao-chia* unit was replacing the *li-chia* in importance and taking over many of its functions. See Hsiao Kung-ch'üan, *Rural China*, p. 60.

140 For successive tax quotas, see Appendix I.

Ch. 4 LINEAGE ORGANIZATION AND SOCIAL STRUCTURE

1 *Chang STP* (T. 656), 26.1b–2b.

2 *Ibid.*, 26.3b–4a; see also *Heng-ch'an so-yen* (Appendix III).

3 *Chang STP* (T. 656). 26.3a–b.

4 *Ibid.*, 2.8a–b.

5 *Ibid.*, 26.4b.

6 *Ibid.*, 2.15b–17b; *MS.* 281.3160–1.

7 See note 5, above.

8 *Yao STP* (T. 428). 1.1a.

9 *Ibid.*, first preface.

10 Cf. Hui-chen Wang Liu, 'An Analysis of Chinese Clan Rules', in Nivison and Wright, eds., *Confucianism in Action*, pp. 63–96, especially p. 64.

11   *Yao STP* (T. 428), first preface.
12   *Ibid.*, second preface (1661), pp. 3a—b. See also above, Chapter 2, note 74; Chapter 3, note 26.
13   *Chang STP* (T. 656), third preface (1666), p. 1b.
14   *Ibid.*, second preface (1609). Very common also in all these prefaces is the idea that virtue and generosity on the part of forebears will mean success for their descendants. For other examples of such reasoning see P'an Kuang-tan, *Ming-Ch'ing liang-tai Chia-hsing ti wang-tsu* (Shanghai, 1947), pp. 114—16, and Hu Hsien-chin, *The Common Descent Group in China and its Functions* (New York, 1948), pp. 109—10.
15   This land is listed as ritual land in *Chang STP* (T. 656), 21.12a—13a, but in *ibid.*, 26.22b, it is stated that the income from it was used to aid members. As will be seen in the second part of this chapter, it was rare in T'ung-ch'eng for the functions of ritual and charitable land to be clearly distinguished. Many instances of this are noted by Shimizu Morimitsu in *Chūgoku zokusan seido kō* (Tokyo, 1949), pp. 15—20.
16   *Chang STP* (T. 656), 26.9a.
17   One of Chang Chien's sons, Chang Shih-chi, was a *sheng-yüan* who built up his small inheritance of property by 'careful calculation'. On one occasion when a powerful man encroached on his land he recovered it by getting together some other local *sheng-yüan* to go and fight for it. See *ibid.*, 26.15b—16a.
18   *Ibid.*, 26.11a, 22b; *TCCCC*, 4.7a—b. At this stage some of them may have moved to the city, for Chang Shih-wei was a member of the seventh generation, and in *Chang STP* (T. 656), 21.50a, it is stated that they lived at their original home at Chang-chia-p'ang from the second to the seventh generations.
19   *Ibid.*, 26.11a.
20   *Ibid.*, 3.16b—19a.
21   See Chapter 2, above.
22   *Chang STP* (T. 656), first preface (1618).
23   These details are taken from a rather full account of Chang Ping-i by Chang Ying himself, in *ibid.*, 26.21b—26a. On his property see the translation of *Heng-ch'an so-yen* (Appendix III).
24   Chang Ying stresses the connection in a preface which he wrote for the Wu genealogy, reprinted in his *Tu-su-t'ang wen-chi*, 4.31a—32a (in his collected works). His mother was given a biographical entry in *TCHC* (1827), 20.30a.
25   *Chang STP* (T. 656), 3.10b—12b. The first of these girls has a biography in the collection *Kuo-ch'ao hua-shih*, 17.3a; the second produced a collection of poetry that was honoured with a preface by Chang Ying (reprinted in *Tu-su-t'ang wen-chi*, 5.27a—28b). Chang Ping-wen's wife was from the Fang lineage and his other daughter was married into it, to a son of Fang K'ung-chao. Cf. Chapter 2, above.
26   This is illustrated by Fang Hsüeh-chien's story in *T'ung-i hsü*, 2.5a, of a Yao woman in the sixteenth century who hanged herself after her husband's death, because the strict code in which she had been brought up permitted no alternative.
27   *Chang STP* (T. 656), 4.9a—b.
28   Chang T'ing-yü, *CHYWT*, 15.27a.
29   *Chang STP* (T. 656), 21.12b—13a.
30   *Ibid.*, 26.22b.
31   *Yao STP* (T. 428), second preface (1661), p. 3b.
32   *Ibid.*, chin-yüeh, 1a.
33   *Ibid.*, 1a—b. Mention of the death penalty, as will be seen later, occurs quite frequently in other T'ung-ch'eng genealogies, a fact commented on by Taga Akigorō, *Sōfu*, p. 19; he finds it to be rare in other places, as does Hui-chen Wang Liu in *Clan Rules*, p. 38.
34   *Yao STP* (T. 428). 22.15b. He very probably carried out routine management of

lineage affairs; as will be shown, this task was far from being monopolized by men of distinction.

35 *Ibid., Hsien-te chuan*, 2.8a–10b; *TCCCC*, 6.13b–15b; also Chapter 2, note 118, above. For more on Yao Sun-fei's chequered career at the end of the Ming, see Beattie, 'Alternative'.

36 *Yao STP* (T. 428), second preface (1661). The Yaos, to judge from occasional references to it, also acquired common property, but unfortunately, unlike almost every other T'ung-ch'eng lineage, did not print records of it in their genealogy; presumably these must have been kept separately.

37 *Chang STP* (T. 656), third preface (1666).

38 *Ibid.*, fourth preface (1666). Other local families are referred to, not by name, but by place names traditionally associated with them, such as Kuei-lin for the Fangs (after Fang Yu, *chin-shih* 1457, who had been prefect of Kuei-lin in Kwangsi).

39 *Ibid.*, 26.23a; fourth preface (1666), pp. 3a–4a.

40 *Ibid.*, 26.29b.

41 The fullest account of Chang Tsai is by Chang Ying, in *Tu-su t'ang wen-chi*, 9.14a–16a; see also *TCCCC*, 7.36b–37b, and *Chang STP* (T. 656), 27.3a–4b.

42 See for example *ibid.*, 21.12a. All information on the purchase and management of common landholdings is derived from the list in this chapter.

43 *Ibid.*, 28.12b–13a.

44 *Ibid.*, 27.7b. Chang Chieh also wrote out instructions for his descendants, with the title *Chia-chü so-yen*.

45 *Ibid.*, 21.14b.

46 *Ibid.*, 27.10b–11a.

47 This is confirmed by some modern studies, for instance, Chow Yung-teh, *Social Mobility in China* (New York, 1966), pp. 115–16. He considers that the division of a family between town and countryside was a deliberate stratagem to secure its power.

48 See translation of *Heng-ch'an so-yen* (Appendix III) for all details of Chang Ying's own property; also *TCHC* (1827), 20.32a, on his illness.

49 Chang T'ing-yü, *CHYWT*, 15.3a. On the upbringing of Chang Ying's wife, see Chang T'ing-yü, *Ch'eng-huai-yüan yü*, 2.7a–b. Frugality was a common trait in her family. Her grandfather, Yao Chih-ch'i, was a magistrate who refrained from enriching himself in office; on his death he left a request that contributions towards his funeral expenses should be used instead to buy land to support his orphans. See *TCCQC*, 5.5a.

50 Chang T'ing-yü, *CHYWT*, 15.21a–b. Yao Wen-jan deliberately budgeted a certain amount of his income for charitable purposes, including help to relatives by marriage. His association with Chang Ying at the capital is shown by the fact that the latter was ordered to attend him during an illness. See *Yao STP* (T. 428), *Hsien-te chuan*, 2.16b,17b.

51 Chang T'ing-yü, *CHYWT*, 15.21a; *CS*, 507.5509. According to *CHYWT*, 15.4a, while Chang Ying was at home in 1668–70, in mourning for his father, the family was impoverished, but it is hard not to suspect exaggeration in such statements.

52 Hummel, *Eminent Chinese*, p. 413.

53 Chang T'ing-yü, *CHYWT*, 15.26a; Chang Ying, *Tu-su-t'ang wen-chi*, 8.2a–3b.

54 Mentioned in *Heng-ch'an so-yen* (Appendix III).

55 *TCCCC*, 8.2a; Chang Ying, *Tu-su-t'ang wen-chi*, 8.4a–5a; other houses which he owned are also described in this chapter, but it is clear that his property was not vast. For comparison, it is worth noting that his contemporary Hsiung Tz'u-li, whose property seems to have been even less, was still said to have been comfortably off. See Spence, *Ts'ao Yin*, pp. 230–1.

56 Chang T'ing-yü, *CHYWT*, 15.22b. A count of the donations of ritual land listed in

his name in *Chang STP* (T. 656), Ch. 21, shows that they totalled around 60 *mou*. The rules of compilation of 1748 however (*ibid.*, *fan-li*, 5a) refer to charitable land which he founded but which does not seem to be separately listed in later editions.

57 *Ibid.*, 21.16a–b; Chang T'ing-yü, *CHYWT*, 10.35a–36a.
58 *CHYWT*, 15.22a.
59 See especially *Ts'ung-hsün chai-yü*, p. 12.
60 *Ibid.*, p. 23.
61 *Ibid.*, p. 25.
62 *Ibid.*, pp. 12–13.
63 *Ibid.*, p. 16.
64 *Ibid.*, pp. 25–6.
65 *Ibid.*, pp. 22–3.
66 *TCHC* (1827), 20.32a; *CS*, 507.5509.
67 *TCCCC*, 8.19b.
68 *CS*, 268.3921; *Chang STP* (T. 656). 27.21b–25a.
69 *Ibid.*, 5.31a–34a; *CSLC*, 14.35a.
70 *Chang STP* (T. 656), 5.35a–39a; *CSLC*, 14.35b.
71 His career is outlined in Hummel, *Eminent Chinese*, pp. 54–6.
72 *TCCCC*, 9.20a. Chang T'ing-yü's nepotism is commented on briefly by Robert M. Marsh, 'Bureaucratic Constraints on Nepotism in the Ch'ing period', *JAS*, 19 (1960), 117–33, on p. 131, but he seems to underestimate its importance.
73 *TCCCC*, 8.34a–b. On Wang I-tai see also end of Chapter 3, above.
74 *TCCCC*, 9.4a–b. One of Ma Ch'i-ch'ang's own family was also recommended for this by Chang T'ing-chuan. See *ibid.*, 8.5a.
75 See for instance his preface to the genealogy of the Chous of Yao-shih in 1731, in which he mentions that he had been chief examiner when one of the family passed the *chin-shih* exams in 1724 (the man was subsequently given office). This could be another way in which patronage was exercised. See *T'ung-ch'eng Yao-shih Chou-shih Shang-i-t'ang chih-p'u* (C. 291), seventh preface (1731), pp. 1a–b.
76 Hummel, *Eminent Chinese*, p. 55; Ho Ping-ti, *Ladder*, p. 138. For the text of the memorial and the emperor's reply see *CSLC*, 18.45b–46b.
77 *TCCCC*, 8.18a.
78 *Chang STP* (T. 656), 28.28b.
79 *Ibid.*, 28.11a.
80 *Ibid.*, 28.23a.
81 *TCCCC*, 8.11a.
82 *Chang STP* (T. 656), Ch. 21, *passim*.
83 *Yao STP* (T. 428), 5.7a–b; Chang T'ing-yü, *CHYWT*, 9.16a.
84 *Yao STP* (T. 428), *chia-kuei, passim*. It should be noted also that members' disputes over property were to be adjudicated by the branch heads and elders (p.3b).
85 *Ibid., Hsien-te chuan*, 3.19a–b.
86 Chang T'ing-yü, *CHYWT*, 9.16a–17a.
87 *Chang STP* (T. 656), *fan-li*, 7b. Chang T'ing-chuan was also involved in the management of their land.
88 They did however specify (*ibid.*, 4b–5b) that details of all joint property were henceforward to be entered in the genealogy.
89 The Yaos by 1796 were said to number over 1,700 male members; see *Yao STP* (T. 428), third preface, p. 5b. A century later the Changs were still only 'over 1,000' (though this was after the Taiping rebellion); see *Chang STP* (T. 656), 1.6b.
90 *Ibid.*, 28.1a–b.

91 On his decline in favour, see Hummel, *Eminent Chinese*, pp. 55–6.

92 *Chang STP* (T. 656), fifth preface (1747), p. 3b.

93 All Ho Ping-ti's statistical data on the Changs are presented in *The Ladder of Success*, p. 139, table 17. Not all his counts are accurate; for example, there were four high-ranking officials in the third generation, not three. He discusses the family's 'downward mobility' on pp. 138–41 and 149–50.

94 *Ibid.*, p. 141.

95 Hsü Ta-ling, *Ch'ing-tai chüan-na chih-tu* (Peking, 1950), pp. 97 ff., shows that the price of the lowest 'expectant' provincial office fell from 180 to around 40 taels in the course of the nineteenth century. On the price of degrees see also Ho Ping-ti, *Ladder*, p. 34.

96 All these calculations are based on information in the biographies of the individuals concerned, in *Chang STP*.

97 One of Ho Ping-ti's observations in *Ladder*, pp. 138–40, is that, in addition to their fall from high office, there was a steady process of 'biological decline' at work among great families, though he feels that the Changs do not show this as severely as some others. I have made a detailed survey of Chang Ying's male descendants (allowing as far as possible for deficiencies in the data in the genealogy), of which only the results can be summarized here. It shows that in four generations average life span declined from 54 to 44 years, rates of reproduction from 4.16 to 2.3 surviving children, and incidence of childless marriages increased from nil to 18.9%; these latter two trends are again rather more pronounced among the descendants of Chang T'ing-yü. A very similar picture is found among the descendants of Yao Wen-jan. It is doubtful whether Ho Ping-ti's explanation, that a family's vitality was sapped by continuous, extravagant dissipation, is entirely adequate, in view of my findings on the Changs' life style. It may be that all this was related to a general decline in the whole area, caused by overcrowding and falling living standards. This seems to be the explanation favoured by Yüan I-chin, who detected similar trends in a whole lineage in Kwangtung; see his 'Life Tables for a Southern Chinese Family from 1365 to 1849', *Human Biology*, 3 : 2 (1931), 157–79. The Changs and Yaos are likely to have enjoyed rather higher living standards than the general population, however, so perhaps Fei Hsiao-t'ung is right in claiming that the reason lay in the system of upbringing and education in this social group, especially the avoidance of all physical labour, which made the offspring physically 'weak, slender and sometimes sterile'. See 'Peasantry and Gentry', p. 12.

98 *Yao STP* (T. 428), *Hsien-te chuan*, 3.14b.

99 *Ibid.*, fourth preface (1795).

100 *Ibid.*, sixth preface (1839).

101 *Ibid.*, *Hsien-te chuan*, 3.28a. See also Yao Ying's essay on the family's remarkable record in the examinations over nearly 400 years (in *Tung-ming wen-chi*, 15.5a–7a, in his collected works), in which he emphasizes the importance of never relaxing efforts to build up their literary tradition.

102 *Yao STP* (T. 428), 24, addenda, pp. 1a–b.

103 *Chang STP* (T. 656), *fan-li*, 9a–12a. In *ibid.*, 13a, it is stated that there were eight branches tracing their descent from Chang Ch'un in the sixth generation.

104 See the prefaces to these two works. (It seems incidentally that there was some local resentment at Chang Jo-t'ing's promotion to the office once held by Yao Wen-jan. See *TCCCC*, 8.15b–16a.)

105 *Chang STP* (T. 656), 21.48a–53a.

106 The contrast was not so sharp with grave land (presumably cheaper); before 1747, 37% of acquisitions were donated by individuals, and after that date, 25%.

107 All these statements are based on the records of land in *Chang STP*, Ch. 21, which seem to have been kept with scrupulous care. There is, admittedly, no mention of

the charitable land said to have been founded by Chang Ying (see note 56, above); it is possible that this latter was not recorded separately from the ritual land.

108 Names of managers and benefactors are noted along with the details of the plots which they purchased or presented.

109 *Chang STP* (T. 656), 8.52a–53b.

110 *Ibid.*, 15.17a–b.

111 *Ibid.*, 15.15b–17a, 12b–13b.

112 *TCCCC*, 4.8a.

113 This finding is broadly confirmed by Freedman, *Lineage Organization in South-Eastern China* (London, 1958), pp. 73–4, 130.

114 *Yao STP* (T. 427), postface to Ch. 24. On Yao Chun-ch'ang (Ma Ch'i-ch'ang's father-in-law) see *TCCCC*, 10.29a.

115 *Chang STP* (T. 656), 1.5b–6b. There were loud protests on this occasion from many members who found that some details of their families had accidentally been omitted. Clearly kinship spirit was still strong if inclusion in the genealogy was felt to be of such importance.

116 In *ibid.*, 24.1a, it is admitted that the family's greatest days were in the Yung-cheng and Ch'ien-lung reigns, now long past.

117 See the postfaces to these works.

118 See his preface, p. 1b.

119 *Chang STP* (C. 510), 24.20a.

120 *Yao STP* (T. 428), 24, addenda, pp. 7a–b; *Chang STP* (C. 510), 1.7a.

121 Ma Ch'i-ch'ang, writing in the early twentieth century, invariably listed the Changs and Yaos among the four greatest lineages of the county (the other two being the Fangs and the Tsos); see *TCCCC*, 2.15a.

122 Those in Japanese libraries are listed on pp. 212–13 of Taga Akigorō's work. There are approximately ten times as many genealogies available for T'ung-ch'eng as for any other county in Anhwei.

123 *Chang STP* (T. 656), fourth preface (1666), p. 5b; Chang T'ing-yü, *CHYWT*, 8.1b (preface to a Wang genealogy).

124 In general the genealogies of T'ung-ch'eng seem to be free from many of the limitations which J. M. Meskill argues can detract from their historical value (her generalizations appear to be based mainly on Taiwanese genealogies, which are probably not so good). See 'The Chinese Genealogy as a Research Source', in Freedman, ed., *Family and Kinship in Chinese Society* (Stanford, 1970), pp. 139–61.

125 Liu, *Clan Rules*, p. 98. Freedman, *Lineage Organization*, pp. 46ff, seems to make the same assumption.

126 This supports the hypothesis of Meskill, 'Chinese Genealogy', p. 141, that initially the genealogy created the kinship group, rather than vice versa.

127 *TCCCC*, 3.4b–7b; *T'ung-pei Chao STP* (T. 977), 21, *ch'ung-shih*, 4b–6b.

128 *Ibid.*, 27, *pei-chi*, 3a–6a.

129 *P'an STP* (C. 818), *chiu-p'u fan-li*, 1a–b, and *hsiu-tsu p'u-t'ieh*; *ibid.*, 1, *lieh-chuan*, 4a–5b.

130 There are only two more P'ans in the list of the county's *chin-shih* winners; as it is an uncommon surname they were probably from this lineage.

131 *Tung-lou Wang STP* (T. 65), 1.4a–5a.

132 *Wan-T'ung Chang STP* (T. 677), 1, *wei-chuan*, 1a–2a.

133 *Tso STP* (T. 126), 2, *t'iao-yüeh*, *chia-hsün*.

134 See note 121, above.

135 See Chapter 3, note 53, above.

136 *P'an STP* (C. 818), *chiu-p'u fan-li*, 2b–3b.

137 *Tai STP* (T. 1136), *ch'ien-hsiu p'u-hui fei pien-yen*, 1b.

138   This statement is based on a survey of the dated prefaces of all the genealogies, usually, though not invariably, reprinted in each successive edition.

139   *P'an STP* (C. 818), *chiu-p'u fan-li*, 1b–2a. See Chang Ying's preface to his collected poetry, in *Tu-su-t'ang wen-chi*, 4.21a.

140   *P'an STP* (C. 818), 1, *chia-hsün*.

141   *Yao-shih Chou-shih chih-p'u* (C. 291), *ch'ung-ch'ih chia-kuei hsü* (1661), 1b–2a.

142   *Hu-chang* in T'ung-ch'eng, unlike other places (cf. Liu, *Clan Rules*, p. 101), seems to mean lineage head, not branch head, for *hu-chang* and *fang-chang* occur regularly in the same lineage.

143   *Tai STP* (T. 1136), *chia-kuei*, 47a–b.

144   *T'ung-pei Chao STP* (T. 977), *chia-kuei*, 12a–b.

145   *Kuan-shan Kao STP* (C. 404), 1, *ch'i-chia t'iao-kuei*, 1a.

146   *Wang STP* (T. 315), *chia-kuei*, 37a. Hu Hsien-chin, *Common Descent Group*, p. 127, does cite a case from T'ung-ch'eng in which the *tsu* head was required to have official rank, but this seems quite exceptional. It should be noted that her translations of these rules are sometimes very loose.

147   *P'an STP* (C. 818), 1, *chia-hsün*, 8b–9a.

148   *Tung-lou Wang STP* (T. 65), 1, *chü-yüeh shih-t'iao* (1805), 1a. For degree-winners see *TCHC* (1827), Ch. 7.

149   *Kuan-shan Kao STP* (C. 404), 1, *p'u-shuo*, 1a–3a.

150   *Ibid.*, 1, first preface.

151   Chang T'ing-yü, *CHYWT*, 8.1a–2b.

152   Cf. note 15, above.

153   Liu, *Clan Rules*, p. 29, finds that comparatively few of the lineages in her sample have detailed rules on common property, whereas in T'ung-ch'eng the majority do, another sign of their general organizational strength. That managers should be well-off was stipulated, for example, by the Lis (T.298), quoted by Taga Akigorō, *Sōfu*, p. 714.

154   *Tung-lou Wang STP* (T.65), 1, *chü-yüeh shih-t'iao* (1805), 3a; Fang Pao, *Wang-hsi hsien-sheng ch'üan-chi, chi-wai-wen*, 8.13b. Shimizu Morimitsu, *Zokusan seido*, p. 177, finds much the same with regard to salaries.

155   *P'an STP* (C. 818), 1, *chia-hsün*, 9b.

156   *Yao-shih Chou-shih chih-p'u* (C. 291), 2, *Chou-shih tz'u-t'ang chi-ch'an chi*, 2a; *ibid.*, *Shang-i-t'ang chia-kuei t'iao-li*, 4b.

157   *Yen-p'ing Li STP* (T. 288), final chapter, pp. 10a–b. They insisted on dismissal of corrupt managers at a public assembly of the lineage.

158   See Twitchett, 'Fan Clan', *passim*. In T'ung-ch'eng the supervision of common property seems to have been more effective than Liu, *Clan Rules*, p. 106, finds it to have been in general, even if a certain amount of discreet peculation was probably tolerated.

159   *Tung-lou Wang STP* (T. 65), 1, *i-tzu*, 1a–3a.

160   *Wan-T'ung Hu STP* (C. 361), *chia-kuei*, 6a–b, 7a–b.

161   See Appendix II, below. It is not usually possible to tell in an individual case whether land was bought with funds raised in this way or with donations from members, and one cannot therefore estimate the relative importance of the two methods. For a useful discussion see Shimizu Morimitsu, *Zokusan seido*, pp. 96ff.

162   They were certainly on a much smaller scale than in parts of south China, where anything from 30% to 70% of cultivated land in a county might be under lineage ownership. See C. K. Yang, *A Chinese Village in Early Communist Transition* (Cambridge, Mass., 1959), p. 42.

163   The Fans of Soochow had of course done this but it seems to have become progressively rarer. See Shimizu Morimitsu, *Zokusan seido*, pp. 148–53.

164   *Ts'ang-chi Sun SCP* (T. 553), 30, *chia-kuei* (1732), 1b.
165   Hugh D. R. Baker, *A Chinese Lineage Village: Sheung Shui* (London, 1968),
       p. 94, has observed this method of finance being used by lineages in the New
       Territories of Hong Kong (though the levy here is merely on persons, not on
       land).
166   *P'an STP* (C. 818), 1, *chia-hsün*, 9a. The method may have been used even in the
       Ming; the Ch'ens claimed that in 1581 they exacted 1 *hu* of rice from each adult
       male to form a common treasury and to buy land. See Ch'en STP (T. 760), final
       chapter, *kung-t'ien chi*, 1a.
167   *Tai STP* (T. 1136), *ch'ien-hsiu p'u-hui fei pien-yen*, 3a–b.
168   *Yao-shih Chou-shih chih-p'u* (C. 291), 2, *Shang-i-t'ang chia-kuei t'iao-li*, 6b.
169   *Ibid.*, 1, *Shang-i-t'ang hsü-hsiu chih-p'u t'iao-li*, 3a–b.
170   *P'an STP* (C. 818), final chapter, appendix to the rules of compilation of the
       Tao-kuang edition (1846).
171   Obviously Meskill's statement 'Chinese Genealogy', p. 141, that 'the genealogies
       are proof mainly of the wealth of some editors, rather than the degree of prior
       organization of the kinship group', does not apply here.
172   Cf. Liu, *Clan Rules*, p. 30.
173   *Tai STP* (T. 1136), *chia-kuei*, 51b–52a. The Chus obtained backing for their
       rules from the local magistrate. See Hsiao Kung-ch'üan, *Rural China*, p. 357.
174   *T'ung-pei Chao STP* (T. 977), *chia-yüeh*, quoted by Taga Akigorŏ, *Sŏfu*, pp.
       738–9.
175   *Ts'ang-chi Sun SCP* (T. 553). 30, *chia-kuei* (1732).
176   Cf. note 33, above.
177   *T'ung-pei Chao STP* (T. 977), *chia-yüeh*, quoted by Taga Akigorŏ, *Sŏfu*, p. 740.
178   *Wan-T'ung Hu STP* (C. 361), *chia-kuei*, 8b.
179   *TCCCC*, 1.9a. This kind of strategic intermarriage was common in other places
       where lineage organization was highly developed, for instance in Hui-chou, where
       it was stated in the mid sixteenth century: 'In arranging marriages, the poor do
       not mate with the rich nor the humble with the honourable.' See *Hsin-an ming-
       tsu chih*, first preface, p. 1b. See also P'an Kuang-tan, *Chia-hsing ti wang-tsu*,
       pp. 120–30.
180   *Yao-shih Chou-shih chih-p'u* (C. 291), 2, *Chih-hsüeh-t'ang hsüeh-t'ien chi* (1821),
       1a.
181   *Wan-T'ung Hu STP* (C. 361), 23.49b; *P'an STP* (C. 818), 1, *chia-hsün*, 4a–b.
182   Liu, 'Analysis', p. 81, confirms that the promotion of education was generally
       looked on as one of the most vital functions of the lineage.
183   This often extended to relatives by marriage. Tai Ming-shih was educated in his
       youth by his aunt's husband, Yao Wen-ao; see *Yao STP* (T. 428), *Hsien-te chuan*,
       1.5b–6b.
184   See for example *Ch'eng STP* (T. 881), 1, *chia-kuei*, 7a.
185   *Wan-T'ung Chang STP* (T. 677), 1, *lai-yü*, 1a–b.
186   *Tai STP (T. 1136), chia-kuei*, 49a–b.
187   *T'ung-pei Chao STP* (T. 977), *chia-kuei*, 14a–b.
188   *Wan-T'ung Hu STP* (C. 361), 23.48b–49a.
189   See Chapter 2, note 90, above for the correlation between lineage organization
       and academic success in the case of Hui-chou. Competition for power and prestige
       between lineages was frequent elsewhere, and in south China often took violent
       forms. See Freedman, *Lineage Organization*, pp. 106–13; Hsiao Kung-ch'üan,
       Rural China, pp. 361ff.
190   See Chapter 2, note 138, above, The Ch'ens were anxious that members who did
       go in for trade should give it up as soon as they had made a reasonable profit; see
       Ch'en STP (T. 760), 1, *chia-cheng*, 5b–6a.

191 *Ibid.*
192 See Appendix II.
193 Quoted by Taga Akigorò, *Sôfu*, p. 740.
194 *Ch'i STP* (T. 957), *chia-kuei*, quoted by Taga Akigorò, *Sôfu*, p. 767.
195 *Tai STP* (T. 1136), *chia-chieh*, 44a–b.
196 See, as one example, *P'an STP* (C. 818), 1, *chia-hsün*, 8a–b.
197 *Tung-lou Wang STP* (T. 65), 2, *Lu-kang kung hsü*.
198 Yao Yung-p'u in 1929 stated that a lineage might then number between 1,000 and 10,000 persons, see *Ma STP* (T. 495), first preface, p. 1a. The case of T'ung-ch'eng does not support the claim of Hsiao Kung-ch'üan, *Rural China*, pp. 357ff. that lineage organization was generally declining in the second half of the nineteenth century.
199 *Ts'ang-chi Sun SCP* (T. 553), 30, note appended to *chia-kuei* (1732).
200 Hsiao Kung-ch'üan in *Rural China*, Ch. 8, tends to emphasize the negative effects of lineage organization on rural control, though he admits, on p. 357, of some exceptions, of which T'ung-ch'eng affords an example.
201 Ma Ch'i-ch'ang quite often observes, for instance in the case of the Fangs, *TCCCC*, 9.14a–b, that some branches did better in the long term than others. Some of the remoter branches of the Changs appear to have declined into obscurity; see *Chang STP* (T. 656), 1.4a. It should be noted that almost all notable officials and men of distinction from T'ung-ch'eng appear to have come from well-organized lineages.
202 Hu Hsien-chin, *Common Descent Group*, p. 78, notes a strong correlation between growth of common property and educational success.
203 Freedman, *Lineage Organization*, p. 128, broadly agrees with this.
204 Twitchett, 'Fan Clan', p. 133, comes to the opposite conclusion. Several other authorities are however agreed that some joint property was essential to a lineage's continued existence. See Fei Hsiao-t'ung, 'Peasantry and Gentry', p. 5; Freedman, *Lineage Organization*, pp. 127–9; and Jack M. Potter, 'Land and Lineage in Traditional China' (in Freedman, ed., *Family and Kinship*, pp. 121–38), p. 127. The evidence from T'ung-ch'eng supports the latter view, though it does not appear that the strength of the lineage here necessarily correlated directly with the size of the property.

Ch. 5 CONCLUSION: LAND AND LINEAGE IN CHINESE SOCIAL HISTORY

1 That a degree was not always necessary for the possession of elite *social* as opposed to legal status has been ably pointed out by Frederic Wakeman, Jr, on pp. 12–14 of his essay 'High Ch'ing: 1683–1839' in James B. Crowley, ed., *Modern East Asia: Essays in Interpretation* (New York, 1970).
2 *Chang STP* (C. 510), 1.15a.
3 Ho Ping-ti, *Ladder*, p. 141.

APPENDIX II. NOTES ON CONDITIONS OF LANDOWNERSHIP IN T'UNG-CH'ENG

1 See Appendix III, note 65.
2 Yao Wen-jan, *Yao Tuan-k'o kung wai-chi*, 18.6a–b.
3 See Chapter 3, note 94, above.
4 Listed in *Chang STP* (T. 656), 21.12a ff.
5 Huang, *Taxation*, Ch. 4.
6 *TCHC* (1696), 1.12a–13b.
7 See note 2, above.
8 Ku Yen-wu, *Jih-chih-lu*, 10.17a; Fang Pao, *Wang-hsi hsien-sheng ch'üan-chi, wen-chi*, 17.6a.
9 Perkins, *Agricultural Development*, pp. 318–20.

10   Huang, *Taxation*, Ch. 4.
11   See Chapter 3, note 45, above.
12   *TCHC* (1827), 2.1a—3b, 21b.
13   Huang, *Taxation*, Ch. 4.
14   *Ibid.*
15   Yang Lien-sheng, *Money and Credit in China* (Cambridge, Mass., 1952), p. 101,
      cites a case in Hunan in 1825 where investment in irrigated land brought a return
      of just under 7% on capital. J. L. Buck in the 1920s concluded from a survey of
      farms in seven different provinces, of which Anhwei was one, that the average
      annual return on capital investment for the landlord was then 8.4%. See J. L.
      Buck, *Chinese Farm Economy* (Chicago, 1930), p. 158.
16   Chang Ying, *Ts'ung-hsün chai-yü*, p. 10.
17   P'eng Hsin-wei, *Huo-pi shih*, p. 561, reconstructs grain prices for the entire dynasty.
18   Ho Ping-ti, *Studies*, pp. 217—19, and Li Wen-chih, 'T'u-ti chan-yu', pp. 85ff.,
      give many examples. See also the case of Sung-chiang prefecture cited in the
      present work, Chapter 1, note 36, above.
19   Li Wen-chih, 'T'u-ti chan-yu', p. 97, describes the importance of usury to land-
      owning families in Pao-shan *hsien*, Kiangsu, in 1823; it enabled them to avoid
      heavy losses in years of bad harvests.
20   Yang Lien-sheng, *Money and Credit*, p. 98.
21   See Chapter 2, note 79, above, and *Chang STP* (T. 656), 27.10b—11a, biography
      of Chang Chia.
22   For one of the most explicit statements of it see the rules of the Changs of Lien-
      ch'eng, *Wan-T'ung Chang STP* (T. 677), 1, *chia-hsün*, 14a—b. Shimizu Morimitsu,
      Zokusan seido, pp. 100—5, shows that this type of reinvestment by lineages
      became very common practice in the Ch'ing.
23   *Mu-shan P'an STP* (C. 818), 1, *chia-hsün*, 9a—b.
24   Fang Pao, *Wang-hsi hsien-sheng ch'üan-chi*, *chi-wai-wen*, 8.11b—12a. The land, the
      extent of which is unknown, was actually in the Nanking area, but the family
      was a branch of the Fangs of T'ung-ch'eng and still had property there also.
25   *T'ung-pei Chao STP* (T. 977), *chia-yüeh*, quoted by Taga Akigorò, *Sòfu*, p. 740.
26   For a summary of the concept of joint family property and rights of pre-emption
      by relatives see Schurmann, 'Property Concepts'; also Li Wen-chih, 'T'u-ti chan-yu',
      pp. 89—92, for its effects in restricting the free sale of land in the Ch'ing.
27   Niida, *Dorei nòdo-hò*, pp. 473—5.
28   See for instance a deed of sale of land by members of the Kuang family, mother,
      sons and grandfather, to the Tung lineage organization in 1632; the father was
      stated to have died shortly before. *Tung STP* (T. 929), 5, *ch'i-shu*, 1a—2b.
29   *Ma STP* (T. 495), preliminary chapter 7, *t'ien-shan-ch'i*, 6b—7b.
30   *T'ung-pei Chao STP* (T. 977), *chia-yüeh*, quoted by Taga Akigorò, *Sòfu*, p. 740.
      See also end of Chapter 4, above.

APPENDIX III. TRANSLATION OF "HENG-CH'AN SO-YEN"
(Remarks on Real Estate) by Chang Ying

The date of composition of *Heng-ch'an so-yen* is never stated, but it is most
likely to have been written in 1697, as Chang Ying refers to it at the end of the
first chapter of his essay collection *Ts'ung-hsün chai-yü*, which he wrote in the
autumn of that year 'during a period of temporary retirement from court'. It
would seem reasonable to assume that *Heng-ch'an so-yen* was also written during
this rare respite from official life. It cannot have been much earlier, as he does
speak, towards the end of it, of his experiences and observations of 'the past
fifty years'. If he is reckoning roughly from his adolescence in the late 1640s
and early 1650s, this would also put the date of writing somewhere in the late
1690s.

The text used here is, for convenience, that reprinted in *Ts'ung-shu chi-ch'eng, ch'u-pien*, 977. There are no problems of textual transmission, all available versions being (so far as I know) identical, with the single exception of that given in Ho Ch'ang-ling's *Huang-ch'ao ching-shih wen-pien*, 36.45b–46a, which has been condensed and rearranged. I am grateful in particular to Professor Piet van der Loon of Oxford University for help on one or two points of translation. Any remaining inaccuracies are my own.

1 On the historical background to Chang Ying's views, see Chapter 1. 'Paths between fields' refers to the paths created between private landholdings when the well-field system of state ownership was finally abolished, supposedly by the state of Ch'in in the fourth century B.C.

2 Mencius, 3A.3. The passage reads, in the translation of D. C. Lau (*Mencius*, Harmondsworth, Middlesex, 1970, p. 97), 'Those with constant means of support will have constant hearts, while those without constant means will not have constant hearts. Lacking constant hearts they will go astray and get into excesses, stopping at nothing.' The phrase *heng-ch'an*, 'constant means of support', was invariably taken to refer to land and thus became a synonym for real estate, hence the title of Chang Ying's essay.

3 Mencius, 1A.3. 'If the mulberry is planted in every homestead of five *mou* of land, then those who are fifty can wear silk; if chickens, pigs and dogs do not miss their breeding season, then those who are seventy can eat meat; if each lot of 100 *mou* is not deprived of labour during the busy seasons, then families with several mouths to feed will not go hungry.' See Lau, *Mencius*, p. 51.

4 Mencius, 6A.7. 'In good years the young men are mostly lazy, while in bad years they are mostly violent.' See Lau, *Mencius*, p. 164. The word *lai*, which is here translated 'lazy', also means 'dependable' or 'to be relied on', and it is in this sense that Chang Ying takes it. .

5 Mencius, 7B.28; Lau, *Mencius*, p. 199. Chang Ying frequently garbles or truncates his quotations. This one he renders as: 'The treasures of the princes are three: land'! Any Chinese reader would of course have been able to supply the rest of it automatically. Chang Ying's near contemporary, Chang Li-hsiang, author of the famous agricultural treatise *Pu-nung-shu*, quotes it in a similar context and explains: 'This applies also to the households of officials and common people. For them "government" means family regulations, "land" means landed property, and "the people" means hired labourers and tenants.' See his *Yang-yüan hsien-sheng ch'uan-chi*, 50.19a.

6 Su Shih or Su Tung-p'o (1036–1101) seems to have been one of the few poets whom Chang Ying considered worth reading; see *Ts'ung-hsün chai-yü*, p. 23.

7 This line occurs in the poem 'Travelling to the Chin-shan monastery', in *Su Wen-chung kung shih-chi*, 7.1a-b. The poet describes his journey down river to this famous monastery, situated on an island in the Yangtze, apparently without regret that its waters are carrying him so far from his former home. Chang Ying misquotes the line, giving *ch'ü*, 'leave, get away', instead of *kuei*, 'return'.

8 The actual title of poem is 'Going by boat from Chin-shan to Chiao-shan', in *Su Wen-chung kung shih-chi*, 7.1b. Chang Ying again misquotes, giving *ch'ü* instead of *t'ui*, 'retreat, withdraw'. The implication of the line, which is lifted completely out of context, is that it is better not to yearn for worldly possessions like land when circumstances prevent one from having them.

9 The lines quoted here are actually from another poem with a similar title: 'Written on a painting entitled "Misty Yangtze and Folded Hills" in the collection of Wang Ting-kuo', in *Su-Shih shih-hsüan*, (Peking, 1957), p. 212. A complete translation is given by Burton Watson in *Su Tung-p'o; Selections from a Sung Dynasty Poet* (New York, 1965), pp. 110–11. One *ch'ing* equals 100 *mou*.

10   Yang-hsien is the present I-hsing county in Kiangsu. The poet had been out of
      favour and 'exiled' from court in the 1080s. Giving up hopes of resuming his
      career, he began to look around for a place to buy land and retire to. In 1083
      he wrote:

            This fall I began talks to buy some land;
            If I build a house it should be done by spring.

      See Watson, *Su Tung-p'o*, pp. 96–7. His fall from grace was a temporary one
      however, and he did not end his days in the countryside. Cf. note 41, below.
11   Lu Yü-lin cannot have risen very high in his career, because he is not listed in any
      of the biographical indexes for the Ch'ing dynasty. Kuei-te is a prefecture in
      Honan, and in *Ho-nan TC*, 36.1b, he is stated to have been a *t'ung-p'an* or second-
      class sub-prefect there from 1682 to 1703, a remarkably long term of office.
      He was a *chien-sheng* from Ch'ang-chou in Chiangnan (the present Wu-chin
      county in south Kiangsu), which is at variance with Chang Ying's statement that
      he was a Chekiang man. In either case, he was from the lower Yangtze region, the
      commercial heart of China, and thus presumably knew what he was talking about.
12   It had long been recognized that commercial enterprise brought far greater
      returns than landowning. In the Han dynasty there was a common proverb: 'For
      a poor man who wants to become rich, farming is not as good as crafts, and crafts
      are not as good as trade. To prick embroidery is not as good as leaning on the
      market gate'; see *Han-shu*, 91.3687. Ku Yen-wu once quoted a similar opinion
      offered by a Soochow man at the end of the Ming Dynasty: 'Agriculture gives a
      one-fold return on capital and needs most labour of all, therefore fools do it. Manu-
      facturing provides a two-fold profit and requires a great deal of labour; clever
      fingers do it. Trade brings three-fold returns and little labour is involved, so
      intelligent people do it. Illegal salt dealing gives five-fold profits and requires no
      labour at all; powerful and unscrupulous people do it.' Quoted by Hatano,
      Kogyoshi, p.1.
13   Rent payment, except in periods of extreme distress, seems traditionally to have
      been regarded as a moral duty. Many peasants, even in the 1930s, still felt this:
      'We are good people. We never refuse to pay our rent. We cannot steal even when
      we are poor. How then can we refuse to pay rent?' See Fei Hsiao-t'ung, *Peasant
      Life in China* (London, 1939), p. 189. The people of T'ung-ch'eng were described
      in the early nineteenth century as being 'very meticulous' over rent payments;
      see *TCHC* (1827), 3.15a. Rent resistance probably did become more common in
      the late Ch'ing as economic conditions worsened, but seems still to have been the
      exception rather than the rule.
14   Chang Ying here must have been quoting the Odes from memory, for he again
      lifts short lines and phrases out of context and quite often gets them wrong,
      which does not make his citations easy to identify. Reference will be made to the
      text and translation of the Odes given by Bernhard Karlgren in *The Book of Odes*
      (Stockholm, 1950), and also to Arthur Waley, *The Book of Songs* (second ed.,
      London, 1954).
15   A harvest-time sacrificial ode, number 209, the first line of which is: *Ch'u ch'u
      che tz'u*, 'Dense grows the tribulus', hence the title that is commonly given to it.
      See Karlgren, pp. 161–3; Waley, pp. 209–11.
16   Ode 212. The first line is: *Ta t'ien to chia*, 'The big fields give a heavy crop'.
      The subject is the planting of the new crops and the subsequent prayers for a
      good harvest; see Karlgren, pp. 166–7; Waley, pp. 171–2. This contains the
      famous lines: 'It rains on our common fields and then on our private fields',
      which were interpreted by Mencius (3A.3) as confirmation of the operation of
      the well-field system.

17 The term 'the descendant', *tseng-sun*, occurs frequently in Ode 212 and also in
    211, 'Wide Fields' (Karlgren, pp. 164–6; Waley, pp. 169–70) and elsewhere.
    It may well imply hereditary ownership of land by the enfeoffed nobles of the
    Chou, though Waley, p. 169, considers it simply an allusive term for the sacrificer
    referred to in these odes.

18 This line is from Ode 210 (Karlgren, p. 164). Waley translates, p. 212:

> Truly, those southern hills –
> It was Yü who fashioned them;
> Those level spaces, upland and lowland –
> The descendant tills them.
> We draw the boundaries, we divide the plots,
> On southern slopes and eastern we set out acres.

19 The first two of these phrases are from Ode 211 and actually read 'Our fields are
    good, that is the happiness of the husbandmen' and 'We invoke the Father of
    Husbandry, to pray for sweet rain, to increase our glutinous millet and our
    panicled millet'; see Karlgren, pp. 165–6. The last is from Ode 209 and reads
    'Our granaries are all full, our stacks are numbered in millions'; see Karlgren, p.
    162; Waley, p. 209.

20 From Ode 211: 'The descendant is not annoyed, for the farmers have worked
    hard'; see Karlgren, p. 166; Waley, p. 170.

21 This line occurs twice in Ode 211; for the first occasion see above, note 20.
    The second time is at the end of the Ode: 'The panicled millet and the glutinous
    millet, the rice, the spiked millet, they are the happiness of the husbandmen.' See
    Karlgren, *Odes*, p. 166, and also Waley, *Songs*, p. 170, who renders the line 'the
    labourers are in luck'.

22 This appears to be a paraphrased version of some lines towards the end of Ode
    211, which Waley, p. 170, loosely translates as follows:

> Here comes the Descendant,
> With his wife and children,
> Bringing dinner to the southern acres.
> The labourers come to take good cheer,
> Break off a morsel here, a morsel there,
> To see what tastes good.

23 From Ode 210: 'By the boundaries and divisions there are gourds; we cut them
    up and pickle them, and present them to the august ancestors; the descendant
    will have long life and receive Heaven's blessing' (Karlgren, p. 164).

24 There appears to be an elaborate pun in this sentence. *Liu-feng* means both 'the
    sound of music carried on the wind' and 'good customs handed down by ances-
    tors', while *lo* or *yüeh* is 'pleasure' or 'music'.

25 Chang Ying was not the first to castigate extravagance in these terms. In 1667
    Hsiung Tz'u-li (1635–1709), then a junior official at court, had used similar
    phrases in his famous memorial directed against corruption in official life under
    the Oboi dictatorship: 'The cost of one fur garment exhausts the property of an
    average man and that of a feast consumes a whole year's expenditures . . . this is
    the reason why people experience hunger and cold and why thieves and lawsuits
    flourish.' See Hsiao I-shan, *Ch'ing-tai t'ung-shih*, 1,432. Possibly these were
    cliches at the time. Hsiung Tz'u-li had incidentally been one of Chang Ying's
    instructors in the Han-lin Academy from 1670 onwards and three years later had
    recommended him as the most suitable person to carry on regular discussions of
    the classics with the Emperor. See Chang T'ing-yü, *CHYWT*, 15.4a–b. The
    T'ien-kung k'ai-wu, a treatise on technology written in the 1630s, has a note on

the cost of fine fur: 'The long-haired variety of black sable is so valuable that merely an over-cap made of it is now worth some fifty taels of silver.' See *T'ien-kung k'ai-wu*, translated by E-tu Zen Sun and Shiou-chuan Sun (University Park, Pennsylvania, 1966) p. 67.

26 In *Ts'ung-hsün chai-yü*, p. 10. Chang Ying mentions that the actual price of grain in T'ung-ch'eng at this time was 4 *ch'ien* (i.e. 0.4 tael of silver) per *shih*, remarkably low even for the K'ang-hsi reign, when the average was nearer 0.7 tael. For more on grain prices, see Chapter 1, above, and Appendix II. The folly of extravagance is a theme that also recurs constantly throughout *Ts'ung-hsün chai-yü*.

27 Shensi province in the northwest had long been suffering from economic depression; it was there in the 1620s that the great peasant revolts of the late Ming had started. See Li Wen-chih, *Wan-Ming min-pien* Shanghai, 1948), pp. 15–32. Drought and famine seem to have been endemic there, and some of the disasters of the nineteenth and twentieth centuries claimed many millions of lives. Confirmation that Shensi peasants sold much-needed grain to pay for manufactured and luxury goods from other provinces comes from a commentator on Ku Yen-wu's *Jih-chih-lu*. Observing that all their silks and cottons are bought from the south-east he adds: 'The peasants there have not enough to eat, yet they sell their food grain in order to get clothing material.' See *Jih-chih-lu chi-shih*, 10.19b.

28 The saying is actually from the *Shu-ching* (Book of Documents). It occurs in the section entitled 'Chiu Kao' (Warnings on liquor). Karlgren, in *The Book of Documents* (Stockholm, 1950), p. 43, translates: 'I say, in our people's guidance, you youngster should economize the products of the soil (sc. not make too much wine of the grain); then their hearts will be good and they will willingly listen to the regular instructions of their grandfathers and fathers.'

29 During periods of shortage or famine, sale of grain at fair prices on a rationing system was organized by the local authorities and by private individuals. A detailed account of the system as it operated in the Ch'ing is given by Hsiao Kung-ch'üan in Ch. 5 of *Rural China*. In T'ung-ch'eng, philanthropic activity of this kind seems to have been considered by wealthy families a reliable way both to enhance their prestige and to ward off resentment against them; many examples are mentioned in the course of Chapters 2, 3 and 4, above. One of Chang Ying's brothers, Chang Chieh, while a teacher in the Soochow area, had been able to organize relief during a local famine in 1679, because of his experience in such matters in T'ung-ch'eng. He had men and women receive twice daily allowances from different granaries, and thus 'saved many lives'. See *Chang STP* (T. 656), 27.8a.

30 Chang Ying here reflects the fundamental attitude of the Chinese (and indeed any) peasant towards the land. Villagers in south Kiangsu in the 1930s still expressed very similar opinions about its security: 'Land is there. You can see it every day. Robbers cannot take it away . . . Men die but land remains.' See Fei Hsiao-t'ung, *Peasant Life*, p. 182. Land could however be encroached on by others, as Chang Ying later admits. (A *chün* is a weight of 30 *chin* or catties, a *chin* being approximately 1⅓ pounds.)

31 This statement was generally true of Chang Ying's home area, where most great families managed to recover their land after the mid-seventeenth-century revolts. See Chapter 2, above.

32 Cf. note 12, above. For a discussion of the returns to be had from land, see Appendix II.

33 Hsin-an is the old name for Hui-chou prefecture in southern Anhwei. According to the author of the late-Ming encyclopedia, *Wu-tsa-tsu*: 'Those renowned for their wealth to the south of the Yangtze are from Hsin-an, and to the north of it

from Shansi. The great merchants of Hsin-an deal in fish and salt and have acquired fortunes of up to a million taels of silver; those with only two or three hundred thousand only count as middling merchants. The Shansi merchants deal in salt or silk, or go in for reselling or the grain trade. They are even wealthier than the Hsin-an merchants.' Quoted by Fu I-ling, *Shang-jen*, p. 54. On the scrupulous business ethics of the latter, see *ibid.*, pp. 66–7. Cf. also Chapter 1, pp. 10–11, above and note 16 to Chapter 1.

34 Mortgage in China took two principal forms. The first, *tien-tang*, simply involved the transfer of a piece of land in exchange for a sum of money. The original owner could redeem the land, virtually without time limit, on repayment of the cash; the lender took the produce on it in lieu of interest. Chang Ying, though he uses the term *tien-chih*, appears to mean the second, which resembled the western form of mortgage. Here the land did not change hands but was simply the security for a loan at a high rate of interest, and for a short period. When lineages in T'ung-ch'eng lent their surplus funds at interest they seem often to have insisted on the borrower putting up land as a security; see *P'an STP* (C. 818), 1, *chia-hsün*, 9a–b. For discussion of mortgage see H. McAleavy, 'Dien in China and Vietnam', *JAS*, 17:3 (1958), 403–15 and P. Hoang, *Notions techniques sur la propriété en Chine* (Shanghai, 1897), pp. 7–8. On interest rates see Yang Lien-sheng, *Money and Credit*, Ch. X.

35 This passage is slightly obscure, and in my translation I have accepted the suggestions kindly offered by Professor Yang Lien-sheng, expanding slightly for the sake of clarity.

36 The implications seem to be, both that it is difficult for a scholar to attempt to play the role of a loan shark for very long, and also that he should not go on risking his capital in this way but should put it into something solid at the first opportunity. (Cf. the injunction by the Ch'en lineage that members who went in for trade should give it up as soon as they had made a reasonable profit; see *Ch'en STP* (T. 760), 1, *chia-cheng*, 6a.) Chang Ying had something of an obsession over the risks of moneylending, and reiterates his views in *Ts'ung-hsün chai-yü*, p. 16: 'When it comes to raising one's family fortunes through usury, it is only very poor gentlemen who can manage it to any extent. But for rich and honourable people there is no better way than this to incur hatred and enmity, censure and resentment.' He advises that loans should definitely not be made to people like porters, pedlars and hired labourers, who cherish great resentments over small sums and will go to all lengths to defame the lenders. Moneylending could always be hazardous, from the point of view of recovering the loans, but it may be that landowners in T'ung-ch'eng were particularly nervous about it in the aftermath of the mid-seventeenth-century revolts. It was too lucrative ever to be abandoned, however, and throughout the Ch'ing it remained a major means of multiplying agricultural income. For further discussion, see Appendix II.

37 In general, cultivation became much more intensive and varied in central and south China throughout the Ming and Ch'ing, on which see Chapter 1. For details of agricultural development and crops in T'ung-ch'eng itself at this time, see Chapter 2.

38 Though Chang Ying here reflects the conventional Confucian anti-commercial bias, his earlier remarks on the merchants of Hsin-an and Shansi suggest that his real concern was with the risks of trade, and that he did not disapprove of the profits as such.

39 Literally 'compare the long and adjust the short'. The idea seems to be to use what you have in excess to make up what you are short of.

40 Lu So-shan is in fact Lu Chiu-shao, a late-twelfth-century scholar who lived in

retirement at So-shan in Kiangsi and was famous for the strict way in which he ran his household, and for his views on family finance. For his biography, see *Sung-shih*, 434.9b–10a. His scheme of budgeting must have had considerable appeal in T'ung-ch'eng, for it is quoted in extenso in the rules of at least one lineage, the Kueis; see *T'ung-i Kuei STP* (C. 475), *chia-fan*, 40a, 41a. It is interesting that contributions to the lineage are taken so much for granted as to be put in the same category as taxation. 'Making expenditure on the basis of income' or 'measuring expenditures against revenues' (*liang-ju wei-ch'u*) occurs in the *Li-chi* and was a traditional tenet of Chinese public, and indeed private, finance. Though the rule was reversed at the beginning of a dynasty when new tax rates were fixed, it is in general true to say that there was no annual budgeting in the modern sense and that there was envisaged a static budget in which more or less fixed revenues determined the amounts of expenditure. For a brief but illuminating discussion of this, see Yang-Lien-sheng, *Studies in Chinese Institutional History* (Cambridge, Mass., 1963), pp. 88–9.

41 Chang Ying refers to Lu So-shan's method of economizing several times in *Ts'ung-hsün chai-yü*, though without adding anything to what is said here. In a rarely reprinted appendix to the latter work, in which he discusses at length the importance of frugality in all aspects of life, he mentions that he was also impressed with a basically similar method of budgeting practised in the eleventh century by Su Shih, who 'made up packages of 150 cash and every day merely used up one of them according to plan, never breaking into that reserved for the next day'. See *T'ung-ch'eng liang-hsiang-kuo yü-lu*, 2.23b. Su Shih himself gives the following account of his economies, in a letter written c. 1080 when he had been exiled from court to Huang-chou: 'When I first arrived in Huang-chou I was very much worried about how I would get along, since my salary had been cut off and my household is a fairly large one. However, by practising the strictest economy, we managed to spend no more than 150 cash a day. On the first of each month I get out 4,500 cash and divide it up into 30 bundles, which I then hang from the rafters of the ceiling. Every morning I then take the picture-hanging rod and fish down one bundle, and then I put the rod away. I also keep a large section of bamboo in which I put anything left over at the end of the day, so I will have something to entertain visitors with. This is a method my friend Chia Yün-lao taught me . . .' See Watson, *Su Tung-p'o*, p. 78.

42 This resembles Su Shih's method, as quoted above, and also illustrates Chang Ying's concern for the general well-being of his kinsmen. It is interesting to find that his mentor and relative by marriage, Yao Wen-jan (on whom see in particular Chapter 3), did actually put such a scheme into operation. He divided the surplus from his regular budget into four parts, each allocated to a certain category of charitable acts (including help to the orphans and widows of relatives and friends, and aid with weddings and funerals); his total outlay on this was several hundred taels a year. See *Yao STP* (T. 428), *Hsien-te chuan*, 2.16b–17a, and note 50 to Chapter 4, above.

43 Chang Ying does not exaggerate when he says that the expense of weddings might reduce a family to bankruptcy. In China a wedding or funeral was one of the most tangible ways of expressing social prestige, and such occasions in gentry families always involved much ostentatious display. They could easily ruin those families that had high status but only moderate wealth. Chow Yung-teh points out, pp. 125–6, that funerals actually caused worse problems than weddings, as the latter could at least be planned in advance, and he cites cases in which families were forced to raise loans and sell land in order to finance a funeral. There was even a proverb: 'The deceased does not eat any rice but half the family property will be gone.' Even peasant families spent much of their income on

this kind of thing. J. L. Buck estimated in the 1930s that a wedding on average cost about four months' net income of a farm family, and a funeral about three months'. In every area of his survey the cost of a wedding exceeded the total value of a labourer's yearly earnings. See Buck, *Land Utilization*, pp. 467–70. That some of Chang Ying's social circle were capable of taking a more rational view of such matters is however shown by the case of his wife's grandfather, Yao Chih-ch'i (1562–1609), the magistrate of Hsiang-t'an in Hunan. On his death he left a request that contributions towards his funeral expenses should be used instead to buy land to support his orphans. See *TCCCC*, 5.5a.

44 This far-sighted attitude seems to have been common among T'ung-ch'eng land-owners. Yao Wen-jan, in his instructions given to his sons when he divided some property among them, emphasized the importance of setting aside some of the rent income to be used for improvements to the land itself, and distinguished explicitly between landlords who merely bought land as a security and those who managed it so as to get the maximum from their investment. See Yao Wen-jan, *Yao Tuan-k'o kung wai-chi*, 18.6a–b. Another example is that of Chang Ying's relative, Chang Shu (1645–1732). He had little success in the examinations and so left the city to live on his estate in the hills, which he spent the rest of his life improving. 'Through his efforts on what had originally been marshy land, annual yields of rice were doubled, and the family property continually increased in value.' See *Chang STP* (T. 656), 28.8a–b.

45 Landlords may well have regarded tenants with greater apprehension in the after-math of the seventeenth-century revolts; their status did improve in the Ch'ing and it may have become harder to turn them off the land. For a brief outline of this question see Chapter 1. Unfortunately there is little direct evidence on the subject from T'ung-ch'eng, though there is no sign that rent resistance ever became a serious problem there. Cf. note 13, above.

46 This is probably a quotation but the source remains unidentified. 'Late crops' must mean the winter crop of wheat or barley.

47 The provenance of the first two phrases is unknown. The third comes from Ode 291, which actually says nothing at all about fertilizers or manure. The stanza reads: 'Their hoes pierce the ground, to clear away *t'u* plants and smartweed. The *t'u* plants and smartweed decay, the millets become luxuriant.' See Karlgren, *Odes*, p. 251.

48 Methods of fertilizing land, especially for the growing of commercial crops like cotton and tobacco, were considerably developed in the Ming and Ch'ing. For discussion, see Rawski, *Agricultural Change*, pp. 44–6; Ch'en Heng-li, *Pu-nung-shu*, pp. 158–60, 231–2; Li Chih-ch'in, 'Shang-yeh-hsing nung-yeh', p. 343.

49 That is, the landlord's rent income will be halved. In theory this could only happen with share rent (normally about half the crop). If the rent was a fixed amount it was supposed to be paid in full, regardless of the state of the harvest (for an example of a contract stipulating this see Niida, *Dorei nōdo-hō*, p. 519), but in practice this no doubt proved impossible to enforce. In T'ung-ch'eng, to judge from the deeds preserved in genealogies, a fixed rent was almost always imposed. Cf. note 64, below.

50 The control of servants seems to have been a perennial problem. Chang Ying in *Ts'ung-hsün chai-yü*, p. 5, devotes an essay to the subject, in which he advises against keeping too many of them as they will then shirk their duties and be hard to handle. He observes that when the family fortunes are flourishing they take advantage of its power and influence to do all kinds of illegal things, and thus arouse great enmity, but if the family's wealth and position deteriorate they become rebellious and treacherous. He concludes that the few servants that are indispensable 'should certainly not be selected from the clever and crafty'

and that they should be made to 'manage their own livelihood, to prevent the evils of time-wasting and eating without working'. His rather earlier contemporary Chang Li-hsiang had in 1661 summed it up regretfully: 'I should say, from observation of present customs, that there are no good servants, and their masters suffer great harm from having them, yet circumstances are such that they cannot do without them.' He, like Chang Ying, felt that they should be made to support themselves, and proposed that each be given a plot of land from which to provide his own food and clothing. See *Yang-yüan hsien-sheng ch'üan-chi*, 19.26a. In *ibid.*, 50.19b, he catalogues their misdeeds, which included illicit sale of their master's land, changing boundaries and appropriating rent for themselves. Very many lineage rules in T'ung-ch'eng include strongly-worded instructions that servants were to be made to show due respect to family members and to outsiders, and not to assert themselves. See end of Chapter 4, especially note 196.

51 Chiangnan, technically speaking, means the two provinces of Kiangsu and Anhwei, but is here probably used loosely of the whole lower Yangtze region, where irrigation works had been extensively developed from Sung times onwards, and which became in consequence the major rice-producing area of China.

52 This metaphor, *fou-t'u ho-chien*, is somewhat obscure. It does occur in a passage from the *Wu-tai-shih*, quoted in *P'ei-wen yün-fu*, 1481.2, where it means literally: 'He who builds a pagoda must also finish it off', i.e. see a job through to the end. In the present context it could perhaps imply that an entry in the accounts indicating the use of a 'few stones' for repairs is a pretext for claiming that the whole job is finished.

53 Chiang-ning in the Ch'ing signified the prefecture of Nanking. Many families in T'ung-ch'eng, including the Changs, must have been well acquainted with this general area, because they had taken refuge there during the revolts of the 1630s and 40s. See Chapter 2.

54 The major ponds constructed in T'ung-ch'eng in the fifteenth century were indeed very shallow in proportion to their size; they were anything from 500 to 6,000 feet long but only 10 or so feet deep. See *TCHC* (1490), 1.17b–19b. For the history of irrigation projects in the county see Chapter 2, above.

55 This seems to be Chang Ying's only statement on the extent of his own property. Presumably these 1,000 *mou* were additional to whatever he may still have retained of his father's bequest, on which see below, note 65. In *Ts'ung-hsün chai-yü*, pp. 16–17, he says, with considerable understatement: 'All I am leaving to my descendants are a few patches of barren land; it is very wild and neglected and there is constant worry over flood and drought. The annual income from it is merely enough to stave off hunger and cold and to support a wife and children. Playthings and amusements cannot be managed.' In fact this was a fairly sizeable holding by the standards of the times (cf. Appendix II) and Chang Ying lived very comfortably in his old age. See Chapter 4, pp. 97–8.

56 On rents and yields in T'ung-ch'eng, and elsewhere, see the discussion in Appendix II.

57 As was explained in Chapter 3, there seems to have been no effective reclassification of land in T'ung-ch'eng after the sixteenth century, and it is probable that owners of land officially graded as low-quality (and therefore lightly taxed) would stand to gain considerably from any improvements they might make to it.

58 On Master Tung-ch'uan, namely Chang P'eng, a fourth-generation ancestor of Chang Ying, see the beginning of Chapter 4. He became extremely prosperous, and on his death-bed left the following instructions: 'My land is not at all fertile but it is where the fields, houses and tombs of my forebears are, and I am afraid that some powerful family might seize it. Let me be buried in the east garden, so that they may not covet it.' His family biographer comments: 'His tomb is on the left

side of the present ancestral home' (which was preserved continuously in the family thereafter). See *Chang STP* (T. 656), 26.4a. It was apparently a common tactic for a man to bury his dead on a piece of land to which he wanted to stake a claim; Imabori Seiji cites some cases of tenants doing this in the Ch'ing, in 'Shindai no kōso ni tsuite', p. 52. One of the Changs in the sixteenth century had to use force to resist encroachment on his land; see Chapter 4, note 17.

59   As was shown in Chapter 1, there was probably a growing tendency towards absentee landlordism in the Ming and Ch'ing, certainly in the highly-urbanized lower Yangtze valley. Chang Ying was not the only one to disapprove of wealthy investors who took no interest in their property except as a source of income. Chang Li-hsiang (who was from north Chekiang) had earlier castigated absentee landlords in very similar terms: 'Their thoughts do not extend to matters like rain and sun, their feet never tread the boundaries of the fields . . . They cannot distinguish one path from another nor differentiate one kind of grain from another . . . They live at ease in deep seclusion, supported by the income of their land, and practically do not know what farming is . . .' See *Yang-yüan hsien-sheng ch'üan-chi*, 19.21a–b. Such behaviour seems to have been less common in T'ung-ch'eng, however, if Chang Ying's own family are any guide. See the first part of Chapter 4, and also note 44 above.

60   Presumably the implication is that those who think it beneath them to take an interest in their property risk being reduced to beggary.

61   This theme runs throughout *Ts'ung-hsün chai-yü* (especially pp. 15–17). For a discussion, see the first part of Chapter 4.

62   Without knowing the quality of the land and current prices it is impossible to work out the area Chang Ying had in mind, though it is useful to know that he expected a net return of 5% or less on capital investment (on this see Appendix II). What is most interesting is to find that it was possible to live in the city with the rather modest income of 100 taels per year, and that even with less it was still possible to live like a gentleman in the countryside. Many of Chang Ying's own relatives, as was shown in Chapter 4, actually did this, a fact which suggests that the style of life of the average member of the local elite (as opposed to persons in office) could have been less extravagant and less expensive to finance than has often been assumed. A substantial holding of land does seem to have been essential however; Chang Ying in *Ts'ung-hsün chai-yü*, p. 15 says that poor scholars without property who are forced to make a living from teaching can barely support themselves and their families.

63   This is Chang Ying's elder brother, Chang Tsai (1616–93), on whom see first part of Chapter 4, and especially note 41.

64   In T'ung-ch'eng land deeds, including those of the Changs' own ritual land, rents are given either as 'nominal rent' (*o-tsu*) or 'actual rent' (*shih-tsu*). The latter evidently signified the amount of rent to be collected in practice, while the former was a nominal quota and usually entailed some reduction. Cf. Hoang, *Notions techniques*, p. 34.

65   It seems to have been quite common for a man to divide some of his land among his sons long before his death. Yao Wen-jan did this (see note 44, above) and it was recommended in the rules of at least one lineage (see Appendix II). In 1648 Chang Ying's father, Chang Ping-i, had four surviving sons (the eldest having died in 1638), so if all received the same amount, as was customary, the total given to them would have been over 1,400 *mou*. In 1664, three years before Chang Ping-i's death, there were six sons, and the total distributed at that time would thus have been over 900 *mou*. Chang Ping-i's total holdings could therefore originally have been over 2,300 *mou*.

66   Chang Ying had married in 1653 at the age of 15, but at that stage remained in

his father's household. He would have been 20 when he first set up house on his own, after which his finances began to deteriorate. See Chang T'ing-yü, *CHYWT*, 15.3a, and first part of Chapter 4.

67 Owing to the death or flight of many of the population during the revolts of the 1630s and 40s, land in T'ung-ch'eng must have been in fairly abundant supply at this time. Its price was probably further depressed by low grain prices, the result of generally good harvests after 1647. See Chapter 2, p. 47.

68 Taking the metropolitan examinations, which necessitated a journey to Peking and quite a lengthy stay there, was a costly business. This is why many T'ung-ch'eng lineages attempted to assist members with examination expenses (on which see second part of Chapter 4) and why public-spirited men like Yao Fen donated land to the county for this purpose (see Chapter 2, note 151).

69 Much the same point was succinctly made by a Kiangsu peasant in the 1930s: 'The best thing to give to one's son is land. It is living property. Money will be used up but land never.' See Fei Hsiao-t'ung, *Peasant Life*, p. 182.

70 This must refer to the fact that land was not freely alienable; its sale was hindered by the rights of relatives to invervene, and to demand compensation if it were purchased by an outsider. See Appendix II.

BIBLIOGRAPHY

ABBREVIATIONS

AM	*Asia Major*
BSOAS	*Bulletin of the School of Oriental and African Studies*
CHYWT	*Ch'eng-huai-yüan wen-ts'un*
CS	*Ch'ing-shih*
CSLC	*Ch'ing-shih lieh-chuan*
CYYY	*Bulletin of the Institute of History and Philology, Academia Sinica*
FEQ	*Far Eastern Quarterly*
HC	*hsien-chih*
HJAS	*Harvard Journal of Asiatic Studies*
HY	Harvard-Yenching Institute Library
JAS	*Journal of Asian Studies*
JK	Jinbun Kagaku Kenkyûjo, Kyoto University
LC	Library of Congress
LSYC	*Li-shih yen-chiu*
MS	*Ming-shih*
STP	*-shih tsung-p'u/-shih tsu-p'u*
TB	Tòyò Bunko, Tokyo
TC	*t'ung-chih*
TCCCC	Ma Ch'i-ch'ang, *T'ung-ch'eng ch'i-chiu chuan*
TCHC	*T'ung-ch'eng hsien-chih*
TK	Tòyò Bunka Kenkyûjo, Tokyo University
TMITC	*Ta-Ming i-t'ung-chih*

I. PRIMARY SOURCES

Genealogies

This is not a complete listing of the surviving T'ung-ch'eng genealogies, but includes all those consulted in the course of this study. They are numbered according to their listing in Taga Akigorò, *Sòfu no kenkyû*. Numbers beginning with T. refer to genealogies in Japanese libraries, which are to be found in the main body of the catalogue, pp. 80–186. Numbers beginning with C. refer to those in Columbia University East Asian Library, listed on pp. 370–450. They are given here in alphabetical order, by surname.

Chang STP 張 氏 宗 譜, 1890, T.656.
Chang STP 張 氏 宗 譜, 1933, C.510.
Chang STP 張 氏 宗 譜, 1902, T.658.
Wan-T'ung Nan-wan Chang-shih chung-hsiu tsung-p'u 皖 桐 南 灣 張 氏 重 修 宗 譜, 1924, T.676.

Wan-T'ung Chang STP 皖 桐 張 氏 宗 譜 , 1827, T.677.
T'ung-pei Chao STP 桐 陂 趙 氏 宗 譜 , 1883, T.977.
Chao STP 趙 氏 宗 譜 , 1884, T.987.
Ch'en STP 陳 氏 宗 譜 , 1868, T.757.
Ch'en STP 陳 氏 宗 譜 , 1877, T.760.
Cheng STP 鄭 氏 宗 譜 , 1897, T. 1072.
Wan-T'ung Ch'eng STP 皖 桐 程 氏 宗 譜 , 1924, T.878.
Ch'eng STP 程 氏 宗 譜 , 1867, T.881.
Ch'eng STP 程 氏 宗 譜 , 1921, T.882.
Ch'i STP 齊 氏 宗 譜 , 1919, T.957.
Chiang-shih chih-p'u 姜 氏 支 譜 , 1846, T.419.
Chou-shih chih-p'u 周 氏 支 譜 , 1925, T.359.
T'ung-ch'eng Lien-hsi Chou STP 桐 城 濂 西 周 氏 宗 譜 , 1931, C.290.
T'ung-ch'eng Yao-shih Chou-shih Shang-i-t'ang chih-p'u 桐 城 鷂 石 周 氏 尚
　　義 堂 支 譜 , 1894, C. 291.
Liu-feng Chu STP 柳 峯 朱 氏 宗 譜 , 1873, T.160.
Wan-T'ung Fang STP 皖 桐 方 氏 宗 譜 , 1929, T.11.
Wan-T'ung Hu STP 皖 桐 胡 氏 宗 譜 1880, C.361.
Hu STP 胡 氏 宗 譜 , 1905, T.462.
T'ung-hsi Hu STP 桐 西 胡 氏 宗 譜 , 1904, T.466.
Miu-Hu STP 繆 胡 氏 宗 譜 , 1909, T.1114.
Huang STP 黃 氏 宗 譜 , 1797, T.837.
Huang STP 黃 氏 宗 譜 , 1873, T.838.
Lu-ch'eng Huang STP 鹿 城 黃 氏 宗 譜 , 1890, T.844.
Hung STP 洪 氏 宗 譜 , 1913, T.445.
Jao STP 饒 氏 宗 譜 , 1897, T.1201.
T'ung-ch'eng Mei-ling Kan STP 桐 城 梅 嶺 甘 氏 宗 譜 , 1905, C.75.
T'ung-ch'eng Kuan-shan Kao STP 桐 城 官 山 高 氏 宗 譜 1755, C.404.
Kao STP 高 氏 宗 譜 , 1869, T.505.
T'ung-i Kuei STP 桐 邑 桂 氏 族 譜 , 1874, C.475.
Lung-ho Li STP 龍 河 李 氏 宗 譜 , 1848, T.298.
Yen-p'ing Li STP 延 平 李 氏 宗 譜 , 1896, T.288.
Liu STP 劉 氏 宗 譜 , 1870, T.1015.
T'ung-ch'eng Ma STP 桐 城 馬 氏 族 譜 , 1929, T.495.
Mao STP 毛 氏 宗 譜 , 1807, T.18.
Mao STP 毛 氏 宗 譜 , 1901, T.19.
Miu STP 繆 氏 宗 譜 , 1869, T.1112.
T'ung-ch'eng Mu-chan P'an STP 桐 城 木 山 潘 氏 宗 譜 , 1928, C.818.
Ts'ang-chi Sun-shih chia-p'u 蒼 基 孫 氏 家 譜 , 1922, T.553.
Wan-T'ung Hsiang-shan Tai STP 皖 桐 香 山 戴 氏 宗 譜 , 1868, T.1136.
T'ang STP 唐 氏 宗 譜 , 1870, T.529.
Ts'ai STP 蔡 氏 族 譜 , 1897, T.1046.
Ts'ao-shih chih-p'u 曹 氏 支 譜 , 1850, T.691.
Tso STP 左 氏 宗 譜 , 1849, T.126.
Tsou STP 鄒 氏 宗 譜 , 1923, T.953.
T'ung-ch'eng Tung STP 桐 城 董 氏 宗 譜 , 1906, T.929.
Tung-lou Wang STP 東 樓 王 氏 宗 譜 , 1874, T.65.
Wang STP 王 氏 宗 譜 , 1895, T.45.
T'ung-ch'eng Wang STP 桐 城 王 氏 宗 譜 , 1866, C.44.
Kao-lin Wang STP 高 林 汪 氏 宗 譜 , 1882, T.315.
Wang STP 汪 氏 宗 譜 , 1900, T.316.
T'ung-ch'eng Wu-chia-tzu Wu STP 桐 城 吳 家 粢 吳 氏 宗 譜 , 1875,
　　T.240.

Wan-T'ung Yang STP 皖 桐 楊 氏 宗 譜 , 1872, C.722.
Yang-shih chih-p'u 楊 氏 支 譜 , 1894, T.920.
Ma-hsi Yao STP 麻 溪 姚 氏 宗 譜 , 1878, T.427.
Ma-hsi Yao STP 麻 溪 姚 氏 宗 譜 , 1921, T.428.
Nan-yang Yeh STP 南 陽 葉 氏 宗 譜 , 1891, T.938.
Lu-Yeh STP 陸 葉 氏 宗 譜 , 1866, T.814.
Yen STP 嚴 氏 宗 譜 , 1904, T.1208.
Yin STP 殷 氏 宗 譜 , 1916, T.601.

Other sources
Locations of rare works are indicated in parentheses. Dates given are those of
printing, not compilation.

An-ch'ing fu-chih 安 慶 府 志 , 1721 (HY).
An-hui TC 安 徽 通 志 , 1877; reprinted, Taipei, 1967.
Chang Li-hsiang 張 履 祥 , *Yang-yüan hsien-sheng ch'üan-chi* 楊 園 先 生 全 集
    1871; reprinted, Taipei, 1968.
Chang T'ing-yü 張 廷 玉 , *Ch'eng-huai-yüan wen-ts'un* 澄 懷 園 文 存 , 1891;
    reprinted, Taipei, 1970.
    – *Ch'eng-huai-yüan yü* 澄 懷 園 語 , in *T'ung-ch'eng liang-hsiang-kuo yü-lu.*
Chang Tseng-ch'ien 張 曾 慶 , comp., *Chiang-yen ssu-shih shih-ch'ao* 蔣 延 四
    世 詩 鈔 , 1893 (HY).
Chang Ying 張 英 , *Heng-ch'an so-yen* 恆 產 瑣 言 , in *Ts'ung-shu chi-ch'eng,*
    ch'u-pien, 977.
    – *Ts'ung-hsün chai-yü* 聰 訓 齋 語 , in *Ts'ung-shu chi-ch'eng, ch'u-pien*, 977.
    – *Tu-su-t'ang wen-chi* 篤 素 堂 文 集 , in *Chang Wen-tuan chi* 張 文
    端 集 , 1897 (LC).
Chi T'ung-ch'eng Fang Tai liang-chia shu-an 記 桐 城 方 戴 兩 家 書 案 ,
    in *Ku-hsüeh hui-k'an* 古 學 彙 刊 , ed. Li Ch'ing 李 清 , 1912–13.
Chiang-nan An-hui ch'üan-t'u 江 南 安 徽 全 圖 , 1896 (HY).
Chiang-nan TC 江 南 通 志 , 1738; reprinted, Taipei, 1967.
Ch'ien-shan HC 潛 山 縣 志 , 1920 (TB).
Ch'ing-ch'ao hsü-wen-hsien t'ung-k'ao 清 朝 續 文 獻 通 考 , ed. *Liu Chin-*
    tsao 劉 錦 藻 , 1936 ed.; reprinted, 1955.
Ch'ing-shih 清 史 , Taipei, 1961.
Ch'ing-shih lieh-chuan 清 史 列 傳 , 1928; reprinted, Taipei, 1964.
Chung-hua min-kuo k'ai-kuo wu-shih nien wen-hsien 中 華 民 國 開 國 五 十
    年 文 獻 , 1st collection XIII, Taipei, 1963.
Fang Hsüeh-chien 方 學 漸 , *T'ung-i chi hsü* 桐 彝 及 續 , 1883 (TB).
    – *Erh-hsün* 邇 訓 , 1883 (JK).
Fang Pao 方 苞 , *Wang-hsi hsien-sheng ch'üan-chi* 望 溪 先 生 全 集 , in
    Ssu-pu pei-yao.
Fu-she hsing-shih chuan-lüeh 復 社 姓 氏 傳 略 , 1831; reprinted, Hangchow,
    1961.
Han-shu 漢 書 , Peking, 1962.
Ho-nan TC 河 南 通 志 ; reprinted, Taipei, 1969.
Hsin-an ming-tsu chih 新 安 名 族 志 , 1551 (*Rare Books of the National Library*,
    Peking, no. 916; microfilm).
Huai-ning HC 懷 寧 縣 志 , 1915 (JK).
Huang-ch'ao ching-shih wen-pien 皇 朝 經 世 文 編 , ed. Ho Ch'ang-ling
    賀 長 齡 , 1886.
Ku Yen-wu 顧 炎 武 , *Jih-chih-lu chi-shih* 日 知 錄 集 釋 , ed. Huang
    Ju-ch'eng 黃 汝 成 , in *Ssu-pu pei-yao.*

Kuei-ch'ih HC 貴 池 縣 志 , 1883 (HY).
Kuo-ch'ao hua-shih 國 朝 畫 識 , ed. Feng Chin-po 馮 金 伯 and Wu Chin 吳 晉 , 1831.
Lü-chiang HC 廬 江 縣 志 , 1885 (TB).
Ma Ch'i-ch'ang 馬 其 昶 , *T'ung-ch'eng ch'i-chiu chuan* 桐 城 耆 舊 傳 , 1911; reprinted, Taipei, 1969.
Ming shih 明 史 ed. Chang T'ing-yü et al.; reprinted, Taipei, 1962.
Pei-chuan chi 碑 傳 集 , ed. Ch'ien I-chi 錢 儀 吉 , 1893.
Po-yang HC 鄱 陽 縣 志 , 1824 (TB).
Shu-ch'eng HC 舒 城 縣 志 , 1907 (TB).
Su Shih shih-hsüan 蘇 軾 詩 選 , ed. Ch'en Erh-tung 陳 邇 冬 , Peking, 1957.
Su-sung HC 宿 松 縣 志 , 1929 (TB).
Su Wen-chung kung shih-chi 蘇 文 忠 公 詩 集 , ed. Chi Yün 紀 昀 , 1834.
Sung-shih 宋 史 , *Po-na-pen*.
Ta-Ch'ing chi-fu hsien-che chuan 大 清 畿 輔 先 哲 傳 , ed. Hsü Shih-ch'ang 徐 世 昌 , n.d.
Ta-Ch'ing Sheng-tsu Jen-huang-ti shih-lu 大 清 聖 祖 仁 皇 帝 實 錄 ; reprinted, Taipei, 1964.
Ta-Ming hui-tien 大 明 會 典 , 1587.
Ta-Ming i-t'ung-chih 大 明 一 統 志 , 1849.
Tai-Ming-shih 戴 名 世 , *Nan-shan chi* 南 山 集 ; reprinted, Taipei, 1970.
– *Tai Nan-shan wen-ch'ao* 戴 南 山 文 鈔 , Taipei, 1956.
T'ai-hu HC 太 湖 縣 志 , 1922 (JK).
T'ung-ch'eng HC 桐 城 縣 志 , 1490 (*Rare Books of the National Library, Peking*, No. 758; microfilm).
T'ung-ch'eng HC 桐 城 縣 志 , 1696 (LC).
T'ung-ch'eng hsü-hsiu HC 桐 城 續 修 縣 志 , 1827 (TB).
T'ung-ch'eng liang-hsiang-kuo yü-lu 桐 城 兩 相 國 語 錄 , comp. Chang Tseng-ch'ien 張 曾 慶 , 1880 (JK).
T'ung-ch'eng Yao-shih pei-chuan lu 桐 城 姚 氏 碑 傳 錄 , comp. Yao Yung-p'u 姚 永 樸 , 1905 (JK).
T'ung-ling HC 銅 陵 縣 志 , 1930 (TB).
Wang-chiang HC 望 江 縣 志 , 1768 (TB).
Wu-wei chou-chih 無 為 州 志 , 1803 (TB).
Wu-yüan HC 婺 源 縣 志 , 1882 (TK).
Yao Nai 姚 鼐 , *Hsi-pao hsüan ch'üan-chi* 惜 抱 軒 全 集 ; reprinted, Hong Kong, 1959.
Yao Wen-jan 姚 文 然 , *Yao Tuan-k'o kung chi* 姚 端 恪 公 集 , 1683 (LC).
Yao Ying 姚 瑩 , *Chung-fu-t'ang ch'üan-chi* 中 復 堂 全 集 , 1867 (HY).
Yeh Meng-chu 葉 夢 珠 , *Yüeh-shih-pien* 閱 世 編 in *Shanghai chang-ku ts'ung-shu* 上 海 掌 故 叢 書 , 1936.
Yeh Ts'an 葉 燦 , *Fang Ming-shan hsien-sheng hsing-chuang* 方 明 善 先 生 行 狀 , in Fang Ch'ang-han 方 昌 翰 , *T'ung-ch'eng Fang-shih ch'i-tai i-shu* 桐 城 方 氏 七 代 遺 書 , 1888 (HY).

II. SECONDARY WORKS

Baker, Hugh D. R., *A Chinese Lineage Village: Sheung Shui,* London, 1968.
Beattie, H. J., 'The Alternative to Resistance: The Case of T'ung-ch'eng, Anhwei', in J. D. Spence and J. E. Wills, Jr, eds., *From Ming to Ch'ing: Conquest, Region and Continuity in Seventeenth Century China*, New Haven (forthcoming).
Brunnert, H. S. and Hagelstrom, V. V., *Present Day Political Organization of China*, Shanghai, 1912.
Buck, J. L., *Chinese Farm Economy,* Chicago, 1930.
– *Land Utilization in China*, Nanking, 1937.

Chang Chung-li, *The Chinese Gentry*, Seattle, 1955.
   – *The Income of the Chinese Gentry*, Seattle, 1962.
Ch'en Heng-li 陳 恆 力, *Pu-nung-shu yen-chiu* 補 農 書 研 究, Peking,
   1958.
Ch'ing-shih-lu ching-chi tzu-liao chi-yao 清 實 錄 經 濟 資 料 輯 要,
   comp. Nankai Ta-hsüeh Li-shih-hsi 南 開 大 學 歷 史 系, Peking, 1959.
Ch'ing-tai pei-chuan wen-t'ung-chien 清 代 碑 傳 文 通 檢, ed. Ch'en
   Nai-ch'ien 陳 乃 乾, Peking, 1959.
Chow Yung-teh, *Social Mobility in China*, New York, 1966.
Chu Shih-chia 朱 士 嘉 (ed.), *Chung-kuo ti-fang-chih tsung-lu* 中 國 地 方
   志 綜 錄, 2nd ed., Shanghai, 1958.
Ch'ü T'ung-tsu, *Local Government in China under the Ch'ing*, Cambridge, Mass., 1962.
Ch'üan Han-sheng 全 漢 昇, 'Mei-chou pai-yin yü shih-pa shih-chi Chung-kuo wu-
   chia ko-ming ti kuan-hsi' 美 洲 白 銀 與 十 八 世 紀 中 國 物
   價 革 命 的 關 係, *CYYY*, 28 (1957), 517–50.
Combined Indices to Eighty-Nine Collections of Ming Dynasty Biographies, Harvard-
   Yenching Index Series, No. 24, 1935.
A Concordance to Meng-tzu, Harvard-Yenching Index Series, Supplement 17, 1941.
Elvin, M., 'The Last Thousand Years of Chinese History: Changing Patterns in Land
   Tenure', *Modern Asian Studies*, 4:2 (1970), 97–114.
Fang Chao-ying 房 兆 楹 and Tu Lien-che 杜 聯 喆, *Tseng-chiao Ch'ing-
   ch'ao chin-shih t'i-ming pei-lu* 增 校 清 朝 進 士 題 名 碑 錄,
   Harvard-Yenching Index Series, Supplement 19, 1941.
Fei Hsiao-t'ung, *China's Gentry*, Chicago, 1953.
   – *Peasant Life in China*, London, 1939.
   – 'Peasantry and Gentry: An Interpretation of Chinese Social Structure and its
   Changes', *American Journal of Sociology*, 52 (1946), 1–17.
Feuerwerker, A., ed., *History in Communist China*, Cambridge, Mass., 1969.
Freedman, M., *Chinese Lineage and Society: Fukien and Kwangtung*, London, 1966.
   – *Lineage Organization in Southeastern China*, London, 1958.
   – ed., *Family and Kinship in Chinese Society*, Stanford, 1970.
Fried, Morton H., *Fabric of Chinese Society*, New York, 1953.
Friese, Heinz, *Das Dienstleistungs-System der Ming-Zeit (1368–1644)*, Hamburg, 1959.
Fu I-ling 傅 衣 凌, *Ming-Ch'ing nung-ts'un she-hui ching-chi* 明 清 農 村 社
   會 經 濟, Peking, 1961.
   – *Ming-Ch'ing shih-tai shang-jen chi shang-yeh tzu-pen* 明 清 時 代 商 人
   及 商 業 資 本, Peking, 1956.
   – *Ming-tai Chiang-nan shih-min ching-chi shih-t'an* 明 代 江 南 市 民 經
   濟 試 探, Shanghai, 1957.
Fujii Hiroshi 藤 井 宏, 'Shinan shōnin no kenkyū' 新 安 商 人 の 研 究,
   Tōyō Gakuhō, 36:1–3 (1953), 1–44, 32–60, 65–118.
Goodrich, L. Carrington, *The Literary Inquisition of Ch'ien-lung*, Baltimore, 1935.
Grimm, Tilemann, *Erziehung und Politik im Konfuzianischen China der Ming-Zeit
   (1368–1644)*, Hamburg, 1960.
Hatano Yoshihiro 波 多 野 善 大, *Chūgoku kindai kōgyōshi no kenkyū* 中 國 近
   代 工 業 史 の 研 究, Kyoto, 1961.
Hexter, J. H., 'The Myth of the Middle Class in Tudor England' in *Reappraisals in History*,
   London, 1961, pp. 71–116.
Ho Ping-ti, 'Early-Ripening Rice in Chinese History', *Economic History Review*, 9:2
   (1956), 200–18.
   – *The Ladder of Success in Imperial China*, New York, 1962.
   – 'The Salt Merchants of Yang-chou: A Study of Commercial Capitalism in Eighteenth
   Century China', *HJAS*, 17 (1954), 130–68.
   – *Studies on the Population of China, 1368–1953*, Cambridge, Mass., 1959.

Hoang, Pierre, *Notions techniques sur la propriété en Chine avec un choix d'actes et de documents officiels*, Shanghai, 1897.

Hosono Kōji 細 野 浩 二 , 'Min-matsu Shin-sho Kōnan ni okeru jinushi doboku kankei'·明 末 清 初 江 南 に おけ る 地 主 奴 僕 関 係, *Tōyō Gakuhō*, 50:3 (1967), 1–36.

Hsiao I-shan 蕭 一 山 , *Ch'ing-tai t'ung-shih* 清 代 通 史 , Shanghai, 1927; reprinted, 5 vols, Taipei, 1962–7.

Hsiao Kung-ch'üan, *Rural China: Imperial Control in the Nineteenth Century*, Seattle, 1960.

Hsü Ta-ling 許 大 齡 , *Ch'ing-tai chüan-na chih-tu* 清 代 捐 納 制 度 , Peking, 1950.

Hu Hsien-chin, *The Common Descent Group in China and its Functions*, New York, 1948.

Huang, Ray, 'Fiscal Administration during the Ming Dynasty', in Hucker, ed., *Chinese Government in Ming Times*, pp. 73–128.
   – *Taxation and Governmental Finance in Sixteenth-Century Ming China*, Cambridge, 1974.

Hucker, Charles O., ed., *Chinese Government in Ming Times: Seven Studies*, New York, 1969.
   – *The Censorial System of Ming China*, Stanford, 1966.
   – 'Governmental Organization of the Ming Dynasty', *HJAS*, 21 (1958), 1–66.

Hummel, A. W., ed., *Eminent Chinese of the Ch'ing Period*, 2 vols., Washington, D.C., 1943–5.

Ikeda On, 'The Decline of the T'ang Aristocracy', draft chapter for the *Cambridge History of China*, forthcoming.

Imabori Seiji 今 堀 誠 二 , 'Shindai no kōso ni tsuite' 清 代 の 抗 租 について, *Shigaku Zasshi*, 76:9 (1967), 37–61.

Index to Thirty-three Collections of Ch'ing Dynasty Biographies, Harvard-Yenching Index Series, No. 9, 2nd. ed., Tokyo, 1960.

Karlgren, Bernhard, *The Book of Documents*, Stockholm, 1950.
   – *The Book of Odes*, Stockholm, 1950.

Kracke, E. A., Jr, 'Family vs. Merit in the Examination System', *HJAS*, 10 (1947), 103–23.

Kuhn, Philip A., *Rebellion and its Enemies in Late Imperial China*, Cambridge, Mass., 1970.

Kusano Yasushi 草 野 靖 , 'Daitochi shoyū to tenko sei no tenkai' 大 土 地 所 有 と 佃 戸 制 の 展 開 , in *Sekai Rekishi*, IX, 345–82, Iwanami Kōza, Tokyo, 1970.

Lang, Olga, *Chinese Family and Society*, New Haven, 1946.

Lau, D. C., tr., *Mencius*, Harmondsworth, Middlesex, 1970.

Li Chih-ch'in 李 之 勤 , 'Lun ya-p'ien chan-cheng i-ch'ien Ch'ing-tai shang-yeh-hsing nung-yeh ti fa-chan' 論 鴉 片 戰 爭 以 前 清 代 商 業 性 農 業 的 發 展 , in *Ming-Ch'ing she-hui ching-chi hsing-t'ai ti yen-chiu* 明 清 社 會 經 濟 形 態 的 研 究 , Shanghai, 1957, pp. 263–357.

Li Wen-chih 李 文 治 , 'Lun Ch'ing-tai ch'ien-ch'i ti t'u-ti chan-yu kuan-hsi' 論 清 代 前 期 的 土 地 佔 有 關 係 , *LSYC*, 5 (1963), 75–108.
   – *Wan-Ming min-pien*, Shanghai, 1948.

Liang Fang-chung, *The Single Whip Method of Taxation in China*, Cambridge, Mass., 1956.

Liu, Hui-chen Wang, 'An Analysis of Chinese Clan Rules: Confucian Theories in Action', in D. S. Nivison and A. F. Wright, eds., *Confucianism in Action*, Stanford, 1959, pp. 63–96.
   – *The Traditional Chinese Clan Rules*, New York, 1959.

McAleavy, Henry, 'Dien in China and Vietnam', *JAS*, 17:3 (1958), 403–15.

Makino Tatsumi 牧 野 巽, *Kinsei Chūgoku sōzoku kenkyū* 近 世 中 國 宗 族 研 究, Tokyo, 1949.

Marsh, Robert M., 'Bureaucratic Constraints on Nepotism in the Ch'ing Period', *JAS*, 19 (1960), 117–33.

   – *The Mandarins: The Circulation of Elites in China, 1600–1900*, Glencoe, Ill., 1961.

Meskill, Joanna M., 'The Chinese Genealogy as a Research Source', in Freedman, ed., *Family and Kinship in Chinese Society*, pp. 139–61.

Ming-jen chuan-chi tzu-liao so-yin 明 人 傳 記 資 料 索 引, Taipei, 1965–6.

Muramatsu Yūji 村 松 祐 次, 'Shindai no shinshi – jinushi ni okeru tochi to kanshoku' 清 代 の 紳 士 — 地主 におけるる土 地 と 官 職, *Hitotsubashi Ronsō*, 44:6 (1970), 24–52.

   – 'A Documentary Study of Chinese Landlordism in Late Ch'ing and Early Republican Kiangnan', *BSOAS*, 29 (1966), 566–99.

Nakayama Mio 中 山 美 緒, 'Heng-ch'an so-yen ni tsuite' 恒 産 瑣 言 につ いて, *Tōyō Gakuhō*, 57:1, 2 (1976), 171–200.

Niida Noboru 仁 井 田 陞, *Chūgoku hōseishi kenkyū: tochi-hō, torihiki-hō* 中 國 法 制 史 研 究, 土 地 法, 取 引 法, Tokyo, 1960.

   – *Chūgoku hōseishi kenkyū: dorei nōdo-hō, kazoku sonraku-hō* 中 國 法 制 史 研 究, 奴 隸 農 奴 法, 家 族 村 落 法, Tokyo, 1962.

P'an Kuang-tan 潘 光 旦, *Ming-Ch'ing liang-tai Chia-hsing ti wang-tsu* 明 清 兩 代 嘉 興 的 望 族, Shanghai, 1947.

Parsons, James B., 'The Ming Dynasty Bureaucracy: Aspects of Background Forces', in Hucker, ed., *Chinese Government in Ming Times*, pp. 175–231.

   – *Peasant Rebellions of the Late Ming Dynasty*, Tucson, Arizona, 1970.

P'eng Hsin-wei 彭 信 威, *Chung-kuo huo-pi shih* 中 國 貨 幣 史, Shanghai, 1954.

Perkins, Dwight H., *Agricultural Development in China, 1368–1968*, Chicago, 1969.

Potter, Jack M., *Capitalism and the Chinese Peasant*, Berkeley and Los Angeles, 1968.

   – 'Land and Lineage in Traditional China' in Freedman, ed., *Family and Kinship in Chinese Society*, pp. 121–38.

Rawski, Evelyn S., *Agricultural Change and the Peasant Economy of South China*, Cambridge, Mass., 1972.

Schurmann, H. F., 'Traditional Property Concepts in China', *FEQ*, 15: 4 (1956), 507–16.

Shang Yen-liu 商 衍 鎏, *Ch'ing-tai k'o-chü k'ao-shih shu-lu* 清 代 科 舉 考 試 述 錄, Peking, 1958.

Shiba Yoshinobu, *Commerce and Society in Sung China*, tr. M. Elvin, Ann Arbor, 1970.

   – 'Urbanization and the Development of Markets in the Lower Yangtze Valley', paper for Sung II Conference, Feldafing, Germany, Aug.–Sept. 1971.

Shimizu Morimitsu 清 水 盛 光, *Chūgoku zokusan seido kō* 中 國 族 產 制 度 考, Tokyo, 1949.

Shimizu Taiji 清 水 泰 次, *Mindai tochi seido shi kenkyū* 明 代 土 地 制 度 史 研 究, Tokyo, 1968.

Skinner, G. William, 'Marketing and Social Structure in Rural China', *JAS*, 24:1 (1964), 3–43.

Smith, T. C., *The Agrarian Origins of Modern Japan*, Stanford, 1959.

Spence, Jonathan D., *Ts'ao Yin and the K'ang-hsi Emperor*, New Haven, 1966.

Sun, E-tu Zen, 'Mining Labor in the Ch'ing Period', in A. Feuerwerker, R. Murphey and M. C. Wright, eds., *Approaches to Modern Chinese History*, Berkeley and Los Angeles, 1967, pp. 45–67.

   – and Sun, Shiou-chuan, *T'ien-kung kai-wu: Chinese Technology in the Seventeenth Century*, University Park, Pennsylvania, 1966.

Taga Akigoro 多 賀 秋 五 郎 , *Sōfu no kenkyū* 宗 譜 の 研 究 , Tokyo, 1960.

Tamai Zehaku 玉 井 是 博 , *Shina shakai-keizai shi kenkyū* 支 那 社 會 經 濟 史 研 究 , Tokyo, 1942.

Tawney, R. H., *Land and Labour in China*, London, 1932.

Twitchett, D. C., 'A Critique of Some Recent Studies of Modern Chinese Social-economic History', *Transactions of the International Conference of Orientalists in Japan*, 10 (1965), 28–41.

– 'Documents on Clan Administration: I. The Rules of Administration of the Charitable Estate of the Fan Clan', *AM*, 8 (1960–1), 1–35.

– 'The Fan Clan's Charitable Estate, 1050–1760', in D. S. Nivison and A. F. Wright, eds., *Confucianism in Action*, Stanford, 1959, pp. 97–133.

– *Land Tenure and the Social Order in T'ang and Sung China*, London, 1962.

– 'Merchant, Trade and Government in Late T'ang', *AM*, 14:1 (1968), 63–95.

Wakeman, Frederic, Jr, 'High Ch'ing: 1683–1839', in James B. Crowley, ed., *Modern East Asia: Essays in Interpretation,* New York, 1970, pp. 1–28.

– 'Localism and Loyalism during the Ch'ing Conquest of Kiangnan: The Tragedy of Chiang-yin', in F. Wakeman, Jr and C. Grant, eds., *Conflict and Control in Late Imperial China*, Berkeley and Los Angeles, 1975, pp. 43–85.

Waley, Arthur, *The Book of Songs*, 2nd ed., London, 1954.

Wang Yeh-chien, 'The Fiscal Importance of the Land Tax during the Ch'ing Period', *JAS*, 30:4 (1971), 829–42.

Wang Yü-ch'üan, 'The Rise of Land Tax and the Fall of Dynasties', *Pacific Affairs*, 9:2 (1936), 201–20.

Watson, Burton, *Su Tung-p'o: Selections from a Sung Dynasty Poet*, New York, 1965.

Weber, Max, *The Religion of China*, translated by Hans H. Gerth, New York, 1964.

Wei Ch'ing-yüan 衛 慶 遠 , *Ming-tai huang-ts'e chih-tu* 明 代 黄 册 制 度 , Peking, 1961.

Wright, Mary C., *The Last Stand of Chinese Conservatism*, Stanford, 1962.

Wu Han 吳 晗 , *Chu Yüan-chang chuan* 朱 元 璋 傳 , reprinted, Hong Kong, n.d.

Yang, C. K., *A Chinese Village in Early Communist Transition*, Cambridge, Mass., 1959.

Yang Lien-sheng, *Money and Credit in China: A Short History*, Cambridge, Mass., 1952.

– *Studies in Chinese Institutional History*, Cambridge, Mass., 1963.

Yüan I-chin, 'Life Tables for a Southern Chinese Family from 1365 to 1849', *Human Biology*, 3:2 (1931), 157–79.

GLOSSARY

Items appearing in the bibliography, dynasties, emperors, reign titles, year names and very well-known place names have been omitted.

An-ch'ing 安 慶
chan-shih-fu 詹 事 府
Chang Ch'ao-chen 張 朝 珍
Chang Ch'eng-hsien 張 承 先
Chang Ch'i 張 芑
Chang Chia 張 嘉
Chang Chieh 張 杰
Chang Chien 張 漸
Chang Chü-cheng 張 居 正
Chang Ch'un 張 淳
Chang Feng 張 鳳
Chang Feng-i 張 鳳 翼
Chang Han-ch'ing 張 漢 卿
Chang Hsien-chung 張 獻 忠
Chang Hsü 張 緒
Chang Hsün 張 勳
Chang Jo-t'ing 張 若 渟
Chang Ju 張 儒
Chang K'o-yen 張 克 儼
Chang K'uei 張 夔
Chang Li-hsiang 張 履 祥
Chang Liu-chi (Liu-chieh) 張 六 吉（六 皆）
Chang Mu 張 木
Chang P'eng (Tung-ch'uan) 張 鵬（東 川）
Chang Ping-chen 張 秉 貞
Chang Ping-ch'ien 張 秉 謙
Chang Ping-i 張 秉 彝
Chang Ping-wen 張 秉 文
Chang Shao-hua 張 紹 華
Chang Shao-t'ang 張 紹 棠
Chang Shao-wen 張 紹 文
Chang Shih-wei 張 士 維
Chang Shu 張 菽
Chang T'ing-ch'ih 張 廷 瓅
Chang T'ing-ch'ing 張 廷 慶
Chang T'ing-chuan 張 廷 瑑
Chang T'ing-jui 張 廷 瑞
Chang T'ing-lu 張 廷 璐
Chang T'ing-tsan 張 廷 瓚
Chang T'ing-yü 張 廷 玉
Chang Tsai (Hu-shang) 張 載（湖 上）
Chang Tseng-ch'ang 張 曾 敞
Chang Tseng-ch'ien 張 曾 虔
Chang Tseng-i 張 曾 誼
Chang Tsung-han 張 宗 瀚
Chang Ying 張 英
Chang-chia-p'ang 張 家 塝
Ch'ang-chou 常 州
Chao I 趙 釴
Chao Jui 趙 銳
chen 鎮
Ch'en Mien 陳 勉
Ch'en Yü-chieh 陳 于 階
Ch'eng 程
Chi-nan 濟 南
Ch'i 齊
chia 家
Chia-chü so-yen 家 居 瑣 言
Chia-hsing 嘉 興
chia-hsün 家 訓
chia-kuei 家 規
Chiang Ch'en 蔣 臣
Chiang-nan 江 南
Chiang-ning 江 寧
chien-sheng 監 生
Ch'ien 錢
Ch'ien-shan 灊 山
chin 斤
Chin Fu 靳 輔
chin-shen 衿 紳

chin-shih 進 士
ch'ing 頃
Chiu kao 酒 誥
chiu-ts'u k'o 酒 誥 課
ch'iu 垯
chou 洲
chou 州
Chou Ch'i 周 岐
Ch'u 楚
Chu-ch'eng-tsui 竹 城 嘴
Ch'u ch'u che tz'u 楚 楚 者 茨
Ch'u-tz'u 楚 茨
chü-jen 舉 人
ch'ü 去
ch'ü 區
Ch'ü Na-hai 瞿 那 海
ch'ü-t'ou 區 頭
chun-che 準 折
chün 郡
chün 均
chün-t'ien 均 田
chün yao-i 均 徭 役
chung-chung 中 中
Fan Chung-yen 范 仲 淹
fan-li 凡 例
Fang Fa 方 法
Fang Hao 方 浩
Fang Hsiang 方 向
Fang Hsiang-ch'ien 方 象 乾
Fang Hsiao 方 效
Fang Hsiao-piao 方 孝 標
Fang Hsüeh-chien 方 學 漸
Fang I-chih 方 以 智
Fang Kuan 方 瓘
Fang Kuan-ch'eng 方 額 承
Fang K'ung-chao 方 孔 炤
Fang Lin 方 琳
Fang Mao 方 懋
Fang Pao 方 苞
Fang Ta-chen 方 大 鎮
Fang Ta-jen 方 大 任
Fang Ta-mei 方 大 美
Fang Tsung-ch'eng 方 宗 誠
Fang Tung-shu 方 東 樹
Fang Yin 方 邠
Fang Yu 方 佑
Fang Yü 方 瑜
fang-chang 房 長
fen 分
Feng-yang 鳳 陽
fou-t'u ho-chien 浮 圖 合 尖
fu 府
fu-i ch'üan-shu 賦 役 全 書

Fu-she 復 社
Hanlin Yüan 翰 林 院
hao 號
heng-ch'an 恆 產
Heng-ch'an so-yen 恆 產 瑣 言
Ho 何
Ho Ju-ch'ung 何 如 寵
Ho-shen 和 珅
hsiang-chang 鄉 長
Hsiang-shan 香 山
Hsiang-t'an 湘 潭
hsiao-jen 小 人
hsien 仙, 祀
hsien 縣
Hsien-te chuan 先 德 傳
Hsin-an 新 安
Hsiu-ning 休 寧
Hsiung Tz'u-li 熊 賜 履
Hsü Ch'ien-hsüeh 徐 乾 燦
Hsü Kuo-hsiang 徐 國 相
Hu 胡
hu 斛
Hu K'o 胡 翽
Hu Tsan 胡 瓚
Hu Tsuan-tsung 胡 瓚 宗
Hu Yen 胡 儼
hu-chang 戶 長
hua-ting 滑 丁
Huai-ning 懷 寧
Huang 黃
Huang Chen-lin 黃 貞 麟
Huang-chou 黃 州
Huang Wen-ting 黃 文 鼎
huang-ts'e 黃 冊
Hui-chou 徽 州
i 役
i-chuang 義 莊
I-hsing 宜 興
i-kuan 衣 冠
i-t'iao pien 一 條 編
i-tien liang-chu 一 田 兩 主
Jao-chou 饒 州
Kao P'an-kuei 高 攀 桂
Kao Shih-ch'i 高 士 奇
Keng Ting-hsiang 耿 定 向
ko 蒿
Ku Yen-wu 顧 炎 武
ku-t'ou 股 頭
ku-wen 古 文
Kuan-shan 官 山
kuan-t'ien 官 田
Kuei 桂
kuei 蟶

kuei-chi 窺覦

Kuei-ch'ih 貴池

Kuei-lin 桂林

Kuei-te 歸德

kun-tan 滾單

kung-sheng 貢生

K'ung-ch'eng 孔城

lai 賴

li 里

li-chang 里長

li-chia 里甲

liang-ju wei-ch'u 量入為出

Lien-ch'eng 連城

Lien-t'an 練潭

Liu 劉

Liu-feng 流風

Liu Kuang-mei 劉光美

Liu Ta-k'uei 劉大櫆

Liu T'ung-hsün 劉統勳

lo (*yüeh*) 樂

lou-kuei 陋規

Lu So-shan
  (Chiu-shao) 陸校山 (九韶)

Lu Yü-lin
  (Hsün-jo) 陸遇霖 (潤若)

lu-k'o 蘆課

Lü Hsien-chi 呂賢基

Lü-chiang 廬江

Lung-mien 龍眠

Ma Ch'i-ch'ang 馬其昶

Ma Fei 馬騑

Ma Meng-chen 馬孟楨

Ma San-chün 馬三俊

Ma-hsi 馬溪

min-t'ien 民田

Ming shih-lu 明實錄

mou 畝

mu-fu 幕府

Mu-t'ou shan 木頭山

nan-mi 南米

Nan-shu-fang 南書房

Nan-wan 南灣

Ni 倪

Ning-po 寧波

nu-p'u 奴僕

nung-sang 農桑

o-tsu 額租

P'an 潘

P'an Chiang 潘江

P'an Jung-i 潘榮陛

P'an Wei-shan 潘為山

pao-chia 保甲

pao-lan 包攬

Pao-ting Academy 保定書院

Pei-hsia-kuan 北峽關

P'eng Chung-tao 彭仲道

pien-shen 編審

pien-shen t'iao-i 編審條議

po-hsüeh hung-tz'u 博學鴻詞

Po-yang 鄱陽

Pu-nung-shu 補農書

shang-shui 商稅

She-hsien 歙縣

shen 紳

Shen Chiao 沈教

shen-chin 紳衿

shen-shih 紳士

sheng 升

Sheng Ju-ch'ien 盛汝謙

sheng-yüan 生員

shih 石

Shih Lang 石朗

shih-cheng-ts'e 實徵冊

shih-tsu 實租

Shu-ch'eng 舒城

shu-chi-shih 庶吉士

Shu-chou 舒州

Su Shih
  (Tung-p'o) 蘇軾 (東坡)

sui 歲

Sun Chin 孫晉

Sung-chiang 松江

Sung-shan 松山

Ta t'ien to chia 大田多稼

Ta-t'ien 大田

ta-tsao 大造

Tai Chih-fu 戴知富

Tai Chün-ts'ai 戴君采

Tai Ming-shih 戴名世

Tai Nan-chü 戴南居

T'ai-hu 太湖
  (Lake T'ai)

T'ang 唐

t'ang 塘

T'ang-chia-kou 湯家溝

ti 地

tien-chih 典質

tien-p'u 佃僕

tien-shih 典史

tien-tang 典當

t'ien 田

T'ien-ch'eng Academy 天城書院

T'ien-kung k'ai-wu 天工開物

ting 丁

tou 斗

t'ou-hsien 投獻

t'ou-k'ao 投靠
Tseng Kuo-fan 曾國藩
tseng-sun 曾孫
Tso 左
Tso Kuang-tou 左光斗
Tso Kuo-ch'u 左國樞
Tso Kuo-ts'ai 左國材
Tso Liang-yü 左良玉
Tso Lin 左麟
tso-ts'an-cheng 左參政
Tsou 鄒
tsu 族
tsun-chang 尊長
tsung-tzu 宗子
Ts'ung-yang 樅陽
t'u 兔
t'uan-lien 團練
t'ui 退
Tung 童
Tung Ch'i-ch'ang 董其昌
Tung Chung-shu 董仲舒
Tung-lin 東林
T'ung-an 同安
T'ung-ch'eng 桐城
T'ung-hsi shu-yüan 桐溪書院
T'ung-hsiang 桐鄉
T'ung-kuo 桐國
t'ung-p'an 通判
T'ung-pei 桐陂
T'ung-pien jih-lu 桐變日錄
Wa-hsieh-pa 瓦屑壩
Wang (of Kao-lin) 汪，高林
Wang Chao-ling 汪兆齡
Wang I-tai 汪以岱
Wang Kuo-hua 汪國華
Wang Mang 王莽
Wang Ting-kuo 王廷國
Wei Chung-hsien 魏忠賢
Wu 吳
Wu Chin-chao 吳晉昭
Wu I-chia 吳一介
Wu Ju-chi 鄔汝楫
Wu Ju-lun 吳汝綸
Wu Ying-pin 吳應賓
Wu Yüeh 吳樾
Wu Yung-hsien 吳州先
Wu-chin 武進
Wu-hu 蕪湖
Wu-tai-shih 五代史
Wu-tsa-tsu 五雜組
Wu-wei 無為
Wu-yüan 婺源
Yang-hsien 陽羨

Yang Su-yün 楊素蘊
Yao Ch'ih-ch'i 姚之騏
Yao Chih-lan 姚之蘭
Yao Chun-ch'ang 姚濬昌
Yao Fan 姚範
Yao Fen 姚棻
Yao Hsi-lien 姚希廉
Yao Hsi-yen 姚希顏
Yao Hsien 姚顯
Yao Hsü 姚旭
Yao K'ung-ping 姚孔鈵
Yao Lang 姚烺
Yao Nai 姚鼐
Yao-shih 鷂石
Yao Shih-hung 姚士實
Yao Sun-ch'i 姚孫棐
Yao Sun-ch'u 姚孫榘
Yao Sun-chü 姚孫槼
Yao Sun-fei 姚孫棐
Yao Sun-sen 姚孫森
Yao Tzu-yü 姚自廣
Yao Wen-ao 姚文鰲
Yao Wen-jan 姚文然
Yao Wen-lieh 姚文烈
Yao Wen-yen 姚文燕
Yao Ying 姚瑩
Yao Yung-kai 姚永概
Yao Yung-p'u 姚永樸
Yeh Kuei-tsu 葉桂祖
Yeh Ts'an 葉燦
Yen I 嚴頤
Yen-shih chia-hsün 顏氏家訓
Yü Ch'eng-lung 于成龍
yü-k'o 魚課
yü-t'ien 圩田

INDEX

The entry of a single surname refers to the family and/or lineage of that name.

acreage under cultivation, 34, 47, 48, 56, 58, 63–4, 68–9, 74, 85, 87, 134, 163n.5, 164n.7. *See also* land registration

agriculture, commercialization of, 10, 12; intensification of, 4, 7, 10, 144, 146; in T'ung-ch'eng, 28–9, 34, 36, 48, 60. *See also* crops and products

An-ch'ing, 24–7, 53. *See also* Huai-ning

Anhwei, 35, 39, 50

aristocracy, 6–7, 9, 128

branch head, *see fang-chang*

budgeting, 183n.40, 184n.41; Chang Ying's views on, 145–6; *see also* Yao Wen-jan

bureaucracy, 7, 9, 128

Chang, ancestors, 27, 88; branches, 173n.103; common property, 91, 93, 96, 98, 107–10, 119, 135–6, 170n.15, 171n.56, 173n.106; degree and office holding, 3, 37, 40, 51, 89, 91, 103–4, 107–8; discussed by Ho Ping-ti, 162n.144, 173n.93; division between country and city, 96, 106, 170n.18, 150–1; genealogy, 91–2, 95, 98, 102–3, 106, 109–11, 174n. 115; history, 42, 45, 47, 88–111; management, 95–6, 102–3, 106, 107–9, 111, 117; marriage connections, 41, 52, 54, 92–3, 100, 102, 104–8, 128, 170n.25; mortality and fertility, 163n.156, 173n.97; philanthropy, 89, 92, 93, 96; rules, 102; size, 172n.89; social differentiation and kinship spirit, 106–7, 111, 174n.115; tour, 106–7; traditions of austerity, 95–9, 101, 111

Chang (another Chang lineage), 114

Chang Ch'ao-chen, 75

Chang Ch'eng-hsien, 101

Chang Ch'i, 101

Chang Chia, 96

Chang Chieh, 96, 109, 182n.29

Chang Chien, 37, 91

Chang Chü-cheng, 62

Chang Ch'un, 3, 37, 89–91, 93, 95

Chang Chung-li, views discussed, 1, 18–19, 127–8, 130–1

Chang Feng, 89

Chang Feng-i, 160n.117

Chang Han-ch'ing, 156n.11

Chang Hsien-chung, 45, 46

Chang Hsü, 40, 159n.88

Chang Hsün, 53

Chang Jo-t'ing, 106, 108, 173n.104

Chang Ju, 44

Chang K'o-yen, 93

Chang K'uei, 109

Chang Li-hsiang, 155n.35, 179n.5, 186n.50, 187n.59

Chang Liu-chi, 71. *See also* Chang Ping-ch'ien

Chang Mu, 89–90

Chang P'eng (Tung-ch'uan), 31, 89–90, 148–9, 186n.58

Chang Ping-chen, 68, 92, 93, 161n.118

Chang Ping-ch'ien (Liu-chieh), 70–1

Chang Ping-i, 38, 45, 68, 92–3, 95, 137; property, 135, 151, 187n.65

Chang Ping-wen, 39, 41, 92–3

Chang Shao-hua, 108, 110

Chang Shao-t'ang, 110

Chang Shao-wen, 54, 108, 110

Chang Shih-chi, 170n.17

Chang Shih-wei, 91–2

Chang Shu, 185n.44

Chang T'ing-ch'ih, 104, 105

Chang T'ing-ch'ing, 101

Chang T'ing-chuan, 100–2, 104, 105, 172n.87

Chang T'ing-lu, 100, 104, 105

Chang T'ing-tsan, 100, 103–8 *passim*

Chang T'ing-yü, career, 51, 100–1; death, 103; descendants, 104–8; efforts on behalf of lineage, 101–3;